AIM HIGH

THE STORY OF
Major General Gerald Stack Maloney, Jr.
WITH SUSAN D. BRANDENBURG

★ ★

Biographer: Susan D. Brandenburg
Page Layout and Design: Sally Ball Sharp
ISBN: 978-1-958174-09-8

TABLE OF CONTENTS

INTRODUCTION
Thoughts on Turning 90 ...

Dear Chris and Katie and Granddaughter Lillian,

What follows is simply me or what I try to be. An outline for my children in their lives.

I have learned that there is too little time for really important things. There is no time to waste on the petty, the mean, and the foolish.

Joy and trust should be grasped and held firm. Do not embrace a second-rate goal or a half-standard or the cruel and the meaningless.

I embrace the Air Force Motto: "Aim High."

Whether it is people or books or activities, none of us has enough time to make even the best of the above our own.

Never believe and do not let yourself believe that kindness and courage do not count. Now that I have learned how much the spoken word and the things done for others have meant, I regret the words that I have left unspoken and the little things not done.

It is my conviction that things that matter are few and for the most part simple. Love is one. I still don't know what total love means in all of its fullness, but I do know that it is utter trust and utter supportiveness. Any person who has known full and true love has been blessed. This love, too, should be grasped and held firm.

A noble trait is compassion which I think means the ability to suffer with, to understand, or to make allowances for.

We should rejoice in our world with its beauty, its kindness, its bravery, its goodness, its humor and its joy.

We must have the courage to never bend to the ugly, the brutal, the cowardly, the vicious or the negative. The old saying, "Perish the thought," applies to the negative.

To live fully, we should embrace a gallantry of spirit, a kind of indomitable defiance of bad luck or the pain of the world. How about a smiling disdain for the worst life can offer and a quiet resolute reliance on positive thinking?

Much has been said of honor. We must cling to our personal honor in spite of adversity. Personal honor embodies a keen sense of ethical conduct. Our word should be our bond as it is mine. Let it not be corroded in your world.

Lastly, humor and goodness – I lump these together because in every situation, endeavor or person, if I look I can find some humor and some goodness. The trick is to try.

Be the first to find something positive in all aspects of your life. Explore ways to change the negative in your life to a positive.

In closing, I leave you with three simple things you can do today as I do.

1. Every day say something nice to someone. Find a way to honestly compliment someone.

2. Every day do something physical to make your or your family's life better. i.e. change a lightbulb, wash the car, cut the grass, oil a squeaky hinge ...

3. Find a way to make every group you belong to in some way better.

Love,

Dad and Grandpa

October 2020

FOREWORD
Letter from Katie

Dear Dad,

Years ago, you sent me a letter you wrote while on your boat watching the sunset. I've kept that letter of love and support with me always. I wanted you to have such a letter from me, because although we tell each other how we feel, sometimes it's nice to see it in writing.

I am very proud of you for all you have accomplished and for all you continue to do for your family, friends and even for strangers. The life you have carved out for yourself in Florida is so full – full of wonderful people and wonderful opportunities. You are truly surrounded by love. This, of course, is a reflection of the kind of man you are.

I am very proud to be your daughter and I believe I am very much your daughter – in attitude, drive and the ability for compassion. You have been supportive of me my whole life; helping me deal with learning disabilities, letting me go to Europe at age 16 (for art) and 17 (for fun), college, work, divorce and death.

You provided me with the foundation to become the best person I could be and for that I'm grateful.

I am most thankful that we never end a phone conversation without saying "I love you" to each other!

Thank you for being a wonderful father! See you soon …

All my love,

Katie (2012)

Dad's boat "Total Blarney" on which he lived for 8 months in 2001-2.

P.S. I'm not sure how many 56-year-olds spend time target shooting with their 91-year-old fathers – not many, I'm guessing. My love of shooting, sailing, art, home remodeling and history can all be traced back to my childhood. My father is still someone I call to share a boat story, ask advice about a remodel project or just pick his brain about places he's been. Probably our biggest common denominator is our shared learning disability. Coping with dyslexia was far easier than it could have been because I had a parent who had "been there, done that." His outlook was always positive and so was mine. Leading by example, I learned from him perseverance, adaptability, how to embrace change, and, especially, courage. He has been my sole parent for almost twenty years now and I am forever grateful for the relationship we have built as adults. I love you, Dad. (written in May 2022)

FOREWORD II
Letter from Lillian

Dear Grandad,

I wish I had more time with you because I love you very much. We are so far away from each other, but the moments I've had with you in my life have meant a lot to me. I've always loved how exuberant you are – how happy you are when you see me! It's obvious how much you appreciate the time you have with your family. When we're together, you always ask about how I'm doing academically and what my interests are outside of academics – we have good discussions, especially about my interest in music – specifically, jazz. I remember when I was about 12 years old, and you took Dad and me to the University of North Florida to watch the Airmen of Note perform. They were amazing! I'm now in the jazz band at my high school and I play the slide trombone. It's a fun instrument to play and my high school, Barrington, has a good music program – with an emphasis on the arts. Grandad, you always told me to make sure I work on my "extracurriculars," and I do that. I'm now looking into college, as I'm going into my junior year of high school.

Last time we visited in Florida, you and I talked about setting goals. I've heard about setting goals from a lot of people, but your advice was the best. You told me to imagine I was on a beach and there were a lot of little pebbles on the beach that were painful to step on, especially when you're focusing on them. Then you said to imagine a friend with a picnic across the beach and how, when I focus on running toward my friend, the pebbles won't hurt anymore. It was a great analogy about focusing on the end result and getting what you want regardless of the hardships along the way. It was the most profound goal advice I've gotten.

Our talks almost make up for the distance between us. Grandad, you're one of the most patriotic Americans I know, but you did share with me that I shouldn't buy an American car because they aren't that well made any more. You are such an interesting man and you've had an adventurous, productive life, but you stay grounded and appreciate what you've got. I hope you know that I'm so proud of you and I love you so very much.

I can't wait to read your book! It's so impressive that you rose to the rank of Major General and I love listening to your Air Force adventure stories. I remember when I was about 13 and you came to Rhode Island. You were telling the story about flying in Korea and getting lost in a night flight and finally finding your way back to your base. You said you just prayed and that it was divine intervention that brought you safely back. That has always stuck with me. You opened my mind to the possibility of miracles, and I'll never forget that.

I love you, Grandad,

Lillian

FOREWORD III
A Tribute to Dad by Christopher Maloney

Dad has done so many things so well that I was awestruck as a kid. He is a pilot, a world-class marksman, a successful businessman, a leader in the military and the community. He has been a major role-model for me, especially after we both recognized in our mid-forties that we were dealing with disorders (he with dyslexia and me with bipolar disorder). The fact that he was dyslexic and was also missing two digits on his hand and never gave up on his goals of being a fighter pilot - that shows brute-force determination and tenacity. Dad has an indomitable core of strength that is so impressive.

Something most people don't know about Dad is that he has a playful side in the midst of his serious determination to achieve goals. A great example of this playfulness was when Katie and I were very young and we lived in the Newton house … Dad would take us into the finished basement where the light streamed through the windows at a certain time of day - I think it was in the spring. He would catch the stream of sunlight in his wrist watch and it would reflect in a small blob of light on the wall. He would say, in a hushed voice, "The fairy is here." It was like a tiny tinker bell spirit dancing on the wall and he would move it up and down and side to side - we could ask it questions. Up and down meant yes and side to side meant no. But, we had to say please because if we didn't ask politely, the fairy would disappear. We had no idea he was using his wrist watch and this would go on for about 45 minutes. He was not only piquing our imaginations but teaching us manners. He told us the fairy only came at certain times of the year and we met the fairy several times for a few years. That little spirit is still there in the twinkle of his eye.

Dad was also truly dialed into the magic of Christmas when we were children. If you want to see an idealized Christmas morning where you come down the steps and stand on the landing and see the tree and all the presents - he made the magic real when we were young. He was totally into it and loved every minute of it, right along with the rest of us.

Dad's playful side also showed up sometimes on Saturday mornings when we were watching cartoons - like bugs bunny and wily coyote . He would pass the television room, pause at the door, and say I'll just watch for a minute. Then he'd get drawn in and an hour later, he'd still be standing there. He never sat down because this was, after all, kid's stuff!

Speaking of kid's stuff, Dad was always a straight shooter in practical matters as well as with weapons. I remember when my voice was changing and I was going through puberty and getting interested in girls, Mom was pretty nervous about it. Dad stepped in and said, "Hey! He's going through this and you need to let him go through it." He never got hung up on propriety. He's done that with Lillian as well - giving her straight talk about the world and how men can be - and she's grateful to hear it. I'm grateful that they are close enough to talk about important things together.

I remember when he got married a second time, it was a bit of a dark period for me. I didn't like Elizabeth and I told him so. He later told me that it gave him a vantage point he needed. I'm so glad he's in the relationship with Marilyn now. They are inspirational together and it's a wonder to see all of the great things both of them have achieved.

Over the years, there were times when we were lost to each other for periods of time, but no longer. Dad has seen me be a father to Lillian and we've achieved mutual understanding that we lacked for a while. I'm so thankful that we have gotten to this point in our lives. I admire his steely core and in times of adversity, I've always looked up to him and thought of him as my major role model. Today, Dad and I are closer than ever before. I play the drums in a band and recently got a promotion at work - and he's thrilled about what I'm doing. I love his enthusiasm about life in general and the love he's always shown for me. Lillian and I are going to visit in April. We're excited about seeing him again soon.

Dad is an impressive man and I'm so proud to be his son.

FOREWORD IV
Letter from Marilyn

Dear Gerry,

We met at an evening program of the World Affairs Council-Jacksonville. I had been active with the Council since retiring from a 30-year career in the U.S. Foreign Service. You and I and many others were interested in critical issues programs made available through the World Affairs Council. In addition to contacting many of our important and nationally known guest speakers, I helped fundraise to bring them to Jacksonville.

As I got to know you better, I discovered that we had much more in common. You had a United States Air Force background and I came from a Navy family (my father and brother,) as both enjoyed our military contacts. You majored in history as did I. We shared a mutual interest in foreign policy and international affairs programs, both of which developed strong ties with the military and business/professional communities.

It is said that Irishmen always have a twinkle in their eye. You have that, Gerry. Your smile is contagious and lights up everyone around you. People seek out your company and you revel in theirs. You like people!

You are a giver in life at every opportunity; a kind person, sensitive to others, never looking to cast guilt or aspersions. A right of center Republican in your politics, you are well-read (despite your dyslexia) and well-informed on current events. You identify more with the

Confederacy than with the North in the Civil War. In fact, you have an ancestor who was a famous Confederate General, and you are proud of what the Confederate Air Force has done to preserve historic aircraft.

I admire your strong sense of loyalty, service and patriotism. Your volunteer work has been extensive in many organizations including the U.S. Coast guard, when you patrolled regularly with your boat and crew, and also taught certification classes. Even today, you continue to volunteer whenever given the opportunity. You are working now with the AFROTC at Sandalwood High School!

As an avid pilot, boater and marksman, you are always striving to be the best you can be. In politics, you are not a fan of Bill or Hilary Clinton, and admire as heroes such as Winston Churchill and George Patton - both for integrity and courage. We've both admired Fox News commentator and journalist Charles Krauthammer, a deep thinker and one of our World Affairs Council speakers (may he rest in peace).

You and I share a love of reading and enjoy many of the same kinds of biographic, adventure, and mystery novels.

Finally, Gerry - you are a person of faith. You have always seemed happy with your life; loved your mother, admired your father and have been devoted to your children.

Your smile was the first thing that attracted me to you and you've never stopped smiling. You have left a very large footprint on life. Thank you for the support you have always given to me with your service and many friendships. You, Gerry, are very special!

I love you.

Marilyn

CHAPTER 1

CHILDHOOD MEMORIES

We resided in Cambridge, Massachusetts when I was born on October 31, 1930. My mother, Norma Claiborn Maloney, gave birth to me at Massachusetts General Hospital in Boston. My Dad, Gerald Stack Maloney, Sr., was not available during my birth, as he was playing a professional football game. He was an end and a kicker on the New York Yankees football team. The day after my birth, Dad came to see my mother and me. He apologized for not being there because of his football game and asked the doctor how much money he owed him for my delivery. The doctor asked him, "How much did you make yesterday?" Dad answered, "$75.00." The doctor said, "Okay, that's my fee!"

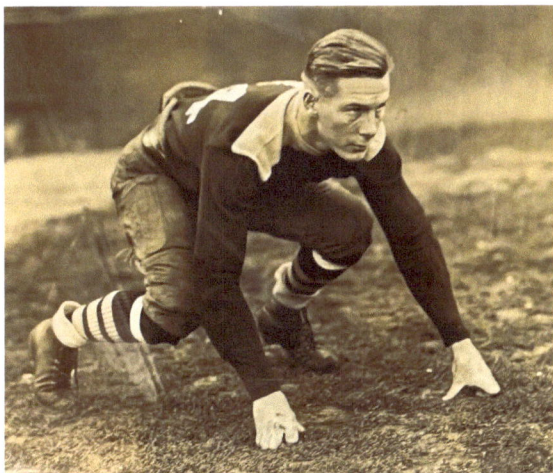

My dad, Gerald Stack Maloney, Sr

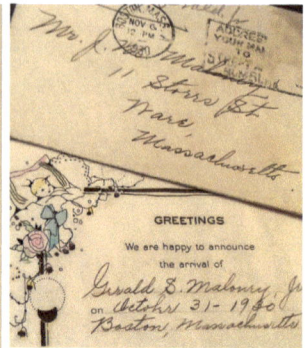

Dear Dad —
Gee but he is a darling. Can't say he is pretty yet. But he has such a cute face and so much personality! Am getting along fine & really think I stood the ordeal better than Gerald did — he is still in a daze. Bestest love,
Norma

GREETINGS
We are happy to announce the arrival of
Gerald S. Maloney, Jr.
on *October 31- 1940*
Boston, Massachusetts

My birth announcement soon went out to family and friends. One special announcement went to my paternal grandfather, James Michael Maloney, in Ware, Massachusetts.

In 1918, an article in the Worcester Telegram and Gazette newspaper lauded my grandfather for his service to the Knights of Columbus during wartime. My father's family were devout Catholics and mother's family were Methodists, so my church upbringing was somewhat sketchy. In the following article, it is mentioned that my grandfather had collected a large number of war souvenirs to send back home. Those souvenirs, stored in our basement for years after my grandfather's death, were destined to play a large role later in my boyhood.

My grandmother, Margaret, died in a gas explosion in 1918 when Dad was still a teenager and his father was in Europe.

...ers Pay Tribute to Local K. of C. Secretary

James M. Maloney Has Been Overseas Nearly a Year and Was With Third Division Most of the Time—Plans To Visit Rome and Ireland Before Coming Back To America

James M. Maloney, K. of C. secretary, who went to France nearly a year ago, is expected home within a month. He is one of the three men who have been selected to remain overseas until the final clean-up of the extensive war activities carried on by the Knights of Columbus in France and with the American army in Germany.

Mr. Maloney has been with the 6th engineers, 3d division in Oetendung, Germany, since shortly after last Christmas.

Previously he had been in Paris and southern France supervising transportation from Bordeaux. While at Oetendung he had one of the largest and best outfitted huts in the division which won him great popularity with the men. His work has been mentioned many times in the regimental and divisional newspapers under the nickname of "Judge." During the winter his large recreation hall was always crowded with soldiers and every evening he staged boxing matches, basketball games or moving pictures, and as soon as the spring arrived arranged outdoor sports.

The Pioneer July 12 said with reference to the Worcester man: "Judge" Maloney, K. C., didn't forget us at the Sixth's big athletic meet on the Fourth. The old lemonade and cakes reminded us of the old circus days and we sure welcome daily issue of newspapers, soaps, cigarets, tobacco and goodies.

The Pioneer July 5 said:
As our activities are all pointed towards an early return to God's country, we are deeply grateful for the splendid work that Brother Maloney of the K. of C. has been doing. His unostentatious way. Ever since his arrival here he has been getting "out" smokes, doughnuts, nuts, kits, reading matter, and...

JAMES M. MALONEY

...better quarters, Hotel sur Post, his untiring welfare work is able to show to better advantage. But even where we look back at his small establishment, way down at the other end of the town, we can't forget that sunny smile and those mysterious bags and bundles of his as he visited the various mess lines, and the "Knights will always have a warm place in our hearts. Maloney has eaten, slept and in truth lived Sixth engineers every minute that he has been with us and we want him to take that big boat ride with us before he settles down in Worcester. Mass.

Dad's older brother was in the Army at Fort Benning, Georgia, so Dad went to live with his mother's sisters until Grandfather returned to Ware, Massachusetts. Grandfather Maloney, whom I barely remember, nicknamed me the Little Corporal.

Dad came from tough stock. His grandfather came over from Ireland during the potato famine in the mid-1800's, settling in Ware, Massachusetts and his father fought in WWI in the American expeditionary forces in France and Germany before returning home to Ware. He was an artist who sketched drawings for the newspaper in pen and ink and owned a printing business. Grandfather Maloney died when I was just a toddler.

I remember going to the hospital with my parents when I was about two years old and looking through a glass window into a room filled with bassinets and babies. My mother pointed to a baby and said, "That's your sister." We never spoke of her again. She didn't come home from the hospital. I later found a grave marker in the Maloney plot that reads *"Jane Maloney – 1932-1932."*

We lived in the bottom half of a two-story duplex on Hilltop Street in Newton, Massachusetts when I was very young. Everett and Helen Cross lived upstairs and have remained good family friends always. I recall being overwhelmed by 4-foot snowdrifts and climbing some of the big trees in that neighborhood. There was an older girl across the street. She was blonde and I had a big crush on her. We once built a snow house together.

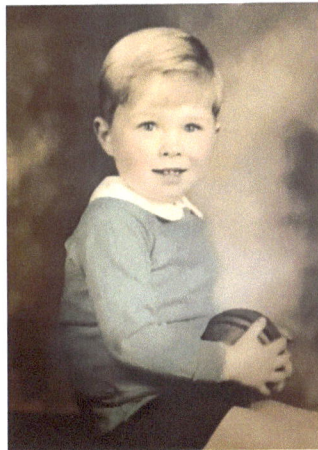

Me as a toddler

I remember that the milk man would deliver Hood Milk by horse and wagon. We'd leave the empty glass bottles on the front porch and he'd pick up the empties and deposit fresh milk. The cream always came to the top. Mmm … delicious!

Another vivid memory that is not as pleasant is when I was wrongly accused of breaking a window in one of the houses down the street. Dad asked me if I had broken it and I told him I didn't know anything about it. The parents all got together and discussed the broken window. What disturbed me was that my Dad sent someone from his company to fix it. That hurt, because I felt he didn't believe me. Dad's company, G. S. Maloney Company, Inc. was a construction company that did a lot of maintenance for the six major oil companies in the greater Boston area.

During the summer of 1936, when I was about 5 years old, we rented an old two-story home in the town of Humarock on the South Shore. In addition to having no indoor plumbing (just an outhouse), the old house had no refrigerator. We fastened our ice box to the back bumper of our car and drove it to Humarock for the summer.

My mother's mother, Grandmother "Ma Ma," came for a visit and caused a great commotion falling down the stairs in the middle of the night on her way to the outhouse. Ma Ma Ella Yancy Claiborn was a good woman who raised ten children including my mother. Her husband, my grandfather, died when he fell from a bridge he had been building with a crew of men.

When we first got to Humarock that summer, Dad told me that by the time we left to go home, he wanted me to be able to run barefoot everywhere. At first, my feet were tender and painful, but I rose to the challenge, practicing all summer. I spent that summer pretty much on my own – learning to swim by dogpaddling. Nobody had much time for me. By the time we were ready to leave, I had toughened up my feet. I ran barefoot back and forth in front of Dad, but he didn't notice. I finally said, "Look, Dad!" but he was not impressed. He'd forgotten his challenge.

By 1937, we could afford a better summer rental house on a hill in Humarock – just one block from the water. We had an 8-foot wooden dingy and Dad installed a center board, a rudder and a mast with a canvas sail and it became a little sailboat. He taught me everything I needed to know about sailing and then I was on my own. Using the bright orange paint that identified Gulf Oil Company stations, Dad had the little dingy painted. So, at 7 years old, I was out in the bay sailing by myself in my bright orange dingy.

My brother Shawn was born in 1935. I have few memories of him except sharing toys at Christmas and riding in our Wills Sainte Claire Touring Car, of which Dad was rightfully proud, having bought the big car when he was a professional football player. It was our family car for a long time.

Wills Sainte Clair touring car with Mom at wheel

Dad drove our family in the Wills Sainte Clair Touring Car from Newton, Massachusetts to New Milford, Connecticut each summer from 1935 to 1940. Our destination was Aunt Katherine Parkhurst's Tinkerbell Farm. Aunt Katherine was my mother's sister. There were no super highways back then and we drove from town to town on secondary roads with little wooden signs that pointed to the left or right when the roads came to an end. Dad followed a rudimentary map and somehow, we never got lost. The touring car had no heater or radio, but we supplemented with blankets and singing. Mom loved to sing as we drove and one of her favorites was the old folk song, *"She'll be comin' round the mountain when she comes ...*" Memories of that drive still warm my heart.

We'd spend a month at Tinkerbell Farm, which sprawled over about 100 acres and featured three barns. I milked cows with Uncle Bill, Aunt Katherine's husband, and sometimes we took a can of milk to the dairy in New Milford, for pay.

There was a gate at Tinkerbell Farm and I would carry a little wooden rifle, marching back and forth like a soldier guarding the

Tinkerbell Farm – Three Barns

gate. When I wasn't marching or milking, I would run through the woods with my dog, Ginger. There was a great hill looking out on the woods and I would sit there, with Ginger by my side, and enjoy the view. Summers at Tinkerbell Farm were a great getaway for me and for Aunt Katherine, who lived the rest of the year at 104 East 81st Street in New York City and worked as an administrator at the Dalton School, one of the finest private schools in the nation. She took me to the Dalton School one day and I was amazed to discover that all of the athletic activities were conducted on the flat roof … there was a basketball court and a playing field, all fenced in far above the City of New York.

My Aunt Katherine was like a second mother to me. She recommended that I attend the Beaver Country Day School for Kindergarten and 1st Grade and I remember carpooling there. It was a girls' school that

Aunt Katherine and me

allowed boys in K-1ˢᵗ grades only. By the end of 1ˢᵗ Grade, all of the other students could read, but I could not.

After we moved to 462 Waltham Street in West Newton, we were a block away from the Davis School, where I repeated 1ˢᵗ grade. I learned to read the words but spent the rest of my schooling, all the way up to 7ᵗʰ grade, scrambling to keep up and pretending to comprehend the thoughts and whole sentences laid out by the words. One day, I was in the library in Waban trying to read a book by Howard Pease about a boy working aboard a tramp steamer when all of a sudden, I realized I was reading whole sentences and understanding them! That was a "red-letter day" for me, as I had just about given up on actually being able to read well. From then on, I enjoyed reading, although I continued to have difficulty with most academic pursuits and didn't learn why until much later in life.

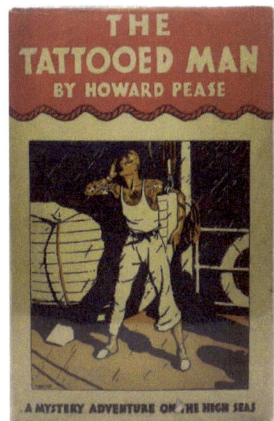

One vivid childhood memory was the day I saw the Hindenburg floating overhead. It was on May 6, 1937, the same day the famous German airship caught on fire and was destroyed when it attempted to dock in Manchester Township, New Jersey, at the naval Air Station Lakehurst. Like everybody else, I ran outside when it went over and remember it being so huge and so low that I felt I could reach up and touch it. It cast a huge shadow and had us speechless as it headed toward New Jersey. Later, when the front page of the newspaper was covered with headlines and photos of the disaster, it seemed unreal to me. I kept thinking to myself, "I just saw that."

Sadly, my next childhood memory is when my little brother, Shawn, drowned on a summer day in 1938. We had rented a summer house at Humarock Beach on Cape Cod Bay and I remember a man running up the hill shouting, "Is anybody missing

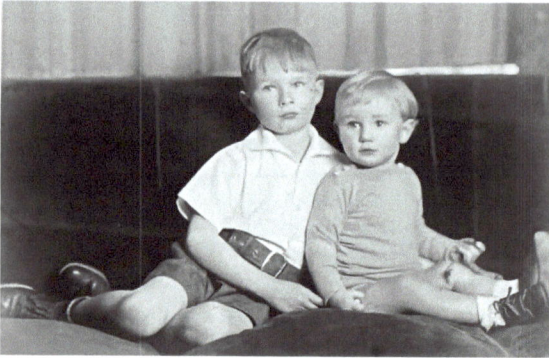

My brother Shawn and me

a boy?" People started running down the hill and I followed them. There were half a dozen people crowded around a tiny boy, my 3-year-old brother Shawn. Firemen were working on him, pushing his chest. I didn't know what to do. I ran back to the house and my mother seemed to be having a nervous breakdown. She was nine months pregnant at the time and later that afternoon, she lost the baby … so she lost two children in one day. Later, the doctor was there with my parents and I peeked in the bedroom but they shooed me away. Nobody spoke to me. I had lost my playmate and brother and I felt terribly alone and sad. Later that same day,

Ginger and me

I went with a friend down to the water. There was a small black bag on somebody's lawn with policemen guarding it and that was my brother Shawn.

I had always been a solitary boy, but that was the day I became an only child – a lonely only child with just one companion – my dog, Ginger.

Having already endured the worst psychological storm a family could encounter, we also were assaulted in September by the Great New England Hurricane of 1938. Historically, the hurricane of 1938 was one of the most destructive and powerful storms ever to strike Southern New England. The Hurricane was responsible for severe flooding in Falmouth and New Bedford, Massachusetts and ultimately resulted in the loss of 564 lives throughout New England.

Dad called to tell us to stay away from the windows. Mother and I cowered in the basement. I played with my electric trains while Mother worked on organizing Cub Scout crafts. She had become the den mother for Cub Scouts and doted on me more than ever now that I was her only child. When I look back, I realize now that Mother's life was filled with tragedy. She lost three children – my sister Jane, my brother Shawn, and the child she was carrying when Shawn died.

Back to the Hurricane of 1938, I remember that we were in the sunroom at our house on Waltham Street when Dad called to warn us, and after the hurricane, I went back in that room and could not see out the windows. A huge tree had fallen next to the sunroom and blocked the view completely. It was a shocking sight to see branches encompassing all the sunroom windows where the sun usually came through.

While Mother's attention was focused on me because I was her only child left, Dad's plans for me intensified now that I was his only son. He had graduated from Dartmouth College and played all east football. I was to do the same. The fact that my grades were not good disappointed him greatly. I appeared to be a smart boy, but I couldn't seem to do well in academic subjects. I had developed a stutter in 1st grade – probably due to being embarrassed at my illiteracy – and Dad had worked feverishly with me to stop the stutter. He sat down with me and told me to bite my words and clench my teeth. Eventually, I no longer stuttered,

but I rarely opened my mouth to talk at all.

Although he took the time to work with me on my stutter, Dad usually didn't have time for me. I would try to perch on the arm of his chair and he'd just keep reading the paper and say, "Lite somewhere, little Maloney!"

If I argued or talked back to Mom, Dad would come home and whip me with a belt or switch. This happened so regularly, and I was told so often to "speak only when spoken to" and "little boys should be seen and not heard," that I learned not to speak up at all. I stopped talking back to anyone in the world! In fact, I was marked down in school because I didn't participate in class discussions. Emotionally, I simply couldn't speak up. My natural impulses had been truncated.

Because I was so quiet and subdued – and because I continued to be challenged by academic subjects - I was mistaken for dumb. I was always the last one chosen for games at school, although I knew I was better coordinated and could play well. I simply stayed quiet, with the exception of having a stubborn streak sometimes. For instance, in elementary school, most of the boys had to wear knickers regardless of the weather. I wore short pants to school when the weather got hot and the other boys urged me to put on my knickers. No way, I told them. I'll wear what makes sense!

In 4th grade, I had trouble with the multiplication tables – I knew them but could only do them by using a method of my own device. I remember I got most of the problems wrong on a test and the teacher was unhappy. Another teacher came in and saw me by myself reworking the numbers. My teacher gestured over toward me in the corner and declared to the other teacher, "He's just dumb." Many years later, after graduating with honors from Stanford, I went right back to that corner and said to the wall, "You see, I'm not dumb." It gave me a great sense of satisfaction.

When I was in prep school, I was taken to Boston University and spent a day doing mental exercises. It finally came out that I had a 146 IQ – just four points away from genius! That was the worst thing that could have happened. Now that my intelligence was confirmed, everyone knew that I was simply lazy – I just didn't study enough. What other explanation could there be?

At this point, I'll explain the dilemma, which will help set the scene for the remainder of this memoir. I didn't learn that I was Dyslexic until I was 40 years old. My daughter, Katie, came home from

My dad – at the cottage on Duxbury Bay

school and told me she had been diagnosed with Dyslexia. My first thought was, "My God! How can a little girl like Katie catch a venereal disease!" When she explained Dyslexia to me, it was as if a light had been turned on. I told Katie, "You are describing your father!" All of the symptoms of Dyslexia where the same symptoms I'd been battling all my life, but nothing was known about Dyslexia back in the years when I was growing up. I was just considered lazy, especially after my IQ was revealed! I've since learned that, given what is known now, many famous people including Leonardo da Vinci, Saint Teresa, Napoleon, Winston Churchill, Carl Jung, Albert Einstein and Thomas Edison, may have been Dyslexic – not bad company to be in, after all!

Speaking of famous people, Refino Tamayo, a famous Mexican artist, taught art early in his career at the Dalton School in New York City. Aunt Katherine invited him to Tinkerbell Farm. We met him there and had dinner with him. I didn't realize then that I was dining with a celebrity.

Later, Dad and I were driving and we came upon a car that

had slid into a muddy ditch. It was Tamayo and his wife, Olga. My Dad and I helped Tamayo push the car out of the ditch and later on, he painted a Christmas card and sent it to Aunt Katherine and painted pictures for both my mother and Aunt Katherine. When my mother and Aunt Katherine died, I got both of those paintings. By then, Tamayo was quite famous and had a museum in Mexico City. I photographed both paintings and sent them to the curator at the Tamayo Museum. He contacted me and requested the "provenance" on the paintings, to which I replied I had met Tamayo more than once, recalled the year and where the pictures had been painted. He was impressed. He said it was rare that paintings came with such a history. I sold both paintings to the museum for $50,000, but I kept the original painted and signed Christmas Card.

Although Dad was obviously disappointed in my academic acumen and was a tough taskmaster as I was growing up, we did have some good times together, too. For instance, Dad annually took me with him to "The Sportsman's Show," which was great fun. There was a good Sportsman's Show in Boston that featured sailboats, camping, fishing, little light planes, etc., and it was a big deal to attend with Dad each year.

In the summer of 1939, we "moved up in the world," renting a house in Green Harbor on the water. It was a big deal to go away for the summer and being on the South Shore of Boston was a sign you had made it in life.

I was nearly ten years old and I moved up, too, from an 8-foot wooden dingy to an 18-foot wooden sailboat, which I sailed in Green Harbor and out into the ocean. The sailboat became part of me – sailing was not something I had to think about. There was no outboard motor. If the wind died, I'd have to wait for it to come up. It was nothing for me to sail against the wind and tide. The town of Green Harbor's marina was mostly a place for lobstermen, and I learned later that the lobstermen kept a keen eye on the lone young sailor.

We put the boat up for the winter and, in the spring, we turned it upside down and I would spend several spring weekends all day in the sun scraping it and cleaning the bottom, caulking it, making the lines right, priming it and getting the boat prepped and ready. Mother drove me to the boatyard in the morning with a bag lunch and she would pick me up about five. That usually took four or five days. Then we would turn the boat over and I would do the same thing on the inside, including sandpapering the paint and repainting it. It was generally two weeks of work before we could put the boat in the water. Dad sailed with me a few times, but most of the time I was on my own.

Me pulling in the anchor on Dad's Nantucket Indian class sailboat, Duxbury, MA 1950

We still had the little orange dingy in Green Harbor and we'd take it out and row about a mile out to fish. That was when I learned that fishing was not for me. We'd row back a mile or

My mother

two to the shore and roll it laboriously up the beach at low tide on two smooth logs. Dad caught fish but I never did. Dad and I did do some good things together, such as going to the Marshfield Fair. The Fair seemed huge to me when I was a boy – with Ferris-wheels, and other rides and, my favorite thing, the shooting gallery.

My mother was always kind to me, although she, too, was concerned about my grades. She was a den mother for my Cub Scout troop, which always met at our house at 462 Waltham Street, West Newton, where we had a basement filled with at least three different American Flyer electric train sets. Dad had his carpenters build big tables for the trains and I fashioned hills and valleys and trees and bushes around the tracks – using chicken wire on wooden platforms, with plaster on the chicken wire and then painting the whole elaborate set-up in shades of green and brown. I loved building things with my hands and using my imagination to make them special. I also loved building model airplanes out of balsa wood, gluing them together and covering them with rice paper, painting them and sticking on insignias. While I struggled in school, I thrived on building model planes, and diorama campsites with hills and streams and forests. People thought so much of them that I actually did a couple of windows for the local bank, and my WWII airplanes were a big hit with my friends. I bought a special type of paper that was luminous when exposed to sunlight and punched out circles with a paper punch, pasting them on the instrument panels of the planes. I sold several of those models to friends. I still have one of my WWII Airplane Models, a USAF -AT 6 (Advanced Trainer).

I remained my own person, too. I remember when some friends were so thrilled to have cigarettes. "Come on," they said,

"Let's smoke 'em!" We crawled behind some bushes which were out of sight of adults and my friends started lighting up the cigarettes. I took a couple of puffs and said, "This tastes terrible! I don't want to do this!" They insisted that I had to do it because "everybody famous was doing it." No thanks, I told them. Never again! And … I never smoked again.

I was ten years old in 1940 when an explosion occurred that could have changed the trajectory of my life dramatically … but

Me with AT-6 Model made in 1951, August 2021

it didn't. Grandpa had sent a large wooden box of memorabilia from WWI to my Dad and it had sat in our basement for many years before Dad decided to open it and see what was inside. It contained rifles, helmets, belts, knives, epaulets, swords, bayonets, pistols (Government issue 1917 – still usable, but rusty on one side). I found a small black box the size of about two cigarette packs with a Skull & Crossbones on it. This intrigued me, so while Dad was busy taking inventory, I snuck the little black box to the kitchen and opened the top, which slid back, exposing a bunch of felt-lined holes. All the holes were empty except one. There was something in it! I turned the box over and out fell a brass cylinder the size of a cigarette. It turned out to be an extremely sensitive landmine detonator. I put the box down and held the cylinder in my hand at chest level. Just the heat of my hand was enough to detonate it and suddenly I was in the middle of an explosion that knocked me back, nearly off my feet. There was a great bang and a bright white flash. I looked down and saw, with horror, that the new Dartmouth shirt Dad had given me was shredded and covered with blood. My first thought was, "Oh no, Dad will be mad." Then I saw that my left hand was also shredded, with parts of my thumb and two fingers gone; the thumb bone actually sticking out of the bloody stump.

I ran to the bathroom and grabbed a towel to cover the wound and put pressure on my wrist to stop the blood pumping (all good Cub Scout First Aid training), and then I looked in the mirror and saw that my face was also a mass of bleeding cuts. In the meantime, Dad ran upstairs from the basement and Mom in from the garden, both of them with shocked expressions on their faces. Dad started to call an ambulance, but I've been told I said, quite calmly, "It will be faster if you drive me to the hospital." They had not seen my hand yet, and the pressure had stopped the bleeding. I was not hurting yet – must have been in shock. I remember we stopped at a red light on the way to the hospital and the lady in the car to the right of us saw me. I'll never forget the look of absolute horror on her face.

We got to the hospital and now I began to hurt. Doctors and nurses worked on me from my waist to my head. A very nice young nurse told me to hold on hard – not let go of her hand. For the first time, my parents saw my mangled hand. Dad's comment was, "Guess you won't play end." (meaning to catch passes on a football team). I spent the next ten days in Newton-Wellsley Hospital. The worst pain I endured was when they changed the bandages.

When I got out of the hospital, we went to Green Harbor for the summer – and I hid my hand for a couple of days – just staying inside and keeping my hand in my pocket when I was outside. Then I looked in the mirror and had some serious self-talk. "You can't do this for the rest of your life," I said to myself. "No hiding anymore!" So, I went about doing what I could do and not worrying about what anyone said about my hand. I treated it just like any other hand. It was a little tender at first, but I ignored it.

There was a doctor who lived next door and I went to see him every week for the rest of the summer. He continued to remove small pieces of shrapnel from my stomach, chest, neck, head and arms. In fact, eighty years later, my body still retains a few pieces of shrapnel. I removed a tiny sliver from my face in December 2020!

On December 7, 1941, I was in the front yard playing with my lead soldiers. I had the soldiers tied to the four corners of a handkerchief. I was rolling up handkerchiefs and tossing them as high as I could, watching them float down like Army parachutes when my friend, Jim, rode up on a bike and told me of the Japanese attack on Pearl Harbor. It was one of life's moments that you never forget.

I made my own toy soldiers. I had a crucible and a bar of lead. I would heat the molten lead in the crucible over our stove and pour it into molds for lead soldiers with guns and helmets (about the size of a finger). I made an old fort out of cardboard that looked like the French Foreign Legion Forts and I played for hours with my regiment of about a dozen or more lead soldiers around the fort. I never had one moment of boredom as a boy. I was alone most of the time and I learned to stay busy.

On Memorial Day at the Davis School, our elementary school principal visited all classes wearing his Army uniform. I remember his highly polished boots and the britches of a Calvary Captain. I was quite impressed.

One sweet and delightful childhood memory was shopping for penny candy at the corner drugstore. In the back of the store was a large glass display case filled with colorful hard candy. A kindly old man with infinite patience would watch my friends and me spending several minutes deciding what we could get for a penny.

Mom and I went to a small clothing store called Barron's in West Newton. The owner, Mr. Barron, was a redheaded guy who was always there. He had dedicated one corner of his store to Cub Scouts and Boy Scouts, and that is where we bought my uniforms. Dad, for some reason, didn't want me to buy these uniforms, so I think they came out of Mom's budget.

Between the ages of 10 and 12, I would take the train into Boston by myself to go to the doctor for sinus treatments, or to the orthodontist's offices. It was about eight miles to Boston on the train, which stopped several times on the way. I was never afraid, although I didn't see other kids my age doing that. I guess my parents trusted me because I also remember going alone to Boston to buy my first suit at about the same age. I came back with a grey/blue double-breasted suit and Mom was disappointed. She didn't like it because it was double-breasted and she felt it was too formal for anything a kid would need. I felt bad about that, as I was proud of buying a suit all on my own.

Me, proud of my double-breasted suit

Grocery shopping back then was a whole different scenario. I went to the A&P with my mother, and she gave the clerk her list. He took the list and went around the store picking up the items while we stayed at the counter. The clerk piled the packages on the counter and then put things in a paper bag while he wrote each item down with a price next to it. Then he added up the total. While this was happening, lo and behold, Mom was adding each item and totaling it up-side down. It amazed me. If Mom could do this, and Dad was a frustrated CPA who could even do more, there was no way any of us could understand my inability to work with figures!

Even after inadvertently receiving my "WWI Injury," I was fascinated when WWII came along. I would often stand on the bluff overlooking Cape Cod Bay and watch the ships forming convoys preparing to go to Europe. One day, as I gazed out to sea, a P-40 Warhawk fighter plane flew along the beach at eye-level.

I was mesmerized. As the plane buzzed around a second time, it was obvious the pilot saw this young boy standing on the bluff watching him. Our eyes met. He waved and I waved back. That was the moment that I knew I wanted to be a fighter pilot – a goal that I eventually achieved.

I was in 6th grade when I saw a squadron of P-38s passing overhead bound for Bedford Airport. Friends and I jumped on our bikes and pedaled as fast as we could go – pretending we were flying airplanes. I distinctly remember leading the way on my bicycle, feeling like I was a fighter pilot. It was exhilarating then – and later, as a Jet Age "Flying Tiger," that same excitement still coursed through my body.

As the war ensued, I saw government posters all over the place – in school, in the library, in the post office – and they were

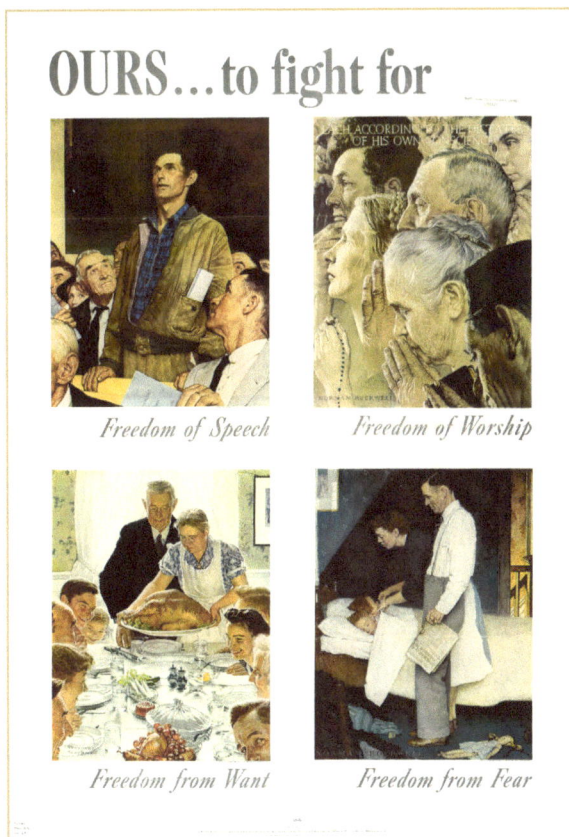

Keep us flying!
BUY WAR BONDS

...because somebody talked!

OURS...to fight for

Freedom of Speech

Freedom of Worship

Freedom from Want

Freedom from Fear

colorful and inspiring. They informed the American public about such things as war bonds, rationing, women in the workplace and the evils of fascism and racism. Some even featured fighter planes on them. Most of them were free and I began to order them from the government agencies regularly. I hung a few of the posters on my bedroom wall. The rest, I kept neatly folded and stored. By war's end, I had accumulated 265 of the posters!

Through the years, I kept that collection of WWII posters in a box and one day, sixty years later, while watching PBS "Antiques Road Show," I saw someone bring in a poster featuring Norman Rockwell's illustration of the Four Freedoms, which the appraiser estimated had a value of $1,500! That was when I realized my collection might be worth something. *See Appendix for copies of these posters.*

We have just begun to fight!

PEARL HARBOR
BATAAN
CORAL SEA
MIDWAY
GUADALCANAL
NEW GUINEA
BISMARCK SEA
CASABLANCA
ALGIERS
TUNISIA

A poster I did not sell and still have

When I brought out the box and spread them around my living room, a neighbor saw them and recommended that I share my collection for an exhibit at the Jacksonville Cummer Museum of Art & Gardens, and this I did in 2010. The exhibit was called "The Art of War." I've since sold most of my collection but still remember the thrill of receiving a new poster in the mail as a boy.

We moved to 592 Chestnut Street when I was in 7th grade. It was a nice house on a quarter acre hill with a terraced front yard that had 100 yards of 6-foot hedges in front. My job was to cut the lawn and trim the hedges nearly every day – spring, summer and fall. I had a 12" hand clipper and a push lawnmower. Dad would not buy a power mower, so I learned to sharpen and repair the push mower. Dad bought that house for $12, 500.00 back in 1943 and it is now worth about $1.7 million.

Maloney home at 592 Chestnut Street

I attended Warren Junior High School for 7th, 8th and 9th grade, barely passing but being promoted each year by the skin of my teeth. Again, my parents and family could not understand why I couldn't seem to get the academic subjects.

As a young teen, around 7th grade, it was pretty obvious that my parents didn't know what to do with me. Once, Dad took me with him in his car when he went to visit some of his friends and he left me in the car all afternoon. Another time, Mom drove to a local golf course to play golf with some of her friends and again, she left me alone in the car all afternoon. Even after I had a license and could drive her car, she often gave me some money and sent me out to a restaurant to buy my dinner and eat by myself. Many years later when I became a parent, I treated my children much differently.

I was in 9th grade at Warren Junior High the first time I kissed a girl. Her name was Helen Sims and we were at the Brae Burn Country Club pond – on the ice on a windy, cold night. That was a big thrill for me.

Another girlfriend, Ann Kimball, lived all the way across town. I rode my bicycle ten miles over to her house often, including some nights. I remember one night her parents had hired a babysitter because she had a young-

My mom and dad

er brother. I got an extension ladder from the garage and climbed up to her bedroom. Those days were innocent … we spent hours kissing and talking and then I rode my bicycle back home in the dark. She is now called Kim Smith and is married to a portrait artist in Cos Cob, Connecticut. They have two boys.

In my early teens, I spent two summer months doing farm work in Natick, Massachusetts. We'd leave home at 6:30 a.m. in the back of a stake-bed truck to work all day with a group of Jamaicans, who had been imported to do farm work because WWII was in full swing and most of the men were in the service.

I got home about 5:30 and then I had a paper route to do on my bike for the next two hours. So, it was a long day, staring at 6 a.m. and finishing around 7 p.m. I remember that all the papers had to land at the front door and it took a lot of practice to do this from my moving bike. If I missed the front door, I had to stop, walk to the front of the house and place the paper by the front door. I saved time by becoming extremely accurate at throwing the paper from my bike and I saved all of the little bit of money I made one summer, giving it to my mother to put in the bank. In fact, I still have the bank book showing a balance of $200!

Later that first summer, we went to the South Shore and I sailed. Dad was in his 40's during WWII and not eligible to go into the service, but he eventually joined the Coast Guard Auxiliary and went to guard the docks one night a week.

CHAPTER 2

HIGH SCHOOL DAYS
NEWTON HIGH SCHOOL & BELMONT HILL PREP SCHOOL

Newton High School was difficult for me. Dad insisted that I take Latin but I simply could not master any part of it, and the correct answer in math always seemed to elude me. Geometry was okay as I could see the problem. I was on the JV football team and doing well, but I was too small for the varsity. I did enjoy football at the JV level, though. Art was my only source of "feel good." I had always been a good artist and many of my pictures were displayed in the front hall cabinets of Warren Junior High.

I was somewhere around the age of 15 when Dad gave me a new single-shot 22 rifle. With fear and trepidation, I went to the local hardware store to buy a box of 22 ammunition, but they sold it to me with ease – no problem. Many years later, when I was on the United States International Rifle Team, I thought about going back to that store and telling them it was a small beginning for a big accomplishment, but I only thought about it.

It didn't take me long to become a crack shot with the 22, and I remember being in a barn loft at Tinkerbell Farm watching a woodchuck sitting atop his hole and spying one of Aunt Katherine's guests crawling across the field toward the woodchuck. He

Tinkerbell Farm, New Milford, Connecticut

was about 50 yards from the woodchuck when he took a shot and missed. The woodchuck disappeared down his hole and I just sat there, amazed that he could miss at only 50 yards.

One time when we were staying at Tinkerbell Farm, I was taken to another farm nearby to help a farmer collect his hay. There were about a dozen kids from other farms and I spent the afternoon pitching hay into wagons. I still smile when I recall the fun of interacting with all those kids. I seldom got a chance to do that when I was a boy.

Early on at Newton High School, we all took some kind of multiple- choice aptitude test and mine came out that I would be good working with my hands. This was inevitable due to my struggles in Latin and math. I went home and told Dad I was probably going to trade school at Newton High. He turned bright red. The next morning, we were on the front steps when the school opened. He told someone there that I was going to enroll in the college courses … or else!

I was tutored every week, sometimes twice a week, in Latin. I still never came close to understanding it or why I had to take it. It led to nothing that I could see, and I still feel that way to this day. I was also tutored in math during the fall, spring and summer. Still, I did the problem formulas perfectly, but came up with too many wrong answers.

One summer I was sent to St. Johnsbury Academy in St. Johnsbury, Vermont to be tutored. Many of the boys there were veterans getting prepped for the education they missed while in the military. I enjoyed the school and met a lot of interesting older guys who told me some good war stories. I don't remember what I studied. The school was run by a Dartmouth classmate of my Dad's.

As a sophomore, I thumbed a ride to high school every day – standing on the same corner and getting picked up by the same people on a regular basis day after day.

Having been held back in 1st grade, I was a year older than my classmates and when I got my driver's license at 16, I became quite popular. Mom had a black 1936 Ford Coupe. There was no backseat, but we could squeeze four in the front seat. Not only could I take my buddies around in the car, but I could now drive to my girlfriend's house instead of riding my bike ten miles back and forth – often in the dark of night! Ann Kimball and I had a great case of "puppy love" for a couple of years. I went to see her in Chatham on Cape Cod in the summers as well. Later, when I was in prep school, Ann went to our sister prep school, Dana Hall. I went to dances with her there and I remember going out to the balcony and kissing her under the moonlight. The mistress hurried out and shooed us back inside. Later, I went back to Dana Hall School as an Asbestos abatement consultant to it for nearly 20 years. A couple of times during those two decades, I stood on that balcony and relived those romantic moments, savoring the memory.

Chores, especially caring for our yard, took many afternoons after school, but I did have time to join the Newton YMCA, where I swam and ran. I soon became a member of Hi-Y and then president of the Newton Hi-Y. During the winters, I was a member of the Newton High School Hockey Team. It was an adequate team and I was just that – an adequate player.

Although I had a number of friends, including Dave Allen, Paul Lynch and Brian Mims, all from Waban, Massachusetts, my first high school years were not a happy experience. When I look back, I remember spending a lot of winters looking forward to summer at Duxbury and sailing when I should have been enjoying every day of life in Newton at high school. I look back and think about those wasted days now.

Finally, when I was a Junior at Newton High School, Dad realized I would not get into Dartmouth with the grades I was making, so he enrolled me in Belmont Hill School, an upscale prep school, as a five-day boarder. I came home on weekends. It was gut-wrenching for me to transfer to a new school and be a boarder. The new school also dealt me a blow, as my grades just weren't up to the standards of Belmont Hill School (BHS). Once again, I was forced to repeat a grade – this time as a Junior in high school.

The math master, Maynard Maxwell, tried to help me. He said, "I know you study because you get the formulas to the problems correct, but I simply don't understand why you get so many wrong answers." When I got time/rate/distance problems wrong, he commented, "Gerry, don't ever try to be a pilot." My God, that was a kick in the gut! All I wanted to be in the entire world was a fighter pilot! He told me once to come back after school and retake the test, taking as long as I wanted. Still, there was no cure for knowing the right answer in my brain and somehow unknowingly transposing the figures as I put them on paper!

The French master, John Henry Funk, also gave me more time, but I simply couldn't understand how all my classmates, starting from zero, could read and speak French in one semester and I couldn't begin to do it. Why? There was a hollow pit in my stomach daily as I entered the French class, knowing I wouldn't understand much.

Several of the teachers and students at Belmont made an impact on my life, both during and after my schooling. For instance, Roger Fenn Duncan, the school's sixth headmaster (1978-79) was the editor of the book *Cruising Maine*. I later gave him my winning Stanford Thesis on the Navy's greatest defeat on Penobscot Bay. He used my thesis in all the later editions of his book. Former classmate Truman Casner, class of '51, had a 42-foot sailboat on which I served as crew to Nova Scotia two summers from New Bedford Yacht Club, Padanaram Harbor, Massachusetts. As an Air Force Academy Counselor many years after graduating from Belmont, I met Erik C. Bertelsen, Jr., director of college counseling and teacher of American History at Belmont Hill, many times over a ten-year period. Prentice C. Downes, physiography teacher as well as coach, was probably the best teacher I ever had, including the professors at Stanford. Downes tested us by giving us several subjects and simply telling us to write all we knew about each. Then he tested us on the extent of our knowledge and graded us accordingly. He was Chief of the Army mapping services in WWII and had climbed Mt. Everest and had been to many other places all over the world. It was exciting to be in his class, which was not about dates and people as much as it was about seizing the moment and discussing adventures! He even canoed across Canada from the Atlantic to the Pacific!

I discovered, to my delight, that at Belmont Hill, I was a good football player! All the players at Belmont Hill School or the other private school leagues were about my size. We had a fair football team and I stood out. I broke my wrist in the Groton game, but it was a spiral fracture and I healed in a couple of weeks.

Belmont Hill School had one of the best hockey teams in the country – with fantastic skaters and puck handlers. I think I was the last man on that team. Most of the guys on the first and second line and defense got hockey scholarships to Harvard, Dartmouth, Yale, Princeton, etc.

Gerry Maloney #23

The ice on our outside rink was too soft for skating when the weather turned warm, so sometimes we went to Boston to an indoor skating rink at odd hours (24/7), as all of the hockey teams rented space to practice there. One night, I was late to practice and as I walked through the hall toward the locker room, a man was blocking my way. I tried to get past him and he kept blocking me until I finally held up my hockey stick and pushed by him. When I entered the locker room, I found a man trying to steal things from the team's civilian clothes. That guy outside was his guard! I was able to chase him away, using my hockey stick and shouting, and I ran out to the rink to tell the coach. He sent all the boys back to the locker room to check their clothes and make sure nothing was stolen. I think I must have gotten there just as he started rummaging, because nothing was taken. For the rest of the day, I was "the Big Cheese."

When the weather was warm and we didn't have an inside rink to go to, I went up to the school rifle range and shot my way

Belmont Hill School Rifle Team

onto the rifle team. I soon became the best shot on the team and the captain. So, my two winter sports were interchangeable. My feeling was that I didn't mind being last man on the hockey team since I was 1st string on the football team and Number One on the rifle team. Dad knew I was too small to play college football and he insisted that I practice hockey more, but I wanted to be on the rifle team. This he was totally against, telling me "You'll never get anywhere with this shooting stuff." He was wrong. He was also wrong about Latin. As I finally learned at 40 years of age, I wasn't lazy or dumb – I was Dyslexic – and neither that nor my mangled hand ever stopped me from aiming high – on the shooting range, in a sailboat, in a fighter jet, or in life.

Dad lived long enough to know the truth about my Dyslexia, but even when I told him, he never apologized for his anger at me. For instance, when I bought one of the first calculators … he was furious, saying he could add and subtract much quicker than that expensive machine!

At Belmont Hill School my best friend was Scott Rambach, also a boarder. His Dad and mine often took turns bringing us to and from school on the weekends. To this day, he remains a good friend.

One day, we had a talk with the headmaster about where to go to college. He asked me where I thought I wanted to go to college and without hesitation, I said, "Dartmouth." After a brief pause, he asked, "Why?" I was taken aback. No one had ever asked me why I wanted to go to Dartmouth. It was just a given. My Dad had taken me to Dartmouth, his alma mater, many times as I was growing up. We followed the Dartmouth football and hockey teams every week. Dad was an All-American End at Dartmouth in 1924/25. I told the headmaster, Mr. Fred Hamilton, that my Dad had sent me to Belmont Hill School so I could go to Dartmouth.

But, that one word – **WHY** – changed my life.

After a short pause, Mr. Hamilton said, "You should figure out where *you* want to go to college. So, go think about it. Now go, you're wasting my time!"

I repaid Mr. Hamilton years later when I was on the committee to pick the most outstanding Belmont Hill School person and I voted in favor of him.

Mr. Hamilton and other faculty members at Belmont Hill

Belmont Headmaster Fred Hamilton

School knew of the tremendous pressure Dad was putting on me. For instance, Dad would tell me on Sunday night, "Remember, you have a math test tomorrow … you'd better study. If you don't pass tomorrow's test, you probably won't get into college. If you can't get into college, where will your life be then?" By the time I got back to school on Sunday night, I'd be physically and emotionally sick all night. A couple of times, I kept the two house-masters up most of the night. I have no memory of how I did on the math tests, but what did matter was that the headmaster and the other faculty knew and understood about parental pressure and were in my corner.

They quietly introduced me to Stanford. I think they thought that was as far away as I could get from my father. I thought that I had discovered Stanford, which was their objective all along (thank you, masters!).

So, winter continued with me playing hockey and shooting, and making good grades except in math and French. With great help from the masters, though, my grades in those two subjects were passing. I spent my winters, as I said, looking forward to summers and sailing.

Sailing was always special to me. You had to really like to sail in those days because it took three and a half hours of preparation and clean-up for two hours of actual sailing. Today, with fiberglass hull and nylon sails, none of this is necessary, but back in the day, the prep was as follows: 1) Get the 2 hp outboard motor and check it for gas; 2) carry the motor to the beach; 3) get the two bags of sails from the house; 4) get the oars; 5) row out to the sailboat which was moored about 200 yards away; 6) fasten the outboard to the big boat; 7) open the bags of sails and put the mainsail on the mast and the gib on the bow; 8) bail out the rainwater with a hand pump; 9) pull up the sails and attach the dingy to the mooring; 10) Go sailing for a couple of hours; 11) come back and secure the sailboat to the mooring - fasten the dingy to the sailboat; 12) remove the sails and stow them in their bags; 13) remove the outboard; 14) put sails and motor in dingy; 15) before leaving, bail water out of sailboat and take inventory of the centerboard, making sure it is up and all lines, halyards and sheets are secured; 16) row back to the beach; 17) take outboard and sails back to house; 18) spread sails on the grass and hose off salt – reverse and hose off other side; 19) hang sails on special clothesline to dry; 20) put outboard in a 55-gallon drum of water and run it for five minutes to get the salt out of it; 21) pull the dingy up on the beach and anchor it above the high tide line; 22) start thinking about tomorrow's sail!

We had a beautiful Nantucket Indian Class Sailboat when I was in my mid-teens and I sailed all over Duxbury and Plymouth Bay. I used to go as fast as I could through the Duxbury marina to the yacht club dock. Then I'd come about and thread through the moored boats and back out into the bay. All my friends from school were in the Duxbury Yacht Club, but Dad refused to join. I yearned to be there, too, and I wanted to show them that I could sail better than any of them. I had a better boat than most of them but I couldn't race because we weren't members, so I spent summers racing as crew for Don Muirhead, a member of the yacht club who owned a boat. We won the division one summer, but I could have won more with my boat – the prettiest and best-handling boat around.

Boating wasn't my only adventure during the summer before my senior year at Belmont Hill School. My friend, Alden Renquist (a descendent of John Alden), and I went on a great adventure to Nantasket Beach. We wanted to ride the world famous Nantasket Beach Roller Coaster, touted to be the biggest, tallest rollercoaster in New England at the time. When we got to the arcade, it was after hours and everything was dark. We saw a ladder going up from the bottom of the rollercoaster. At age 17, we were fearless and invincible, so we promptly climbed the ladder. Getting to the top of the ladder, we realized there were steps up the side of the rollercoaster. We started up and kept going until we reached the top. I'll never forget the exhilaration of standing on the top of the tallest rollercoaster in New England, looking out on the ocean and the lights of the City of Boston, and seeing the guard walking on the arcade. He looked like a little ant. We stayed quiet up there, despite our excitement, and climbed down carefully, finally finding ourselves on the roof of a building. It

The World's Most Famous Roller Coaster in Paragon Park, Nantasket Beach, Mass.

Nantasket Beach Roller Coaster

had a trap door and we opened it. Looking inside, we saw the tunnel of love! We jumped into one of the boats and paddled our way through the tunnel of love, which was completely dark except for a few night lights. At the other end of the tunnel, we were met by the police! Quickly, we back-pedaled into the gloom and climbed out through the trap door and were then taken into custody by the waiting police.

So, the police took us to my car and upon inspection of the trunk, they found two long-handled shovels, a pickaxe and a big saw. "Aha! A whole set of burglary tools!" I had been clearing land on Otis Hill in Hingham for my Dad's construction company, but they were convinced we were crooks. We were taken to the police station and thrown into a jail cell. Our parents were called and our fathers came to pick us up. A week later, our case was arraigned in court. Judge Dewing, who presided, was our close neighbor, so we got off with a warning. The warning didn't phase me, though. There were more adventures ahead. Years later, the Judge's son, Jerry Dewing, was the head of the Veterans of Foreign Wars in Duxbury. He invited me as the Commanding General of the Massachusetts Guard, to lead the 4th of July parade in 1995, which I did. The circle of life goes on.

Leading the 4th of July Parade, Jerry Dewing to my left

In the spring, as a member of the Belmont Hill Sailing team, I went to the national championships held at and hosted by Annapolis (the U.S. Naval Academy) for a week. Belmont Hill had a great captain, Lee Quinn. He led us to the U.S. Championship and we won the Mallory Trophy. This was my first of four national championships in two different sports (one in sailing and three in shooting).

With the headmaster's approval and encouragement, I applied to Dartmouth and Stanford. I was accepted to both. Dad read the Dartmouth acceptance and without talking to me, signed the acceptance and sent in the fee. I opened the Stanford correspondence – saw the acceptance and burst out crying with joy! I signed the letter and sent my own money to Stanford.

This began a terrible tug of war between Dad and me – with Mom in between. Dad had sent notice at my birth to Dartmouth College and signed me up for the Class of '53. Many years later, I saw the note from the Dean, noting me as a future member of the class of '53. Dad had some of his fellow Dartmouth grads stop by to talk to me about how great Dartmouth was and how the school had a wonderful alumni group. They kept coming. I listened politely.

Dad did his best to try and talk me out of Stanford. He pointed out our many trips over the years to Dartmouth and how I knew the place and would feel so at home there. He pointed out that I had never even seen Stanford. I didn't know anyone on the West Coast and didn't know anyone who went to Stanford. Stanford, he said, could not hold a candle to Dartmouth academically. Still, I wanted to go to Stanford.

Finally, he said, "If you go to Dartmouth, I'll pay your way and all your expenses and get you a car. If you go to Stanford, you can pay your own way."

My poor Mom. I think she would have liked to see me get away from my Dad, but Stanford was oh so far away from home. She'd miss me. But she could not overtly commit to this feeling in front of her husband, although she did help me fill out an application for a job at Stanford.

Billings   Dud Richards   Gerry Maloney

While all this drama was happening, I was on the Belmont Hill School crew at Annapolis again at the National Sailing Championships. This time, we came in 2nd in the United States. Dudley Richards was the most capable captain, but the lack

Starting Line   Annapolis Races

Belmont Hill Wins U.S. Title At Annapolis

ANNAPOLIS, Md., June 18, (AP) —Leigh Quinn, 17-year-old yachtsman, won the 14th annual regatta of the Interscholastic Yacht Racing Association for Belmont Hill, (Mass.) School today.

Sailing through rain, Quinn's boat was first home in the final race of a four-day program in which 20 prep schools started.

Skippers and two-man crews from five schools which reached the finals sailed 26-foot knockabouts over a seven-mile triangular course in the mouth of the Severn river.

Belmont Hill won the title and the Mallor Trophy with 33¾ points. Phillips Andover of Andover, Mass., was second with 30.

Order of finish in final race; (with skippers).

1—Belmont Hill, Leigh Quinn; 2-Andover, Palmer Epler; 3-Trinity, John Hutton; 4-St. Andrews, Bob Thomson; 5-Trinity-Pawling, Braxton R. Nagel. Final point standings:
1—Belmont Hill, 33¾.
2—Andover, 30.
3—Trinity-Pawling, Pawling, N. Y., 26¼
4—Trinity, New York City, 25
5—St. Andrews, Middletown, Del., 18
(Brooks of North Andover, Mass., withdrew last night with 12 points. Finalists which withdrew previously were Choate, Deerfield, Tabor and Noble and Greenough).

of wind did us in. Dudley Richards was a good friend. He was on the U.S. Olympic Skating Team. The entire U.S. Skating team was killed in a Swiss Air Airplane crash in Europe. I think of him and our friendship often. He was the first friend to die. I read about the crash in the newspaper and felt

My woodcarving at Belmont Hill, 1950

sick to my stomach. It still makes me sad to think of him.

There is still evidence of my presence at Belmont Hill School, as every senior is required to do a small woodcarving for the walls of the school. My woodcarving was typical of my favorite pursuit – shooting a rifle.

NOTE: In one year, Belmont Hill had two on the U.S. Olympic Hockey Team (The Cleary Brothers), Dudley Richards on the U.S. Olympic Skating Team, and me on the U.S. International Rifle Team.

Mom had her sister, Aunt Katherine, come up from New York

City to bolster her courage when it came time for me to leave for Stanford. They secretly packed for me so Dad didn't see it. They were both afraid of his reaction when the "deed was done," and I was actually gone. When Dad was at work, Mom drove me to the airport; she somber and me excited … looking forward to a new adventure. I was, however, secretly worried about my academic abilities. School was never easy for me, and I knew that Stanford was a top institution. I was deep down

Gerald Stack Maloney, 1950

worried but having the Belmont Hill School work ethic helped me beat down this worry. The masters also seemed to have confidence in me and had expressed it in subtle ways. I left Belmont Hill School with better than adequate grades and a better sense of self-worth. My mother was able to convince Dad to at least pay for my tuition. I was responsible for all the rest.

I was a four-sport athlete, but too small for big time Stanford football and Stanford had no hockey team. Sailing wasn't until spring, so that left my only athletic endeavor as the rifle team. I'd try to do that.

Belmont Hill School graduating class, me (4th row, right) with Dudley Richards next to me

CHAPTER 3

STANFORD
FIRST TWO YEARS MEMORIES

The cheapest flight I could find was in an ad by Irish Air. Never had heard of it before and haven't heard of it since – it was a start-up airline with a couple of old renovated Air Corps C-46's. I bought the ticket myself with my own money and left from New York LaGuardia Airport and flew to Oakland, California. Looking at a map of the U.S., Oakland looked pretty close to San Francisco and Palo Alto. I spent the day at LaGuardia Airport dressed in a charcoal gray suit, oxford cloth button down shirt and a nice rep-tie. The airplane didn't depart until evening. When we left and climbed into the night, I was exhilarated and tingling all over. This was, so far, the biggest adventure of my life!

It was an all-night flight. We landed at Oakland in the morning. It was a warm, September day. I was way overdressed for California weather. Question? How to get to Palo Alto? I took a taxi to the Port of Oakland, then a ferry to San Francisco. I was blown away by an all-new world to me and by San Francisco Bay. The beautiful city and the boats and ships and the bridges – everything was different and new! From San Francisco, how do I get to Palo Alto? So, I was pointed to a bus station. I lugged my suitcase from the San Francisco Ferry to the bus station. It was hot and I was overdressed, but I didn't care. I was immersed in a new adventure.

The bus took me, finally, to Palo Alto, where I found a cab and asked stupidly if he knew where Stanford was. I was greeted by total silence. Of course, everyone knew where Stanford was, but I didn't. I asked another stupid question … if he knew where Toyon Hall was. He simply said, "Of course." I went to the Toyon Hall Office to check in. There was no one around except the lady – house mom. She gave me my room number on the second floor. I went and there was no one there either. I thought, "I must be early." What I didn't know was that the Stanford Welcoming Committee met students arriving by airplane at the San Francisco Airport or met the kids arriving by car and herded all new freshmen to a big freshman rally. No one comes to Stanford by bus – so no one met me.

My first class I signed up for was Air Force ROTC. I remember going to the desk and being proud of myself. I knew that I didn't want to take any math courses. Some freshman courses were mandatory – Western Civilization and a Science Course were mandatory for freshmen. I met my three room-mates, Paul Volk from Los Angeles, Pat Mahoney from San Francisco, and Paul Schwartz from somewhere in California. Pat Mahoney played tour guide and took us out the first couple of nights to show us around Palo Alto and the environs. Everything in California was all new to me. I had no car, so I was dependent on roommates to go anywhere.

The first morning at breakfast, so many freshmen seemed to know one another – much backslapping – everyone seemed to have come from someplace local. I felt down – I didn't know anybody – but that was not a new feeling for me. This was a new school that I'd never seen before, a new area. All these students and their families had gone to a university tour at some time or another, but not me. I felt lost and vowed to myself that I'd make good at this place and make friends.

I don't remember much about my freshman year except that I went to Los Angeles a few times with friends. In Los Angeles, I met Pat Tedford, the love of my life. She was 17 and I was 19. She was a senior at Marlboro Prep School. I thought she was the most beautiful girl I'd ever known. I got along well with her family and they lived in a nice home in Los Angeles. I can't describe exactly why I felt as I did about her, but there was magic. I got rides as often as I could to Los Angeles and double-dated, so we'd have transportation. We went to country club dances and other places in Los Angeles and dated for a couple of years.

Grades … they were difficult. Freshman classes were huge – four or five hundred people would meet in a big hall on Monday to listen to a lecture from a well-known professor. Then the classes broke up on Wednesdays and Fridays into groups of 20 or so for discussion. I was okay on note-taking, but when the examinations came, I had a hard time with the recall, even knowing that I had studied the subjects. I could even close my eyes and see a picture that was on the page I'd studied, but I could not recall the information I knew I had recently read. This was a Dyslexic problem. I can't tell you how frustrating this was – knowing as I walked away from the exam, that I was then able to recall the answers I hadn't been able to recall on the tests. My recall was slow then and it still is.

I wanted to do a sport, so I found out where the university rifle range was. I went there after classes one day. I met the range officer who was an old Army master sergeant. I asked him what to do about getting myself on the rifle team. He directed me to a stack of target rifles, told me to pick one and go site it in. Then he gave me two paper targets with ten bulls eyes on each. He then told me to go shoot. I did. I shot twenty times. I got twenty bullseyes – a perfect score. He viewed my targets and said, "Hmmm, good. You are now on the Stanford Rifle Team."

I then sent for my own rifle. The sergeant said, "Come any time. I'm always around. Later, he then introduced me to the rest of the team – about ten people. One was Jon Lindberg, son of Colonel Charles Lindberg. Another was Derrick Bok, the future president of Harvard University.

I was used to the semester system – two semesters per year. Here, we had the quarter system. Any three quarters constituted a good complete year. I took the summer quarter off. Evidently, I was not required to take any math. I did have to take a science. I dreaded this, since so much of science is memory of a million formulas. I took biology and hated it. Dissecting animals is not my thing. I did, however, pass it. But my overall grades were still not good. Grading was on the curve – so damn many smart kids – always competition. I now realize that ingrained competition was good. It keeps you one step ahead all through life.

The first week of school, I interviewed for a job – filled out the forms and got a job waiting on tables at Branner Hall, a girls' dorm. That took care of my lunch and evening meals. Branner was full of lovely, bronzed, statuesque California girls. I got along well with them – in fact, on their birthdays, each of them got to choose the waiter who would bring them their birthday cake. Then they got to kiss the waiter. I delivered cakes and kisses regularly. I was a waiter at Branner for all four years.

No matter how much I studied, I couldn't seem to be able to get good grades. I was too often on the backside of the curve. I did, however, get all A's in Air Force ROTC. My Dad, a frustrated CPA, insisted I take economics. I did and I flunked it. He still couldn't understand my problems with figures and numbers and neither could I. He insisted I repeat economics. I did this - and had help this time – still flunked it. For my language, I took French, met an understanding teacher in an understanding modern language department, but still, I flunked French. The older grey-haired teacher took me aside and confided to me that they (the modern language department) knew that for some unknown reason, some people could not learn a foreign language. She said they (the foreign language department) had set up a course to help those of us with this unusual problem. She said, "There is no reason an intelligent person like you shouldn't graduate with your foreign language requirement completed." So, she took me up to the foreign language office and they put me in a single class – solo. I was given a French magazine each week and told to read certain chapters in French. At the end of each week, I was quizzed on the content of the magazine. I found that I couldn't hear the language, process it or speak it – I could, however, read it and absorb it. I got reasonably good at this aspect of the course. I completed the two quarters required – so forward thinking of Stanford – they did not know about Dyslexia, which had not yet been identified – but they knew how to teach an individual in a unique way. My hat's off to a big institution for taking a freshman and setting him up in a special class of one.

The Stanford rifle team traveled in an Army ROTC van to other colleges in Northern California. Other teams traveled to Stanford. I ended up with the highest scores on our team. We did okay in the league – I can't remember our league standings. The Air Force ROTC also had a rifle team and I ended up Number one on that team, too. I ended up winning the most points on both teams.

At the end of the year, Colonel Barrett, the professor of Air Science, presented me with a medal for superior marksmanship at a parade. I was the only freshman in the Air Force ROTC to get a medal at that parade.

Colonel Barrett arranged to get me selected Captain of both teams in my sophomore year. So, after knowing no one in my class and having never before seen Stanford, in one year I had gotten a job, made the best university marksman, become captain of two teams, and was pledged by a top Fraternity – Delta Kappa Epsilon (DEKE), but … many of my grades were still not up to par.

Freshman year summer, I was so in love with Patricia that I bummed a ride to Santa Barbara where her family lived. I slept on my fraternity brother, Donald Harcourt's porch nearby. I had no car, so I borrowed a bike to commute to Pat's home. I bor-

Colonel Barrett presenting me with medal

rowed a car from Harcourt (of publishing fame) for some dates. I wandered around in love-infused daze for a month. Then, somehow, I got home. I vowed to come back my sophomore year with a car of some kind and I did get a car cheap – a '41 Ford wagon. The wood was somewhat rotten – but so cheap. I used lots of glue on that car.

Sophomore year began. I moved into the Deke fraternity house and met my pledge brothers, and then went through the usual initiation … a lot of unpleasant, difficult things. I missed work at Branner Hall for the first time in a year and a half, but they understood about fraternity initiation.

Toyon Hall and Branner Hall got together to do Christmas Decorations and since I had worked at Branner Hall as a freshman, I was put in charge – probably because I already knew so many girls there. I met Loni Holmes – and was smitten. We worked together on Christmas stuff and started dating. We dated most of the remainder of the winter. She never returned for

41' Ford Wagon, broken down in Arizona

spring quarter. Her girlfriends said that her old boyfriend came, took her away and married her.

At the end of the first quarter of my sophomore year, I was placed on academic probation. I had a meeting with my faculty advisor and the two options were 1) to leave school and return next year or, 2) stay for the next quarter, but I must make up my entire deficiency in this next quarter. This was not recommended. The faculty advisor said that prep school study habits might help me, but his advice was for me to leave and return the next year. I knew if I left, I would never be able to return, so I had a long talk with myself and decided to stay. I would only study – no dates, no beer, no Friday afternoon parties. I still did not understand that I had Dyslexia.

The probation notice was sent from Stanford to my draft board back in Massachusetts. I had now lost my deferment. This was serious in view of the Korean War. The correspondence from the draft board notified me of my eligibility for the draft. The Korean War was going full-blast. The Deke house president got drafted away from Stanford and into the Army. Not knowing for sure what to do, I took the draft notice to the ROTC headquarters and asked them what I should do. There were 750 guys in my Air Force ROTC Unit – it seemed improbable to me that they would know me from anybody else. At that point, I was only a sophomore. However, I soon found out they did know me – they knew me because I was Captain of the Air Force Rifle Team and their Number One Shooter and I had won their Marksmanship Medal.

I spoke to the Major and gave him the notice and he disappeared into the office. I stood there on pins and needles. What could they do? After a while, the Major came back. They had a plan. We sat down and he asked if I was going to stay that quarter. I said yes. He wanted to know if I really thought I would be able to make up my grade average for reinstatement. I answered yes. So, here was the plan. "We at the ROTC headquarters will sign this notice instead of you. We know this is incorrect. You have two weeks to return this notice. Wait the two weeks. Then mail it back to Massachusetts draft board. Do not use air mail. We figure a week to get there – a week on somebody's desk – a week to get back to you. When the notice comes back, you wait the two weeks to return it – slow mail again – but sign it in the wrong place this time. Another two to three weeks, you get the paperwork done correctly." What a plan! Meantime, I got notice to go to San Francisco for their pre-induction physical. Please note that my grades are vastly improved, having done nothing but study thus far in the quarter - with an A, as usual, in AFROTC.

I drove to San Jose to take a train to San Francisco. A lot of guys were standing around on the train platform ready to go to San Francisco for their pre-induction physicals. The sergeant came up and yelled, "Anybody here in the ROTC?" I very proudly raised my hand. The sergeant said to me, "Okay, form them up and march them to the train." My God, my heart was in my mouth. I'm just a basic cadet – never ordered anyone anywhere yet. But then, none of the guys in the crowd knew that I was scared to death and they wouldn't know if I made a mistake. So, somehow I formed them up and marched them to the train. Wow! I went to San Francisco and passed my pre-induction physical.

Sometime later, I went back to San Francisco and took my pre-induction written test – then back to Stanford. It was almost to the end of the quarter and my induction was imminent – so the colonel called the Dean of Students and asked that I be allowed to take all my exams in the first two days rather than spread out over the whole exam week. Then he and the dean agreed that the professors would immediately correct my exams and telephone the Dean, and the Dean would telephone the results to the colonel immediately. I passed all of my exams – got all A's and B's. The Dean verbally reinstated me. The Colonel sent a telegram to my draft board in Massachusetts that I was reinstated in school and my deferment should be reactivated. Just ahead of the draft! Whooo Hoooo! I felt so grateful to Stanford – that an institution the size of Stanford would go out of its way to help me. Over the next week or so, I began to realize the lengths that all of them went to on my behalf. I'm still awed that it happened. I didn't know then but I know now that it was another instance of a higher power in my life.

The outcome of all the machinations of so many at Stanford to keep me from being drafted was this: Instead of digging four-foot foxholes in the dirt of Korea, I ended up flying a fighter jet 40,000 feet over Korea.

As a sophomore, my grades remained about the same. I remained in the Delta Kappa Epsilon Frat House and was busy with chores as Captain of the University and ROTC Rifle Teams. Among the chores was scheduling firing matches. I went to most of the other colleges in the area and also organized postal matches with teams all around the country. As President of the Rifle Club, I did the usual arranging and get-togethers and letting those interested in just shooting for fun get range time. We always coordinated with the Army Sergeant. Captain Barko, U.S. Army, was in charge of all aspects of the range. The range building and club house was an old WWI Army building originally meant to house the horses.

I met and dated several girls in my sophomore year. I had little to no money. If you had a dime, you could have a coffee date. One cup of coffee cost five cents. I spent a few weekends with friends in San Francisco, and Christmas week found me working for the post office. I got quickly used to the route up and down through the San Francisco hills. I spent Christmas of my sophomore year in San Francisco with Ann Matherson and her family, as I had been dating her through the fall and winter. Her father, a surgeon, was a Reserve Major General assigned to U.S. Army Medical Corps. Ann made no appearance at Spring quarter. It was the old story ... she had gone back to an old boyfriend and eventually married him.

The last week of school, frat elections were held. The new President asked me to be business manager for the house – to collect all dues, buy all food and house supplies, pay the cook, run the new pledges on assigned tasks to keep the house inside and outside. I got free room and board – this was important. I also got $100 a quarter from AFROTC. Now I had basic costs covered.

Books were very expensive. I raided the frat library and could get most books that were only one or two years old for my classes. The rest, I read in the library or borrowed from the library. I may be the only Stanford University Graduate to leave school with no books.

My '41 Ford wagon was reglued wood all over, then repainted to look like new. Compound and wax shine paint worked! I sold the car for decent money.

And so went most of my sophomore year. Near the end of the year, I entered my first outdoor shooting tournament at Santa Barbara. The Semina Nautica Celebration. I borrowed a mat (which all prone shooters lie on) and a 20-power spotting scope. The entry fee, gas, and ammunition took up most of my money, and left none for food. I was able to get some food from Branner

Hall kitchen to travel there. I didn't do well, but I did get three medals. My first three from outdoor tournaments.

At the end of the school quarter, I went home and worked for Gerald S. Maloney Company in construction for the summer and saved all my money.

I looked for another car at home, finding and falling in love with a '48 Lincoln Coupe. You should never fall in love with a car – it clouds your judgment.

I left for Stanford University with Winty Harrington, a Belmont Hill School graduate, in my new car. The Lincoln used so much oil that we had to stop every 200+ miles and refill, buying oil in 3-gallon cans. This time, we went the northern route to Canada – Niagara Falls and back to the U.S. through Windsor and Detroit, Michigan. The Canada rural route was nice. Then we took the famous Route 66 all the way to the West Coast. There was no U.S. route yet. We found all kinds of places to pull over and roll out on the ground beside the car into sleeping bags. We woke up one morning in a pig run – surrounded by pigs. They were only a little annoyed at having to go around us. Another night, we found a rural church open and slept on the carpeted floor. We found out in the morning that it was an African American church. The janitor was friendly.

We stopped in Salt Lake City at a friend's house. The Lincoln's engine erupted and stopped – that was the end of it. Our friends found a Ford dealer with an engine from a wrecked Ford, so we replaced the useless worn-out engine with a relatively new Ford V-8 and set out on our way to Stanford for Junior year.

CHAPTER 4

STANFORD
THE LAST TWO YEARS

Back at school I did the usual sign up for classes, search for books, sign into Branner Hall as a third-year waiter, got the frat house organized, and checked in with ROTC and rifle range sergeant.

During the first week, we had a mixer with girls' house across the street. I met and had immediate chemistry with one of the sophomores. I thought her name was Joan Denny, we had coffee and got acquainted. Soon, the frat brothers were kidding me about dating Jack Benny's daughter – I had no idea! For three days, I thought her name was Denny – not the famous actor/comedian's daughter, Benny. So began thirty-six years of a very intense relationship – more on this later.

Joan Benny, 1953 in Yosemite Valley

Soon, the ROTC Colonel and staff picked me

as the new Cadet Colonel. They interviewed me first. I already knew most of them after two years of being Captain of ROTC Rifle Team and Captain of Drill Team. When they selected me as the new Cadet Colonel, I was aware that it required a lot of extra-curricular work.

Also, at the start of ROTC 3rd year, many of the group are culled and don't go beyond the 2nd year. Still about 750+ cadets were in AFROTC alone – almost the same in Army and Navy. The Korean draft wanted everyone.

Closely interfacing with active-duty officers and sergeants gives good insight into the various workings of a real Air Force Unit. I liked the Sergeants. They help me a lot. My grades continued okay. I had to pick a major and I thought I wanted "industrial design." My interview with the head professor went okay. I was good at art in Junior High and High School. I wrote Dad, feeling good about choice, but Dad immediately wrote back NO. He insisted that I drop this "arty foolishness" or he wouldn't even pay tuition. So, I settled on history. I couldn't do sciences, couldn't seem to memorize hundreds of formulas; it couldn't have anything to do with figures – so history ended up being my major.

Meanwhile, Joan and I became very close. She called her Dad every Sunday night after his broadcast. When Hollywood actors came to San Francisco in person for their stage shows, Jack told them to send Joan two tickets. So, we went to a number of shows in San Francisco, getting third row center seats. It was the usual thing for Joan, but a big deal for me. We usually got invited backstage to have one-on-one with actors. I learned quickly "who's who in Hollywood."

We discussed marriage. I knew I couldn't get married – no money, no job and four years of Air Force coming – but we talked of it. Between Joan, ROTC, shooting, gun club, being house manager and waiting tables at Branner Hall, I was kept busy all of my junior year.

One day I got a call to go see the Professor of Air Science,

Col. Barrett. The Colonel told me that he had just heard about my hand. I showed it to him. I was missing the ends of two fingers and the end of my thumb. He was concerned that I couldn't do all the things a pilot has to do with his hands. He asked me to pick up and maneuver some things on his desk. He saw that I had full use of my hand and fingers. Then, I think, not willing to dismiss me from the flight program himself, he said, "Let's see what the Air Force regulations say." He pulled a blue book of Air Force Regulations off his bookcase. After a couple of agonizing minutes, he found a page on hands. He read aloud to me. "You may be missing the digital extremities of two, but no more than two fingers." He looked at my hand and saw only two digital extremities were missing. I gave a sigh of relief.

Then, looking at my thumb, he turned a few pages and found a reference to thumb. The paragraph said, "You may be missing the digital extremity of one, but only one, thumb, and you must have an operable joint." Looking at my thumb, as I held up my hand, it appeared there was no joint. He looked sad. I think it was because he was about to disqualify me from the flight program. He started to close the book, but before he could say more, I held up my hand and wiggled my thumb joint. He said something I didn't catch because I was so relieved. Then he opened the book of regulations and again read me the page and paragraph on the finger and thumb. He said, "Write these down and keep them always with you. You will be challenged when you go to a new base. The flight surgeons review the history of each new pilot who reports in."

I was challenged, true to his word, at the next two training bases shortly after I reported in. In each case, each flight surgeon expressed surprise that I had gotten that far with, as one put it, only half a hand. In each case, I pulled my notes out and said, "Read this." Thank goodness for Colonel Barrett's warning.

Seemingly, we in the flight program were always taking written tests. I guess I passed them all. One day we all had to complete an extremely comprehensive medical form. It took a couple of hours to complete and I even had to call my Mom about some of the answers. In being completely truthful, I had answered four questions:

Ever faint? Yes

Sinus? Yes.

Back problems? Yes

One other which I can't remember. Yes

A day or so later, a tall Air Force Sergeant who I had never seen before found me and asked me to come meet with him. We went to a quiet corner in an empty classroom. He asked me about fainting. I told him a dentist was drilling a tooth when I was a boy and hit a nerve. I fainted. He asked me how long I was out and I told him a few seconds.

He asked me about my sinus problem – how did I know I had one – and I told him my Mom said I had sinus.

He asked me about my back problems and I told him I had hurt my back in a JV Football game and the doctor said to lay off contact sports for a while. I told him that since then I had played four years of football and four years of ice hockey with no problems.

So, without further ado, he pulled out two blank pages of the medical evaluation and said, "Let's fill out this new questionnaire." I said, "Oh, it took so long to fill out the first one – let's just white it out and change the answers." He looked at me and didn't say anything and let the completed survey fall to the floor. I immediately bent down to retrieve it. To this day, I can see his black boot in front of my face, stomping on the pages on the floor. He said, in no uncertain tones, "Do you really want to be a pilot?" Of course, I replied in the affirmative. Then, he said, we will fill out a new health survey. At that time, I didn't realize that any one of those four things would have disqualified me for flight training. The Sergeant saved my life, so to speak, and I never saw him again. I still wonder where he came from and where he went.

Joan Benny and I got pinned. This was a big deal between two people in the 1950's … don't know about now. That night, while I was working at Branner Hall, I heard all the girls serenading someone. Then I realized they were serenading me about getting pinned to Joan. I don't know how they all seemed to know about it and got themselves organized. I have always remembered that night.

Studies came easier in the third year as I had integrated myself into the academic system. I didn't spend the grinding hours studying as I had previously. The one thing that had plagued me and still did was that during an examination I'd be answering a question that I couldn't recall the answer to. I say, "recall", because I remembered studying that and could even remember the picture or illustration on the page, so I knew for certain that I had recently studied that item. Then – much to my chagrin – the answer would always seem to pop into my head on the way home after completing the exam. Again, part of my Dyslexia is "recall." I have always had the same problem with peoples' names. I can't instantly recall someone's name, but the name pops into my consciousness as I walk away. It was and is very frustrating.

When spring quarter came, Joan didn't return. She called me and said she had gone to NYC and met a tall, dark, handsome rich Jewish man and on the spur of the moment, gotten engaged. She always said nobody in Hollywood liked her mother, Mary Livingston, Jack Benny's wife and partner in his shows. She did this to spite her Mom. She came back to school later for a few days and we carried on as before.

Mr. and Mrs. Jack Benny invited me to the reception. I still have the invitation. I think back, growing up in Junior High and listening every Sunday night to Jack Benny – and as Jack Benny ended his broadcast, he said, "Good night Joanie." I asked my mother who Joanie was and Mom told me the Benny's had adopted a little girl. How could I know that my future would be loosely tied with hers for many more years to come. The wedding was small but the reception was huge. Mr. Benny spent the equivalent of about $500,000 in today's dollars. At the reception, a lady came up to me, introduced herself as Miss Valence. I knew her name, as Joan had often referred to her. She was Joan's governess. She confided in me, "there are three people here who know this whole thing is a farce – you, me and Joan." She said she was glad to meet me, as Joan had often spoken of me. She hugged me and left.

I returned to school with feelings of deep loneliness. It was like I had a heavy knot in my stomach. Joan never lost contact with me. We saw one another many times over the years and in 2021, I was saddened to hear of her passing.

I spent some months during that year earning money painting houses around Palo Alto and Menlo Park. One senior student who had flunked out had organized this little group. He was our salesman, organizer and accountant. He stayed around because he was afraid to tell his parents he'd flunked out. Too bad, because he realy was smart.

I went home to our summer cottage on Duxbury Bay that summer and did a lot of sailing with four friends that I had grown up with – Alden Renquist, a descendant of John Alden who lived in Duxbury (John Alden's house is now a museum); Don Muirhead, with whom I had crewed one summer on his Duxbury Duck class

Beach House – Duxbury Bay

sailboat, who later became a doctor; and Bill Ryer, an MIT Grad who later became an independent consultant.

Our Duxbury Cottage was a 2-story, 5-bedroom summer place built in 1902 – on its own beach on Duxbury Bay – still with its now unused outhouse. Duxbury Bay is the other half of Plymouth Bay. We could stand on the porch and look across the bay and see the replica of the Mayflower on the Dock at Plymouth. Our property was on a farm once owned by Captain Miles Standish, military leader of the Plymouth Colony. His old homestead was two blocks away and now is a small park. The hole which was his cellar is still there.

The property immediately next to us was originally owned and occupied by Elder William Brewster, the spiritual leader of the Plymouth Colony. In fact, the lilacs he brought from Holland and planted are still there and still blooming. They are marked by a granite marker. Across the water directly to the east one mile away is Clark's Isle. This island is named for the Mayflower Boswain who helmed the ships longboat to this isle during a December storm in 1620. He was the first pilgrim to set foot in

Clark's Isle Picnic – 1982 – Maloneys, MacDonalds, cousins

Plymouth. Clark's Isle was also the place where the first Thanksgiving was held.

Every year in August, there is something called the Clark's Isle picnic. There is a big rock in the center of the isle which has been named pulpit rock, so-named because for as long as anyone can remember, a church service has been held there in August yearly. In big letters on the face of the rock is chiseled "Thanksgiving 1621." Many years later, when my family came back from California and lived in Duxbury, our tradition of the Clark's Isle picnic continued.

I always looked forward to spending the day there. There is no electricity, no running water, sewage, or road. There are six to eight houses – all still owned by descendants of the original Plymouth Colony settlers. They are in turn occupied all summer as the original descendants come and go. The same paths still lead to and from the houses and to the wells.

Standish Shore and our cottage have always been a magical place for me and for most of the residents on the end of the point. All the houses on Standish Shore Peninsula, except two, were summer cottages. After Columbus Day all the houses were dark. All the leaves were off the trees – there were no street lights. Occasionally, Dad and I drove to Duxbury in the winter to check on the cottage. I got an eerie feeling throughout my whole body … so dark, so many big trees with a million intertwined black branches forming almost a spider web over and around me. It was a chilling feeling that I remember to this day.

The saddest day of my year was when Dad and I went to close up the house, drain the water and cut off the electricity. We never locked the door. I can still to this day recall the feeling of deep-seated sadness as we departed the house for the year. The next saddest day was when we took the sailboat out of the water for the winter and loaded it on the trailer to tow it home.

The garage had 3 small changing rooms in the back. In the early 1900s, people left the house fully dressed – then went to the rear of the garage and changed from street clothes to bathing clothes and walked across the lawn to the beach.

Dad removed the changing rooms so that our 21' sailboat bow would fit in the garage for its winter storage.

Back at Stanford in my senior year, still steeped in the history at Duxbury, I was destined to receive the highest honors in the country – in history!

My history professor, Dr. Miller, encouraged me to write my thesis about the Penobscot Expedition. He had written one or two history books on the American Revolution, but when I asked him about the Penobscot Expedition, neither he nor Dr. Bailey, the head of the history department, knew much about it – only that it was a military defeat and had been all covered up.

One thing that was not covered up was the court martial of the famous Paul Revere – more about him later. Admiral Saltonstall was the head of the Naval part of the Penobscot expedition which consisted of approximately forty plus ships (many of which were armed privateers). A number of the ships were transports. Many of the soldiers were conscripts – poorly armed and poorly trained. The British had three warships anchored in Castine Harbor, Maine. Admiral Saltonstall refused to risk any of his ships in attacking the three British man-o-war ships even though the Continental Navy had the British out-gunned. The Continental armada cruised around for a week or more before finally discharging the soldiers on to the shore.

The British Commander, General Francis McLean, thought, from looking at the number of ships, that he must be facing 5,000 Continental troops when, in actuality, there were only 2,500. The Continentals approached the partially finished fort and prepared to attack. The British Commander had prepared all of his troops to retreat off the peninsula, and he had the British flag halyards in his hand ready to concede the colors. He told all his troops to fire once at the Continentals in the woods and retreat to the prepared place. The Continentals all fired and then the British fired, and when the smoke cleared, the British were picking up and preparing to retreat when they saw that the Continentals had all run. The British Commander secured the flag and did not concede. The Continentals all reboarded their ships and argued and procrastinated about what to do next.

Twenty-one days after their arrival, a British fleet appeared at the headwaters of Penobscot Bay. This blocked the exit to the ocean and back to Massachusetts. Seeing this, the Continentals and all of their ships headed up the Penobscot Bay to the narrows of the Penobscot River, followed by the British warships. There being nowhere to go, the ships were – one after the other – beached and burned. The crews then commenced the long walk back to Boston. Today, archeologists are still discovering remnants of the fleet.

The Stanford History Department submitted my paper to the National Society of Colonial Dames of America and I was informed by the History Department that I had won the 1954 National Scholarship Award from that organization, which included a $100 check (Big money in those days!)

I also won second place in the Stanford University Speech Contest in 1954 – It was, of course, a speech on Shooting Safety.

The A's I got in ROTC offset the D's I received in some other subjects. The Korean war was over in 1954 when I graduated from Stanford. ROTC knew the Air Force now did not need as many officers, so one of the ROTC Majors took me aside and said, "If you don't want to go in the service at all, we will lose your file." They knew a lot of people would not get commissioned. I said, "I absolutely want to go. I want to be a fighter pilot."

CHAPTER 5

AIR FORCE
1954-1985

Basic Training

I reported to pre-flight training at Lackland Air Force Base in Texas. We had six weeks indoctrination into basic Air Force functions, one part of which was the warning that all the girls from all the little towns where our flight training bases were located would want to marry us and get out of their little towns to travel the world. So, we were warned, "Be careful – you are not the greatest lovers in the world, but you will be pursued for their interests." It was the best advice ever.

Eventually, we got orders to go to initial flight training. I was posted to Hondo Air Base - 40 miles out of San Antonio in the desert – for primary flight training.

We flew Piper Cubs for the first 15 hours. That was an inexpensive way to find out if each person had any ability to fly. I could fly, but I couldn't seem to land. The instructor took extra time with me. He knew I could fly and that I had to learn to land. Learning to fly in three dimensional (the ability to go up, down and sideways) is not like playing a two-dimensional sport. You have to get used to it all. I'd close my eyes and go through all the

Jet Age "Flying Tiger", Korea 1956, my's F-86 Sabre Jet

procedures with my hand on the imaginary stick and go through them and through them and through them … then when he'd say "steep left turn" I knew I could do it. I knew, when I was through with that good instructor, that I could fly.

One time while flying the cub, the tower called all the cubs in the air to say the wind had changed, so the runway had changed. Therefore, we had to establish a new landing pattern. All of the other cubs milled around in the air. No one wanted to be the first to lead in the new landing pattern. "Well," I said to myself, "I know what to do, so I'll do it." I set up the new landing pattern and all the other students followed my lead.

Then we flew the T-6 (we called it the Terrible Texan) – a 1935 prop airplane with a big radial engine. I got in the front seat, looked out on the wings and saw the Air Force insignia, and I knew that I was in a real Air Force airplane. There was a whole scenario of things you had to do to master this type of flying. The instructor tried to make you angry and upset – tried to make you screw up – because if you lose your temper, you're not there anymore. They said 25% of the class would never be able to complete the program and get their wings. There were four people to a table and one instructor. Some mornings, there would be only three people at the table – someone had washed out and was gone. We had to focus on our own flying and not dwell on those who were gone.

We spent a half-day in academics and the other half of the day flying. Academics, as always, were rough, but the flying – oh, the flying – I loved to fly. I loved acrobatics!

There was so much memory in this training. I tried so hard. I wasn't getting good grades and the instructor was unhappy with me. He said, "You have the best education of anybody in this class and you're getting C grades – you need to study more." I'd heard this before. I'd heard it all my life. There was so much to memorize – instruments – emergency procedures, etc. We had thick books in ground school, but somehow – faced with all of these challenges, I was able to pass – I think it was pure perseverance. I wanted so badly to fly. Although I was never an academic, I was a whiz at flying and shooting. I was the last guy to solo in the Cub, but the first officer to finish the T-6 program two weeks early. So, I went out every day by myself and flew acrobatics. The T-6 was fun to fly - it was a forgiving airplane.

We had six more months of training, which would be in jets. They told me to pick three jet bases, but as usual, I didn't get any of the three I picked. Laredo AFB (not my choice) was what I got.

One day, while at the jet base, I went to the range to fire an issue 45 handgun. I had hoped to qualify as an expert and I did. In fact, I did well enough that the base pistol team made me a member. Pretty good, I thought, for a student here to make it to the base team! I practiced with them a couple of times in between my classes and flying schedule. Then I finished up, got my wings, and left before we could do any competitive shooting.

My flying class was the last class to have the old World War II

T-6. The Air Force had upgraded to the T-34s and the T-28s. My jet instructor told us that we might lose half the class because it was a big jump from a 1935 era T-6 to a modern jet.

Unlike my previous caring instructor, this instructor loved to fly the airplane. He would show me a maneuver and then tell me to do it. Usually, I didn't get it right the first time, but instead of letting me do it until I did it right, like my previous instructor, this one would do it two more times himself, which didn't help me at all. I knew I had a good basic grounding in flying – and I was really good in the air – but this instructor landed the airplane every time. Once, I took my hand off the stick at 120 knots on final approach and the stick was moving – I landed it but I could feel his hand on the stick.

When I soloed, I realized that I had never really landed the airplane alone, so I botched the landing. My senior flight instructor knew about the other poor instructor. He said, "Don't worry. I know about that guy. We have to give you a check ride." When we went out for the check ride, he told me, "I'm putting my hands up here, so you can see them, and you will do all the flying." I could see in my mirror that his hands were up and visible all during the flight. I did the air work, landed three times and all was well.

Note: The T-33 was the first jet trainer. Our first jet fighter was the F-80 – a single seat, single engine fighter. The Air Force put a second cockpit in it so the instructor could go up with a new pilot. We went from 60 knots landing approach speed in a T-6 to over 120 knots landing approach speed in a jet. The T-33 was a beautiful plane to fly. We all became capable of all aspects of flying through instrument flying, acrobatics, all emergency procedures, unusual attitudes and so forth.

When I first met my jet instructor, he briefed us on all the aspects of flying that we would be learning. Then he opened a page of our one-inch-thick instruction manual and said, "In six months, you will be able to tell me what's on any given page." I thought to myself how hard it had always been for me to memorize anything, but by the time I graduated, I was nearly as conversant as he predicted. I had 125 hours in the T-6, 120 in the T-33 and 15 hours in the Piper Cub. By this time, we could take off and fly around a half a dozen states at night or in the clouds, and by using only our instruments and never seeing the ground, we'd land where we were supposed to. It was absolutely unbelievable to me that I could do that! During the next several years, I was faced with doing that a number of times. The wonder of it never left me.

Night Flying Training – A Heavenly Intervention

Near the end of jet training, we went out on what is called a "round-robin." What it is – you fly an upside-down triangular course 200 miles in one direction, 200 miles across the top of a triangle, and 200 miles back to the home base. Each student fills out a log of the entire round robin - his compass heading to a town which is usually his first turning point. He then estimates his speed and the time he will arrive and the fuel he should have left. He does this for each of the three segments. Before he takes off, he must have all of the figures and calculations checked and approved by his instructor. This way, he will catch any mistakes the pilot might make. As the student flies, he fills in the actual figures such as the actual time he turned over the first place and how much fuel he actually had. He did this again on the next two segments.

This particular training flight was at night. Each turning point was over a southwest Texas town. In the middle fifties, southwestern Texas was sparsely populated, so at each destination a small lighted town stood out. This usually made a night-training flight easy.

I took off in my T-33, climbed as prescribed, left Laredo AFB behind and headed on my computed compass heading. All calculations were double-checked, the appointed arrival time when

I should have seen the first town. I saw nothing. Everything was dark. At 35,000 feet on a clear night, you should be able to see 100 miles. I saw nothing. A little apprehensive, I turned to my next heading. I wrote down the time I expected to be over this first turn and the amount of fuel. I proceeded on the proper new heading to the next town or turning point. I still saw nothing. I noted my fuel-state, which was exactly as programmed, but I never saw the town. I then, with fingers crossed, turned on a new compass heading for home-base. I still saw nothing. This was very worrisome. I couldn't understand why I had not even seen car headlights on the road. Soon, I saw lights of a city ahead, right on the nose of the airplane. So, exactly on my computed time, I arrived over Laredo AFB, with the exact pre-computed fuel state. I landed. My instructor met me, very happy that I had completed this training flight right on my exact time with the exact correct fuel state.

The next morning, I tried to figure out where I went. Why did I never see anything? I recomputed everything, looking at a map. I should have seen each town which were my turning points. I do not know to this day where I went. Now, after all these years, I see the hand of heavenly intervention. I believe my guardian angel set out to prove to me what he/she could do, and now, years later, I think I understand.

I was academically in the middle of the class when I graduated from flight school. I never sought to be first academically. I graduated with 120 hours of jet time. Before we got our wings, we had a check ride with instruments, a check ride for emergency procedures and a check ride for standardization procedures so that every pilot flies the same way and each knows what to expect of the other. After mastering these and numerous other things, we got our wings.

An example of the training we were put through: while flying in the middle of a loop, the instructor would pull the power from the engine while you were upside down, then scream and yell at you to get you upset and disoriented (if he could) – and say, "What are you going to do – the engine quit!" Per the instruction book, I had to recite the proper procedures of flying with no engine. "The proper procedure is to fly at 150 knots. The glide ratio is 10 to 1 for this airplane. We are at 30,000 feet. We should be able to go 80 miles, taking into consideration the wind behind us. So, we'll have to glide seventy miles or so to our base," which I did.

We also simulated a flame-out landing (no engine) procedure as follows: Arrive over the end of the runway at 6000 feet – hold 150 kts airspeed and begin a left descending turn. If you maintain a proper airspeed and proper bank, the airplane will arrive at the runway ready to land without the use of the engine. The instructor challenged me to save enough speed as we landed so that we could turn off the runway and park. I did. I finished all my checks early again – and went out and did acrobatics every day for ten days.

Everybody in the class receives their wings on the same day. For me, it was the culmination of a lifetime. Now I was an Air Force Pilot. We could pick where we wanted to go. Some picked Germany or Europe, but I picked Korea – and everybody looked at me like "are you nuts?" I was assigned to Korea (K-55). I considered Korea to be where the action was and I was right. They were still shooting at each other, even though we had an armistice. The Air Force was being challenged by the North Korean Air Force. There was not much shooting, but we had to be careful.

A friend on his first flight in Korea in an F-86 went out with a wingman, doing orientations, and they got separated. The leader called radar and asked them to help get them back together. Soon, a voice from North Korea, in perfect English, told the new F-86 pilot to turn right. Then our radar guy said, "Turn left – head South." These instructions from the North Korean Radar and the U.S. Radar totally confused the new pilot in his first Korean orientation flight. Eventually, before he ran out of fuel, he realized-what was happening and turned South. When he did run out of fuel, he was over South Korea when he ejected from his F86. So, chalk one up for North Korea.

On the way to Korea, a couple of WWII captains gave us good advice. They said, "You can talk your way into almost anything overseas – the rules are relaxed." I told them, "We're supposed to go to a fighter squadron." The general who gave us our wings had told us that everybody who gets their wings is going to an operating squadron.

Another pilot and I told the personnel guy at K-55 that all newly-minted pilots were going to get flying assignments – that Brigadier General Lloyd P. Hopwood, Commander of the Air Staff School at Maxwell Air Force Base, Alabama had assured us of this. Previously, not all new pilots got flying assignments right away. Many went on to more schooling for various Air Force specialty jobs. Later, after their administration assignments, they were supposed to get flying jobs. General Hopwood, who spoke to all of us in our graduating pilot class, reiterated that we would all get flying assignments.

We reported to the personnel officer at the base. He wanted to assign us to administrative jobs. We would fly a base T33 just often enough to maintain currency. We argued that General Hopwood promised that we would have 100% flying assignments with an active squadron.

Each time we used the general's name, we scored points. So, the personnel officer said he'd send us to see the Colonel who ran the flying part of the base. We met the Colonel, an older WWII pilot, and he told us we were not qualified to fly the F-86 Sabre Jet. It was the most advanced airplane in the world. All F-86 pilots had to go to a six-month course in the states in order to be qualified to fly with an active squadron, especially in Korea. We again used the General's name on the Colonel and he relented. He said, "The 310th Squadron and the 311th Squadron each need a Squadron Adjutant, so I'll send each of you to a flying squadron as a replacement for their adjutants. If the CO wants to let you fly one of the F-86s then I'll leave that up to him."

I reported to the 311th Squadron. The Squadron Adjutant, a Captain, spent a few days orienting me. The name "adjutant" is an old-school term for a unit administrative officer. As a second lieutenant, I now replaced a captain. I had a lot to learn. This was my first assignment in the real Air Force and I was a little bit lost, however, everyone in the squadron was friendly and welcoming.

Each squadron of single-seat airplanes always has at least one two-seater – this two-seater is used for VIP rides, orientation of new pilots, or to go get parts and so forth. By tradition, I guess, the two-seater - a TF-80 – was assigned to the Squadron Administrative Officer – me. So, the next day, I went over to the flight line and met the TF-80 Crewchief. I watched a Korean artist paint my name on the airplane. Imagine. My own airplane and I was only a newly-minted second lieutenant … an elated second lieutenant!

The TF-80 is the original designation of the airplane now called the T-33. To start the older TF-80, there was a four-step procedure. The old-fashioned start program was as follows and must be rigidly adhered to: to start it, you had to turn on a battery, then flip a switch that started the turbine going, then wait for the turbine to come to 15%, then reach over and flip another switch that was the spark (like a spark plug). Then you flip the fuel switch. If you did this procedure incorrectly, you blew the tail off the airplane. Boom! (seriously, if you operated the fuel first and then the spark, there was too much fuel, and the spark blew the tail off).

After I flew the TF-80 for a couple of months, the squadron CO decided that I was a competent pilot, so I transitioned into the F-86 Sabre Jet. They could have continued letting me fly the two-seat TF-80. I transitioned to the F-86 with OJT (On The Job Training). I got the flight book and I memorized it. An overseas training detachment came to K-55 to update the current fighter pilots. I spent every day in that class and I passed everything. There was, of course, no instructor in the back of the F-86. You got in it and you flew it. When you did maneuvers, you did them alone for the first time. When you landed, you'd better do it right. We had what is known as a blindfold cockpit check, which amounts to somebody sitting outside the cockpit telling you to do this and that, and you must say out loud and point to each instrument and switch that is required to do what he says. It is much like what you do in your own car on a dark night. On each flight, a senior qualified lieutenant or captain would brief me on what we were to accomplish on that flight and would evaluate me upon landing. The squadron didn't have to take on this responsibility, but they did, and I'll always be grateful.

The 58th Fighter Wing had 20-25 pilots in each of 3 squadrons and 24 airplanes in each squadron. The mission of the 58th Fighter Wing was to protect South Korea and provide air defense and offense capability if the North disregarded the armistice. Example: The North Koreans would often get two or three MIG-15's and head south at 40,000 feet at high speed. They would then wait to see how long it would take us to intercept them. We always had two airplanes primed and ready to take off in five minutes or less. The North Koreans were testing our reactions.

One part of our job was to work with the Army's 24th Infantry Division. When they were practicing war games, we became part of their scenario. We (four F-86s) would take off and orbit at a known point near the Army action. At some point, the forward air controller would call us and tell us the compass heading to where the so-called problem was. The squadron call sign was changed monthly – one that I remember was "Goodnight." He would tell us what we were to shoot at and what ordnance (bombs, rockets or guns) he thought we should use. We then appeared and set up a shooting pattern and fired rockets or practiced bombs in coordination with the Army on the ground. This was practice in marksmanship for us and practice in coordination between the Army and the Air Force.

Back to being the adjutant, I had a desk and an office next to the squadron commander. Was this good luck or was I in over my head? I realized I had the least experience of anyone in the entire squadron. A half-dozen of the pilots and department heads were of WWII vintage. Every day at 8 a.m., we had squadron briefing and a weather briefing. I then went to my office hoping I'd know what to do as the administrative arm of the squadron. So, again, I learned on the job.

In the middle of my tour of duty, my squadron went to Taiwan. A little background: The Chinese Communists (we called them Chicoms) on mainland China said that Taiwan belonged to them. The Taiwanese (we called them Chinets – Chinese Nationalists) felt that they had a separate autonomous democratic country and wanted it to remain so. In 1954 the Chicoms made as though they were going to invade two of the Taiwanese Islands just off the mainland coast. These islands were called Quemoy and Matsue.

The U.S. Government had gone on record as standing with the Taiwanese, so to show support for them, our government sent fighter planes and some Navy P2 patrol planes to WS (Willie Sugar) Airbase at Tainan, Taiwan. I was sent ahead of the squadron with Lt. Dutch Holland, a Naval Academy graduate, as the advance party. The advance party is supposed to assess all accommodations for people and airplanes and report back to the U. N. Squadron in Korea. As a young, almost know-nothing second Lieutenant, I found this to be a valuable learning experience. The first night we were there, we were driven to a Chinese hotel. There was no one at what appeared to be the check-in desk. We were just told to go and find an empty room, which we did.

This was on October 31, 1955, my 25th birthday. We went down the street to a teahouse for dinner. While there, I had to use the men's room. There were no men's rooms in China. There was one toilet room for all. With fear and trepidation brought on by my stern New England upbringing, I entered. There was a row

Our huts in Taiwan

of toilets – no stalls – so I dropped my pants and sat. Shortly, in walked a gorgeous, well-dressed oriental woman. She smiled at me and started a conversation. I kept my legs firmly together. There were six or eight toilets in the room and she picked the one next to me. She then pulled up her skirt and sat down and continued to engage me in smiling conversation. I do not have any remembrance of the conversation. Here was a New England boarding school boy in an entirely new environment. I took a deep breath and decided to go with the flow. She finished, pulled down her dress and left … finally. I've never forgotten my introduction to Chinese public restrooms.

Soon, our 311th fighter/bomber squadron came to Willie Sugar Airbase in Tainan, Taiwan. We had about 22 airplanes and the same number of pilots. One of the WWII pilots pointed out the holes in the upper part of one of the hangars and proudly said, "I made those holes with my P-38 during WWII when this place was a big Jap base."

Taiwan was warm and friendly. We all lived in bamboo huts

underneath mosquito netting, about eight pilots to a hut. There was always an armed guard on duty. Each hut had a Chinese custodian of sorts assigned to us. He took care of everything we needed. We had an oriental latrine in the middle of the group of huts. It was, typically, just a slit in the floor over which we squatted. You could get used to anything.

Our Officer's Club was a tiny bamboo building with an outdoor bar and a smiling Chinese bartender on duty every day after our flying. The U.S. Navy had six P2 long range patrol planes hangered at the other end of the runway. We ate breakfast and lunch at the Navy Mess Hall and for dinner, we all climbed into a couple of trucks and drove across the base to the CAT Club (Civil Air Transport). The chef was a beautiful white Russian woman who really knew how to prepare food. Willie Sugar had been a large Jap Airdrome in WWII. They had made berms all around our living area to help protect from strafing American Airplanes. Each pair of our Sabres was enclosed by a high twelve-foot berm on three sides, thanks again to the Japanese. Every other airplane berm was guarded 24/7 by an armed Chinese soldier.

As Americans were somewhat restricted, we could fly all around Taiwan but could not fly toward the mainland beyond the Pescadores Islands in the Taiwan Strait. No one wanted to get shot down and possibly captured by the communists and create some sort of international incident. We did many of the usual things all pilots in the U.S. did – we practiced instrument flying, instrument landings, night flying, radar intercepts, radar flight following, air to ground shooting, air to air shooting. The air to air targets were towed behind my TF-80. The target sleeve was about ten feet by thirty feet – like a big canvas curtain. Each of our 50 caliber ammunition rounds had a different color paint on them. We flew back to base and dropped the sleeve, and the squadron ops officers then counted the holes and matched the color that each bullet left on the sleeve. We then knew which pilot made how many hits, if any.

The Taiwanese squadrons were active in their war with the communists. They flew reconnaissance over the mainland as well as along the coast. A United States Navy P2 Reconnaissance/ Electronics Airplane had been shot down over international waters the year before we got there. One or more high altitude U.S. Supplied U-2s had been shot down in the interior of the mainland. Once a Chinese Navy Cruiser was caught out of its port and we Americans watched as the Taiwanese F-84s and others took off to try to sink it. It was sort of an agreement that each country left each other's ships alone as long as they remained at their docks in port, but to catch one of the communist ships out on a cruise was a cause for a lot of action. The communist cruiser got back into port before anything was done to it.

The USAF Flying regulations were hundreds of pages long. The Chinet's regulations were only a few pages. So, when we flew, there were few restrictions. The other half of the base was occupied by the Taiwanese First Fighter Bomber Group. They all flew F-84s. They also had some four-engine long-range patrol planes, modified from our WWII B-24s. At each mornings' briefing, we were shown a chart of the mainland coast. We saw a daily update on the number of landing craft in the ports and we were briefed on the construction of the port facilities. We also saw the extent of the railroad being built from the interior to the port facilities. The Taiwanese knew that the Chicoms wanted to invade Taiwan but they couldn't think about doing that until several things happened: 1) They had to finish the port facilities from which to stage any kind of invasion, 2) they had to complete the railroad so that they could bring the needed supplies to the coast, and 3) they had airfields, but they had to build all the aircraft support facilities. We were shown this updated information every morning. The Taiwanese flew their four-engine long-range reconnaissance airplanes all along the mainland coast, photographing everything. Then they counted the number of invasion craft and estimated the various construction projects and completion times.

We, the American flyers, were there as a trip-wire. If the Chicoms attacked, they would be attacking Americans. Then our government would have another reason to help the Taiwanese defend their island. Also, by rotating American fighter pilots through Taiwan, the U.S. Air Force would have a trained, experienced group of pilots that could be quickly taken from their bases around the world and sent back to Taiwan, ready to swing into action.

One time, four of our F-86s were assigned to fly cover (protection) for one of the U.S. Navy P2 Long-range surveillance planes. Some had been shot down deep in mainland China. These had been crewed by Taiwanese. One of the U.S. Navy P2s was shot down by the communists over international waters. On this mission, we four flew a few miles off Taiwan but out of sight of the Navy P2. We were, however, within sight of the Chinese radar people. We were part of something larger. Possibly, we were some sort of a warning to the Chinese Communist Air Force about attacking one of our surveillance planes.

Another interesting thing happened with the United States Navy. Someone from the U.S.S. Bon Homme Richard Aircraft Carrier (nicknamed Bonnie Dick), contacted FEAF (Far East Air Force) and said the aircraft carrier, Bonnie Dick, would be traversing Taiwan during several future dates. Would we like to interact with them? My squadron CO said yes. I, as a junior lieutenant, was not part of this, but what happened was … the CO turned the planning over to Captain Andy Anderson. Captain Andy had been a Combat F-86 pilot during the Korean War. He had shot down three Mig-15s. The radar people on Taiwan were informed to watch for the Bonnie Dick when it approached the island. What we did was to send four experienced WWII pilots in our F-86 Sabre Jets out in an easterly direction. Local radar then guided us to the carrier. Well, Captain Andy split the flight – two went high and two went low to wavetop (very low above the waves). They spotted the carrier and raced to it at close to the speed of sound. The two high up Sabres engaged the carrier's combat air patrol (CAP) and while all the Navy eyes were looking up at the two Sabres, one minute later came the two low Sabres. The two low Sabres were lower than the carrier deck. They were evidently unseen by the Bonnie Dick's radar. Our Air Force Sabres pulled up and raced across the carrier deck. They were lower than the superstructure of the ship! The ship's captain actually had to look down to see our two planes as they raced perpendicularly across the flight deck. The two high Sabres got into a position to shoot down the two Navy planes … gun camera film from my two squadron mates plainly showed the Navy planes in a position to be shot down. I can't remember what the carrier broadcast to us or what the air-to-air conversation was. At any rate, age, experience and audacity had won the day!

In mid-February of 1957, we left sunny Taiwan and went back to cold Korea. This was a long flight, all over water. The Air Force had an amphibian rescue airplane (SA-16) cruising along our route to Kadena Air Base, Okinawa, Japan – as a fueling stop halfway from Taiwan back to our base in Korea. The next day, we continued our flight home and landed in Japan for refueling. Later that day, we headed for K-55 Korea. When the squadron arrived back at our base, K-55, I and another pilot were sent two minutes ahead to break the sound barrier over the base. When an airplane flies through the sound barrier, it creates a sound wave that radiates out and, in this case, down. When this sound wave strikes the ground, it creates an extraordinarily loud bang, like a double-thunder clap. This was to announce our homecoming. When you are flying the plane that breaks the sound barrier, you don't feel or hear a thing. The F-86, as it punctures the sound barrier, has a slight right-wing dip … other than that, the only reason we knew we went faster than the speed of sound was that the machmeter went past one. One on the meter was speed of sound. In actuality, our speed was approximately 700 miles an hour.

So much of this time I had been a second lieutenant. Usually, one gets promoted to first lieutenant after 18 months … I had been a second lieutenant for 27 months. I think perhaps the fact that I was on temporary duty on Taiwan caused my promotion orders to go missing. I bought first lieutenant silver bars and carried them around in my pocket so I would have them instantly ready when I got my promotion orders. One day, I mentioned this to my squadron commander. He simply said, "Put 'em on!" So, I hotfooted to the nearest latrine, whipped off my shirt and old gold bars, and immediately pinned on my coveted first lieutenant silver bars. Then I walked proudly around the squadron area. Much to my amazement, nobody noticed. Looking back, I realize my squadron mates saw me as me – not as a newbie second lieutenant.

When I left Taiwan to go back to the U.N. in Korea, I was told to keep my notes and maps on the Taiwan facilities. When I was in Taiwan in 1956-57, I was flying F-86 Saber Jets. The Chinese nationalists had three islands about one and a half miles off the coast of China. I still have my maps. Another one or two USAF squadrons went back a few years later to stop a potential invasion in its tracks. Now, in 2022, I am still constantly being asked to speak on my time in Taiwan, as it has been in the news recently. The Chinese, once again, may invade! I have revealed to a few military friends what I know to be true about what happened in 1958: In 1958, the Chicoms appeared to have amassed enough boats and airplanes to invade Taiwan. Our intelligence people said that invasion was imminent. The U.S., as the Taiwanese protector, acted immediately. The Navy sent the 7th Fleet into the Taiwanese Strait. The USAF sent one-half a squadron of F104s to the island. The F104s were operational the next day. To impress the Chicoms radar, the F104s did what no other airplane in the world could do. They flew absolutely straight up to 50,000 feet! Then they patrolled the Taiwanese Coast at twice the speed of sound! The Chicoms sent 28 bombers to bomb the Taiwanese airfields. They were intercepted by U.S. Navy Fighters. Our fighters shot down all the Chicom airplanes, using our new "sidewinder" missiles. The next day, six more Communist airplanes were shot down. We lost two airplanes. The Communist fleet turned back. I call this the battle that didn't happen because there was no press coverage. Only a few knew what happened, and the reason that the invasion of Taiwan never happened.

History has a way of repeating itself. Below is a map I kept, as instructed:

While I was in Taiwan, our commander coordinated our group of airplanes and pilots with the USAF headquarters and the Taiwanese Air Force. We flew day and night seven days a week and, as fighter pilots, we loved it. After three weeks of this intensive flying, the Taiwanese flew all of us to Hong Kong, gave us the names of tailors and put us up at a hotel. We had one week there. It was a fantastic place. A dollar went a long way. Someone had called ahead and we were met by a group of lovely oriental women. They guided us around Hong Kong and Kowloon as if we were VIP Tourists. After a week, we all had new, beautifully tailored clothing. I had a tailor-made flight suit, a couple of sports coats, four or five shirts

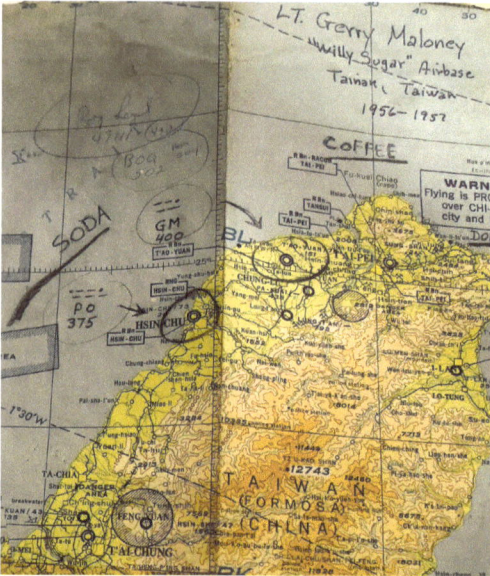

and a suit made of good English fabric. The Taiwanese plane appeared at the Kai-Tac Airport on Sunday afternoon. We all climbed aboard with the promise to see our new girlfriends again in three weeks. On Monday, we went back to intense flying for the next three weeks, and then, back to Hong Kong for a week.

Having all of these tailor-made clothes made me feel like a millionaire. I got to know one Hong Kong tailor in particular and years later, around 1960, he contacted me in San Francisco and we agreed to meet over a drink. He told me that he and his tailor firm were setting up a company in San Francisco whereby people could come and be measured and pick fabrics and the measurements would be sent to Hong Kong. There, they would make the clothes and ship them back to San Francisco, where they could be measured and fitted to the individual. He also asked me, on the side, how to invest in America. We had a long talk about this, and I said I thought he should invest in real estate. This association continued for two or three more years and then I left California for Massachusetts. Some years later, I flew back to California, visited friends in the San Francisco area, and decided to look him up. He invited me to his tailor shop and greeted me with open arms. We sat and talked about Hong Kong and old times and then he thanked me for my advice on real estate. I congratulated him on having a tailor shop in a big 20-story building in downtown San Francisco. "Oh," he said, "I took your advice. I now own this building." The clothes he made for me lasted for decades.

While in Hong Kong, I also met an American who was living there. He befriended me and I think others in our group, as well. He seemed to speak with authority when he said he was watching out for me and for us. That was in 1957, and in the early to middle 1980's, he called me to reintroduce himself. He was in San Francisco for medical evaluation and some operations, I believe, at the Army Hospital in the Presidio of San Francisco. I got him an apartment in Sausalito in my building. He immediately bought enough furniture to furnish his apartment. I am speculating that he was CIA (or some other U.S. Government agency), stationed in Hong Kong, and was very likely charged with looking out for us young American service men. He never said that, but when his medical evaluation and operations were completed, he left and gave me all of his new furniture.

Some extraordinary experiences happened while I was flying in Korea and free China (Taiwan) and here are a few of them:

Stratosphere

One day, I was flying wing on Captain Watson, a WWII fighter pilot. He said, "Let's see if we can get these planes into the stratosphere." The stratosphere begins at 10 miles up – that would be 52,280 feet – the service ceiling of an F-86 is around 48,000 feet. So, we went up and up and up slowly. Control in the thin air got a little sloppy, so we moved somewhat away from a close formation. As we used fuel, we got lighter and after a few minutes, we did manage to get above 52,280 feet. Therefore, we had entered the stratosphere – sort of a milestone for 1956.

The Flight from Hell

We had an instruction book of about 1000 pages and we had to memorize all the aircraft shooting procedures. I went out on the range one day as number four of a four-ship formation to practice machine gunning, rockets and dive-bombs. My first pass was shooting machine guns. There was an electronic dot projected on the windshield as a target site. My left machine gun hung up and wouldn't shoot anymore, and the electronic dot site disappeared. So, I fired the remaining machine gun passes without a site.

On this same flight, we next went to practice shooting high-angle rockets. We had four practice rockets to fire – one at a time. We fired at a circle on the ground. My first pass went fine. On my second pass, the rocket target site disappeared. I had to fire the rocket manually and emergency procedures told me how to do it. I went around again to fire the third rocket. I armed it and pulled the trigger and it didn't fire. I went around a fourth time, manually armed the last rocket and it too didn't fire. Now, I had two hot rockets and a hot armed gun. Not a good feeling.

Dive bomb runs were next, so I set up for dive bomb. Under the wing, we carry a drum with six small bombs in it. The bombs have just enough explosive in each to make a small hole in the ground so you can tell how accurate you are. I released five of those, but on the sixth run, the last bomb would not come out. The flight lead said, "Head out to sea and pull all the G's you can pull and try to thrust the bomb out." I did that, but it still would not release.

So now we got cleaned up (all armament switches off) and headed back to the base. I had two armed rockets and a bomb hanging, plus a hot left machine gun. I was required to fly around the base (obviously, it would not be good to have hot munitions falling on barracks) and be the last in.

I approached the runway. At a certain point over the end of the runway, the pilot brings the power back, opens the speed brakes and makes a 180-degree turn. At the end of the 180-degree turn, the pilot puts the flaps down. Well, at the 180-degree point, I looked at my air speed and I had not slowed down. The speed brakes did not work and I was going much too fast to put the flaps down. So, I pulled up to slow down (this is dangerous at low speed in the pattern), got the flaps down and got back on track for a turn to final. I put the landing gear lever down. Flashing red indicator lights on the panel showed landing gear malfunction (no wheels). At this point, I made a low pass over the runway and they confirmed that no landing gear had lowered. The nose gear door was hanging open, but no nose gear either.

There is an emergency procedure for getting the main gear down. A little T handle is located down between the pilot's legs. By pulling it manually and forcefully, it unlocks the gear on each wing so they can fall down. I had tried this procedure during my first few flights to see what it was like and I couldn't pull the T handle out. My flight instructor had told me, "Not to worry, when the time comes, your adrenaline will take over and you'll have all the force you need." So, I pulled the handle and it was like a hot knife through butter … the wheels came right out! When the up locks are pulled out, the gears can fall down about halfway. Then you have to yaw the airplane so the side load of rushing air pushes the gear fully down and hopefully to a locked position. Then you yaw to the other side to push the other gear down. It is a dangerous maneuver at low speed close to the ground. It worked.

But still, there was no nose gear down. The pressure device to force it out failed. Now, at low speed, low altitude and low fuel, I told myself, "Let me try bouncing the airplane on the runway." I'd seen a guy do this once. He bounced his airplane on the runway and the nose gear shook loose and locked into landing position. Well, I bounced it on the runway, went farther down and bounced it again and still farther down the runway, bounced it again. I thought to myself, "Jeez, I've never done this before!"

At this point, I noticed several firetrucks, a wrecker, an ambulance and the base commander's car lining the runway ... reminders of my serious situation. The tower called and asked what I wanted to do. "Do you want to bail out or do you want to land?" The helicopter was starting in case I bailed out. I thought that if I had a crosswind, my rudder (which sticks up perpendicular) would turn the airplane off the runway. That could be ugly. I did not have any nose wheel steering, so I'd have to use brakes to steer. I tested the brakes and both brake pedals went right to the floor. No brakes.

The tower called again and said the wind was right down the runway, which meant I could keep the airplane straight without nose wheel steering or brakes. No crosswind, so I decided to land. I advised the tower that I would be landing with a hot gun, two hung rockets and a live bomb. As I rounded to final approach, I noticed all of the reassuring people that were lining the runway had disappeared. Weren't they there to help me? I didn't blame them. The 50-caliber machine gun might not fire again or it might fire the one round that was in it or it might fire all hundred rounds and not stop until it melted. If the rockets dropped off, they would arm themselves and do some real damage. And the bomb might fall off. Still, I couldn't help thinking "my life is at risk and they are all gone." But there was no time for thoughts like that. I had to stay totally focused. I had to do everything right.

Bad Day: Left Gun Hung up with 100 Rounds Left in it, Sight Malfunctioned, Rocket Sequence Had Elec Short - 2 Rockets Failed To Fire, One Practice Bomb Hung & Wouldn't Drop, Speed Brakes Failed To open, Gear Wouldn't Come Down. Emergency Gear System Failed, Wheel Brakes Failed, Canopy Failed To open, Utility Hydraulic System Failed.

The last procedure the pilot wants to be sure to do in an emergency landing is to open the canopy and slide it back so he can get out quickly. I flipped the switch for that and it didn't work. Shit! Off to the side of the runway, there was a long black streak where a week before, a guy had run off the runway, crashed and burned to death because he couldn't get his canopy opened.

I landed and the nose went down and struck the runway at probably 100 knots per hour. I came right up out of my seat, within an inch of the gun site. The seatbelt pulled me back. The plane stopped tail up with the nose crunched on the runway. The reason everyone had disappeared from the runway was that procedure required it, which I didn't realize until later. I was new to crash landing. When somebody lands with big problems, and especially with hung ordinance, everyone there to help with emergency equipment goes to the back end of the runway. As you fly over, they accelerate down the runway following you, prepared to do whatever the situation requires.

When the nose went down with a great crunch, the canopy opened. Just about the time I stopped, the fire chief pulled up beside me in his jeep and yelled at me to jump. Unbuckled, I leapt immediately out of the airplane and onto the hood of the jeep which quickly backed away. There was a little fire, but only from hydraulic fluid.

The airplane never flew again but became a "hangar queen" and a reminder. The point of this is training. All this happened rapidly in less than an hour at speeds from 200 to 400 MPH. Fortunately, I had been diligent in studying emergency procedures. Summarizing the problems, they included:

Left gun failure
Gunsight failure
Electric busbar control failure
2 Rockets – failure to deploy
1 Bomb – failure to deploy
Speed brakes – failure to deploy
Main wheels – failure to deploy
Nose Gear – Emergency Operation failed
Utility Hydraulic Pump Failure
Wheel brakes Failure
Canopy Open Failure

Upon later inspection of the aircraft, we determined that the busbar containing all of the electronics that control the shooting was shorting out. The parts that plugged into this from the machine gun shorted out. The rocket controls went for a minute and they shorted out. Then the divebombing controls went for another minute or so and that shorted out. One after another, they just burned out.

Without speed brakes, I was still going extremely fast after I made the initial turn. The speed brakes are like doors on your car – they open from the side of the airplane and they really slow you down. It is just like opening the doors on your car at 100 MPH. The main gear didn't work because the main hydraulic pump had broken. I thought I was so smart, having memorized all the emergency procedures and applied them properly, but upon looking back, I sincerely know God was my co-pilot.

Heavenly Intervention

As in the book, *God Is My Copilot*, I definitely had Him on board one time when I was flying a TF-80, which was our first fighter plane. In the beginning, they put an extra cockpit in because so many guys in WWII had never flown a jet. They made only a few dual seat TF-80s and later called them a T-33 (trainer). In Korea, I was flying one of the original TF-80s fitted with two seats.

I went out to the airplane for a scheduled flight and as I walked around to do my inspection, I noticed that there was hydraulic fluid on the ground in front of the nose gear. I asked a mechanic, "What's this?" and he said, "I just had to fill up one of the cylinders." There is a hydraulic cylinder on each side of the hose gear and the pressure from them makes the nose gear stay straight. I told the mechanic, "You are supposed to wipe up any fluid you spill so we will know if there is a leak." He said, "Sir, we do not have any rags." Well, this was Korea ... the end of the supply chain ... so I took him at his word that it came from the refilling.

I went to fly by myself. When I came back, I was planning to do a "touch and go," meaning that you fly a whole pattern and as you come down toward the runway, you begin bringing the power back just about the time you touch down. Then you roll down the runway, adjust your flaps for takeoff and take off again to do another practice landing and takeoff. I was rolling down the runway bringing the power from idle to take-off power when the airplane suddenly veered left about twenty degrees. I went streaking off the runway and across the dirt toward the rice paddies. I had started to use the right brake to turn back to the runway but realized I might blow a tire on the uneven surface. So, I stomped on the rudder. Using only the rudder, I turned and gained airspeed heading the aircraft back to the runway and keeping the plane from racing into the rice paddies. I managed to get back on the runway, straighten out and take off again. In the process, I broke some runway lights. Flying out, I decided to declare an emergency. In addition to the steering problem, which was bad enough, I did not know how much other damage might have been done. I flew around and recycled the gear a couple of times trying to correct the nose gear angle. Then I made a low pass over the runway. The tower said the nose gear was now down and straight. I stayed out circling around until I used up most of the fuel. If something happened and I had an accident, I did not want a fire. When I was satisfied that the fuel was low enough, I came in and landed. It stayed straight and at the end of the runway, I stopped. They towed it off the field.

During my preflight check of the plane, when I had noted hydraulic fluid spots under the nose gear, the mechanic had told me he had just filled the hydraulic cylinder and it was not leakage. When I took the plane up, it leaked. The nose gear, leaking on one side, could not be kept straight with full pressure from the hydraulic cylinder on the other side. On landing, that imbalanced pressure caused the aircraft to head off the runway at a 20-degree angle. The mystery is what held the nose gear straight on the second landing. It shouldn't have been possible. Heavenly intervention?

I never saw the mechanic again. I don't know where they sent him. Probably to Alaska.

Radio Beacons in the Night

My wingman and I were flying the last patrol of the night in Korea. We took off from our base at K-55 which is just below the DMZ (Demilitarized Zone) to fly to Pusan which is the city at the southern end of Korea, then turn around and fly back. Right after we took off, my wingman said he had an engine problem and needed to go back to the base. Normally I would go back with him but we were still in sight of the field so he went back and I proceeded. It was pitch-black flying in Korea at night in 1956. There was no power in the countryside, so no lights. There were no highways; there were no towns. It was absolutely pitch black ... like stepping into the closet and closing the door. I flew to Pusan and that was lighted because there were some generators there. Then I turned around to head north. All squadron pilots had to memorize the heading and distance for every K site (base). The Air Force gave all of the airfields K numbers (K for Korea) and my site was labeled K-55. Seoul City was K-14. Pusan was another K number. If you had to divert somewhere, there was no time to open a chart and study it. You had to know it. So, I was headed north for K-55. I tuned in the K-55 radio navigation beacon. I did not expect to hear it yet because it was a very low power radio beacon. You had to know where it was. It was used only to get down through the clouds, but my needle responded to a signal straight up north. I tuned in again and listened for the proper identification. My needle continued pointing straight north. I thought this was unusual – that maybe it was bounding off the ionosphere or something. What I did not know was that the North Koreans had set up a radio on the same frequency with the same identification as ours with ten times the power on the radio beacon at K-55 – my home base. It was pulling me north, but it was so close to my heading that I was understandably redirected by it. So, I headed north at 600 MPH. It was pitch black and the only thing I could see was twenty-four round instrument dials in front of me. I re-tuned the thing again, and again I heard the proper identification. After 20 to 30 minutes, something told me I should be there ... I should be there. I looked and couldn't see anything. It was pitch black. I thought ... well, what to do? I made a 90 degree turn and headed west. The needle continued to point off my wing north. Suddenly, the needle moved back down to my nose and in two minutes I flew right over the absolute center of the K-55 runway and landed. From nowhere in the dark night I was now right over the runway. Amazing. The next morning, talking to some of the older senior officers, some of them from WWII, they said I had experienced "heavenly intervention," as had they. There is no way you can figure out some things that happen which are improbable if not impossible; they just do.

Directions from Heaven

Several months later, I was flying back from Japan and the entire peninsula of Korea was covered in overcast from about 500 feet to 15,000 feet. I was number 2. The flight leader had started down and I started down with him. We were making what we call a penetration, meaning you fly over to the radio beacon at a specified air speed and make a specified turn. If you do it correctly, you come out of the clouds at the end of the runway. Heading down, I realized that all of my flight instruments were dead. Flying in clouds, you have to have instruments – you can't see.

The flight leader and I got separated, probably at about 10,000 feet in the clouds. He just disappeared. I knew that my wings were level at that point, so I just gave it power, went up and popped out of the overcast at about 17,000 feet. Then what? How was I going to get down? I didn't have any flight instruments to guide me through the clouds to the runway. The tower called and asked, "Where are you?" I told them I had no flight instruments and was above the clouds. Then somebody said, "There is a hole in the clouds over by the range." I knew where the range was, so I headed for the range and sure enough there was a hole in the clouds. Now, mind you, the entire peninsula of Korea was covered with clouds from 500 or 600 feet to 15,000 feet. Suddenly, there was a hole. With clear weather inside the hole, I could see the ground below. It was like looking through a tunnel. Is that heavenly intervention? In the whole peninsula, a little hole for me? So, I went for the hole and managed to fly down through it and at the bottom, because it was a very low ceiling. I had to fly practically at tree top level. Now, how to get back to the base? I was flying in the general direction of the base but between me and K-55 was a high ridge, so I knew that the base was off to my right, but the tree-covered ridge was between me and the base. So, I tuned into the radio beacon which was a mile off the end of the runway at K-55 in line with the runway. When the needle pointing to the radio beacon was off my left wing, I knew K-55 should be on my right wing. I turned 90 degrees to the right. I had never done anything like this before and there was no precedent for this kind of flying. I didn't have time to dwell on that, but when the navigation needle approached my left wing, the airport should be off the right wing. So, I turned right, shot up over the ridge at 300 miles an hour, held my breath, popped out of the clouds on the other side of the ridge, and behold … there in front of me was the runway. I then proceeded to land visually behind my lead. Later, no one knew who had called to tell me there was a hole. And how would anyone at the base even have known?

During that same time period, two South Korean airplanes were pulled over the border and shot down – they didn't realize where the border was – but other than that – we didn't have any real shoot-em-ups like the Army did.

In Korea, I flew about five times a week – morning, afternoon and evening. We had a target range about 30 miles away and we would go out and practice shooting.

Korea in February was cold, cold, cold. Having been away since October, we had thankfully missed most of the usual harsh Korean winter. I was now no longer a student, so to speak. I

311th Fighter Squadron pilots in front of their quarter, 1956. K55 Airbase, Korea

pulled my weight and was scheduled on operations daily, even though I had the least amount of time or experience in the F-86. As the squadron adjutant, I had a number of collateral duties. I was the fire marshal, the head of the enlisted promotion board, the squadron historian, and a number of other things. In the squadron area, each lieutenant took times being Officer of the Day (OD). On the day it was my time I strapped on a loaded 45 pistol, put on my lieutenant's full uniform and had an armband with OD written on it in big letters. From 5 p.m. after duty hours until 8 a.m. the next day, I guess I was in charge of the squadron, the squadron area, its hangars, airplanes, barracks, officer's club and the sergeant's club.

One very nice thing happened. As I made my rounds in the evening, one of the senior sergeants that I knew from the flight line came to me and invited me and then personally escorted me into the Sergeant's Club. Even as the OD, I didn't have access to their club unless invited. Well, while there, we all got a little better acquainted than we could have done during the daily squadron operations on the flight line. They offered me a beer and I said, "Thanks, but as OD, I'd better not imbibe." I asked for Orange Juice instead. The bartender slyly put vodka in the orange juice and gave it to me. No one was fooled. I felt – and feel to this day – that the sergeants in the squadron knew they could trust me and wanted to interface with me. I still have a warm feeling about this.

The Korean winter and spring went by fast. As the squadron adjutant, I was busy when not flying. The squadron commander Lt. Colonel Back, and I had good vibes with each other. Colonel Back's son was in grad school at Stanford, so we had some common ground.

All squadrons supplied one officer every six months to the U.S. Army 24th Infantry Division on the DMZ (Demilitarized Zone) as air liaison officer. The Air Liaison officer also doubled as a forward air controller. The forward air controller had to be a combat-qualified fighter pilot. The air liaison officer was the U.S.A.F. representative to the Army. I got the job. The Army Air Corps came and picked me up in a little two-seat L-19 Liaison Airplane. We landed on a small dirt strip near the DMZ. I was assigned to the 24th Division Artillery (DIVARTY). I met with four other first lieutenants. At dinner the first night, I was introduced to the Army way as opposed to the Air Force Way … as follows: The lieutenants didn't walk the short distance to the officer's club for dinner. A jeep came to fetch them. As I started to get into the jeep, one of the Army lieutenants said, "What is your date of rank?" To the Army, all lieutenants weren't the same. They went by date of rank. My date of rank was older than any of the other three quarter-mates. Therefore, according to them, I was senior and therefore, I got into the jeep last so that I could be first out when we stopped.

At the officer's club for dinner, everyone was sitting down waiting. At the Air Force Mess Hall, all officers walked in, sat down and ate when we got there – not the Army. We all waited until the Colonel came out of a private back room, followed by some Lt. Colonels. Then, when they all were seated, we lower ranks followed. To my astonishment, the lieutenants, now including me, proceeded by date of rank. I thought "Here we are, a stone's throw from the DMZ with a hostile army right over the hill and we are going through what I consider is utter foolishness." I was then informed that all Air Force fighter pilots attached to the 24th division were called Zoomies – I thought that a good call. Well, for the next month, I was a Zoomie. The food was good when we finally got it. I met a lot of nice young officers. The next morning, I was introduced to my crew. I had a jeep and a driver assigned to me. In addition, I had a communications van with two radio techies. Over the next thirty days, we drove all over the DMZ area.

My job was to call in air strikes from the three fighter/bomber squadrons stationed at K-55. The fighter squadrons were the 69th, the 310th and the 311th. I worked with the infantry as they rehearsed possible war game scenarios. I called in simulated air strikes as the Army needed them. This was good training for the F-86 pilots and the Army, but I must say that the Air Force rocket-firing was extremely inaccurate. The pilots just didn't get enough practice. In real wartime operations, they do this almost every day and hone their skills. Now, they only got to do this every few weeks ... just enough to keep the procedures in mind. They'd be sharp in a couple of days in a real new war. There is a great deal of mechanics involved in aiming at the ground. There is also a learned skill and a substantial bit of art – a fighter pilot has to do it all – fly, navigate and be your own flight engineer, fire machine guns, fire rockets, drop bombs, conquer emergencies, etc. There wasn't enough practice time to produce all of the skills necessary for total proficiency, unless it was wartime.

At the end of a year of flying in Korea, I felt minimally qualified to be a master of all aspects of the F-86 squadron operations. When I left the 24th DIVARTY, I went to say goodbye to the commanding general. He asked me if I'd come back in a jet and make a low pass or something. He said he realized the Air Force frowned on buzzing because it frightened civilians, but he said, with a gleam in his eye, "You have my permission to buzz us." When I got back to the squadron, I resumed all the daily operations. All F-86 flights were scheduled from start to finish with no opportunity to go and buzz the Army. However, a week later, a new pilot reported in, so I used this opportunity to put him in the back seat of my TF-80 and give him a ride to show him around the area. I also took the opportunity to fly up to the headquarters of the 24th U.S. Infantry Division. The officer's club building was on a hill. I approached it from a half-mile away. I was below the building. I flew at it, then curved around to fly beside it. As I flew by, I was below the windows of the building. I pulled up, rolled over and flew down the other side of the building. People raced out of the club. They were looking at me nearly eye to eye as I sped by. It was that low. All of them waved. I waggled my wings as I flew away.

Several days later, when I was on the flight line, an MP came up to me and said, "There was an Army sergeant here asking for you. He says he was your sergeant when you were the forward air controller for the division." I said, "Let him in and bring him to me." The sergeant, who I had gotten to know quite well during my month with him, came with a big grin. He looked in absolute awe at the F-86s he was standing amongst. He said the general had sent him to thank me for the fly-by buzz job. I asked the sergeant if he had a camera and he said yes. So, I helped him get into the cockpit of one of the F-86s. He did. I took his picture, and hopefully, he was one happy dude. I think that to actually sit in the cockpit of the most famous and best jet fighter plane in the world must have been a thrill to him, and now he had a picture to show friends and the two communication techs that he and I had worked with.

As my year in Korea drew to a close, I realized that I was now one of the senior pilots. Considering that when I joined the squadron I was not even a qualified F-86 pilot, now I was made an "element lead." I was no longer forever someone's wing man. Now I could lead at least one other airplane. Now I had a wing man. I thought to myself that I had made considerable measurable progress. In a way, just like I did at Stanford University … in each, I had started on less than zero and now I could feel proud that I had become an integral part of each organization.

I must point out that the type of flying we were doing was somewhat dangerous. The 311th squadron alone lost 15% of its pilots in the year that I was there. Captain DeFreeze crashed on a Skip-bomb mission. He caught a wing-tip during a high-speed low-level turn. DeFreeze was a WWII pilot, and I had just flown with him the day before. Lt. Ford, a Naval Academy Graduate, crashed when a wing tank came off and hit his horizontal tail. The airplane became unstable and hit the ground nearly at the speed of sound. The third fatality was our new squadron commander, a World War II Major. He had a compressor stall, which blew his tailpipe off at low altitude and he crashed. I actually saw him and watched as he crashed. I didn't know how I felt, but I still feel whatever it was in the pit of my stomach.

This Korean assignment was my first assignment in the real Air Force. I had so very much to learn. I had been thrust into an operating squadron in the heart of the cold war in a semi-active hostile environment. By now, I had mastered my job as the squadron adjutant with the help of Master Sgt. Gammons, and I could pull my weight as a combat qualified pilot.

More good things. The Aircraft Carrier, U.S.S. Shangri-la, was due to dock in the port of Yokosuka, Japan. A high school friend sent me a letter asking if we could get together on the Shangri-la when it docked in Japan. I asked the squadron commander, Colonel Back, if I could go and he asked the wing commander if I could go and represent the Air Force. The Wing Commander, Colonel Reinhart, said he would like to go with me. My squadron commander said he'd like to go with me, too. We'd take our two-seater and borrow another two-seater from another squadron. I wrote my friend with this tentative arrangement. He wrote back that the Captain of the Shangri-la requested that our Wing Commander not come as his presence on the ship – per protocol – would require him and his staff to be present. So, the Wing Commander, Colonel Reinhart, couldn't come with me, but my squadron commander, Colonel Back, still was going. So, now we had two two-seater jets, one lieutenant Colonel and three lieutenants. The pilot with me was A. D. Johnson and the pilot with the colonel was Dutch Holland. This was now an official Air Force liaison trip. An okay came back from my Navy friend, Lt. J. G. Brian Mims. On the appointed departure day, we had two planes positioned at the end of the runway for formation take-off. The airplane the colonel was in blew an engine. As his airplane disappeared in smoke, I saw the colonel come out on the wing-tip pointing at us and gesturing that we were to go alone. Both he and Lt. Holland were okay.

A. D. Johnson and I landed at Tachikawa Air Base, Japan. We took a commuter train south to Yokosuka Naval Base. On arrival at the Naval Base, we were treated like dignitaries as we were, in essence, representatives of the United States Air Force, FEAF (Far East Air Force) and Operations in Korea. We were shown quarters on the ship and promptly got lost. The ship was huge. My high school friend took us in hand and showed us around. I got to sit in the Captain's chair. I had my picture taken there. We also toured the flag bridge from which the ship is run. On the flight deck, we also got a tour of various types of airplanes the Navy was using – fighters, bombers, torpedo bombers, long-range surveillance, airborne radar. The airborne radar airplanes could control all the facets of surface and air weapons during a conflagration. We were asked to speak to the pilots about the North Korean tactics, Mig-15 capabilities, the North's radar capabilities, and so forth. This was the official liaison duty for us.

When I look back at my time in Taiwan and Korea, I remember it as the most exhilarating time of my life. I've had two children – two nice wives – graduated from college – and lived a great life, but nothing was as exhilarating as that year of flying fighter planes overseas in the Air Force.

Although I loved my time there, living conditions in Korea were relatively primitive. We lived in a ten-man, one story corrugated hut with sandbags on the roof. My bed was a two inch-by four-inch wood frame with pieces of a rubber innertube stretched across it. Our only furniture was made from numerous wooden boxes. The only heat was from a single pot-bellied stove. The flying was primitive by today's standards, but for me, it was as if I were the bird … a big, beautiful bird.

CHAPTER 6

BACK IN THE STATES

I left Korea in the summer of 1957 and after a short home leave, I reported to Webb Air Force Base in Big Spring, Texas. When I volunteered for Korea, I was told that after my year there, I would receive any assignment I requested. I requested fighter squadrons in Europe or the West Coast of the U.S. The only thing I didn't want was the air training command in West Texas. I got the air training command in West Texas.

When I reported to Webb Air Force Base, the base adjutant got hold of me. He had been in my Air Force ROTC at Stanford. He wanted to speak to me before I went to the personnel office. He told me he might have something interesting for me. He said he'd told the base commander about me and my background. The base commander had said, "Okay," if I wanted the job. The job was a position as a squadron commander. The present squadron commander had become an alcoholic. He had 18 ½ years in the Air Force and the base commander wanted to put him on ice, so to speak, until he got 20 years in and then he could retire with his pension. I would replace him. The squadron was the motor pool squadron. My friend told me that if I remained in the Air Force, as I rose through the ranks, I'd never make full colonel and maybe not even Lieutenant colonel without command experience. He pointed out that I'd have that command experience as a lieutenant – way, way ahead of my contemporaries.

The motor pool squadron was no glamor job, but to have a lieutenant replace a major was a great accomplishment. So, I took the job. The Colonel, the base commander, told me at the next squadron commanders meeting that I was the youngest squadron commander in the entire Air Force. All of the other Air Force Squadron Commanders were majors or lieutenant colonels. I was very nervous at our first base commander's meeting and kept my mouth shut. I sat there and looked at all the brass around me and thought about my two years of minimal experience and wondered how I got there.

As I settled in, I met my first sergeant and the head of maintenance. Between them, they carried the squadron functions until I could get up to speed. Soon I realized that every piece of equipment on the base with a wheel on it belonged to me. Thus, I had an in – so to speak – to the administration of most of the squadrons on the base. I had not been to squadron officer's school. In fact, as only a lieutenant, I was not even eligible for this school. Some months after I got to running the squadron, the Air Force Personnel Center called. They wanted to send me to teach at basic instructor school for beginning jet pilots. I declined, as I was now a squadron commander and there certainly was nothing better than that for a young lieutenant. I was learning leadership sort of blindly, but I always did what I thought was the right thing.

One day, the operations officer, a Major Brophy, called me. The ops officer on the base runs the flight line and has charge of all the airplanes. We had a cup of coffee in his office while we got better acquainted. He said he needed his four-wheel drive go-anywhere vehicle in case there was an airplane accident anywhere on or off the base. He said that vehicle would not start. He then said if that vehicle didn't work, he would take the sedan assigned to him to go to the crash. He said the sedan wouldn't go

Photo of Dad and me in front of a T-33 at Otis AFB, Cape Code, Mass., Dec. 1957

into first gear. He said he had called my scheduling department and had been told that he was on the schedule for next month. He asked if I would help him. He really felt he needed those vehicles. I thought to myself, "Imagine, a major asking a lieutenant for help." I went back to the squadron maintenance shop and got them to repair his two vehicles asap.

After the vehicles were repaired and returned to the major, he called to thank me for the expedited fix. Then he said, "Anytime you want an airplane to go anywhere anytime for as long a time as you can get away, let me know. You got it!" Now, imagine … I'm only a lieutenant – not only am I a squadron commander, I have the use of a jet almost as if it were my own! I flew a few weekends to Stanford Football games in Palo Alto, California. I flew locally every chance I got. There was always a jet ready for me. I asked him if I could take one over Christmas vacation for a week. He said, "Of course. Okay." In fact, he further said, "This is a jet training base, so the students won't be back from Christmas leave until 4 January. There is not much doing here with the students away, so keep the airplane for two weeks and come back on the 3rd of January." So I called my folks in Massachusetts to come and pick me up at Otis Air Force Base on Cape Cod on December 20. Neither Mom nor Dad had ever seen me in a flight suit or an airplane that I flew. Dad and I had our picture taken in front of the jet. I felt proud of myself and my accomplishments. Dad, as far as I remember, never said anything. I hope they were impressed even though the T-33 was only a jet trainer.

Since I loved to fly, and had unlimited use of the T-33, I drove to Otis Air Force Base almost every day and flew up and down the coast for an hour or two.

After about a week, the Otis Air Force Base operations officer came to me and asked if he could help. I said, "Help with what?" I was, of course, polite to a major. He said it seemed to him that every time I departed the base, I had to return ... was I having problems that the base was not able to fix? I told him the base people were great. I just had the airplane for a couple of weeks and so I was just flying it around. He looked incredulous and a little bit exasperated. All he said was, "You certainly must know someone."

Back at Webb Air Force Base, the motor pool squadron had a touch football team. Since they were all black except me, we named ourselves after a famous entertainment group, "The Ink Spots Plus One." We were not a winning team, but we had a good time. They made me quarterback because I was the commander, which, looking back, was not a good decision. I have small hands and don't throw the ball well ... any one of them would have been a better quarterback. This I thought of afterwards, unfortunately.

Another organization I dealt with on the base was the maintenance squadron. They were in charge of maintaining the 100 or so airplanes stationed at Webb AFB. One of my jobs was to write annual justifications for the use of every wheeled vehicle on the base. That included trucks, jeeps, tracked vehicles and a myriad of other equipment. One piece of equipment was an ungainly looking spidery thing on wheels that was used to roll up to and over an aircraft engine. It then hoisted the engine up and out of the back of the airplane. This contraption and the engine were then wheeled away to a maintenance shop to be worked on. Well, the usage book (so to speak) called for a certain number of times of usage in order to justify keeping each piece of equipment. The amount of usage of those contraptions at the Webb Maintenance Hangar was in fact way below requirements.

Previously, my predecessor had fudged the figures. I went to the maintenance squadron commander – a Major – and told him what I was going to do. I said I'd write in my annual justification that, according to the official use requirements, I could not justify each of these pieces of equipment, but that regardless of the Air Force's arbitrary usage assigned to these pieces of equipment, they were indispensable. Each of the 100 or more active Jet T-33's on the base required mandatory periodic engine maintenance. This type of equipment was essential to the base mission, no matter what the usage – and, as the base exists for the airplanes, the specialized equipment required to keep the airplanes flying far outweighed the arbitrary use requirement for this piece of equipment. As the squadron's commanding officer, I directed that we must keep it regardless of its usage value. I wrote this up and reviewed it with the major. He was very pleased, signed it, sent it to headquarters. I never heard another word.

Sometime later, the Major came to see me. He said he had looked up my flying background. He said that he felt that flying overseas in Korea, Taiwan and for the UN had given me a unique background. Therefore, he would like to designate me as one of the his maintenance test pilots. I was very pleased and of course I said yes. I felt extremely special to be one of the few pilots on the base to be offered this opportunity to work with him in this special capacity of flight testing. Most unfortunately, after only a couple of flights, I was mustered out of the active Air Force.

Webb AFB was a jet pilot training base. When The pilots graduate and get their wings, they have never flown in what we call the real Air Force (RAF). Usually there is a time lag of several months before the new pilots get their Air Force assignments.

The Air Force encourages older experienced pilots to take the new pilots up in the back seat of the T-33 jet as they go on various flights around the country. The major did come to see me. He looked up my background of flying in Korean operations with the USAF, the UN, and the Chinese Nationalists. He expressed his thoughts to me that he would like to designate me as one of his maintenance test pilots. Based on this request, I took a new pilot up with me and decided to really fly him around and show him how real flight operations worked.

As an example of USAF Flight Operations, I will go over in detail the second segment of our cross country flying. The first segment of our cross country flying was an uneventful flight from Big Spring, Texas to Chanute AFB in Rantoul, Illinois. The following is a detailed account of the flight from Chanute AFB to Westover AFB and then to Plattsburgh AFB, New York:

Webb AFB - A "Routine" Training Flight - 1958

We had two single-engine jets that day – T-33's – Al, another regular Air Force Pilot, would lead this leg. He needed element lead practice. I needed work on my close formation. Both Al and I had brand new pilots with us in the back seats. We figured very complete flight plans and arrived from Webb at almost identical fuel reserve and ETA at Westover, AFB Massachusetts. We checked Pease AFB weather, filed our flight plan and scurried to our two T-birds.

Specifically, we had begun the flight by getting the weather briefing, which is usual. However, it is not usual to have the weather almost end your flight. On this night we ran a frantic race with the elements, almost landing in Canada, 200 miles from our destination.

The weather forecaster at Chanute Air Force Base, Illinois advised that a continuous line of heavy snow storms was rapidly moving into New England from the Virginias. Our destination was Westover Air force Base, near Boston. The forecaster gave us 3 hours before the storm hit. Our alternate AFB would have to be to the North, ahead of the advancing snow.

We chose Pease Air Force Base at Portsmouth, N.H.

Maintenance delays caused us to lose an hour of precious time.

Our fingers were so numb from cold we were barely able to copy the Air Traffic Control (ATC) flight clearance. I chose "Shorttimer" for our call sign.

"Shorttimer deuce, let's light 'em up," cracked Al.

"Rodge, lead," I snapped.

Instruments checked, radio tested, oxygen working, all switches in order. A motion to the Crew Chief, acknowledged, and the cold, lifeless T-bird became a warm eager adventuress.

"Chanute Tower, Shorttimer was off at 15:15 – good-day" … the sky was crystal clear and cold.

We climbed for 37,000 feet. Al was a little rough and I was rougher on his wing. Due to USAF budget cuts it had been difficult to get two air-planes to go to the same place on any one weekend. Formation practice was difficult to come by.

We leveled at 37,000 feet over Indianapolis. Bob, in the rear seat, and I, practiced close formation. The idea of a night weather letdown at Westover Air Force Base rattled around the back of my head. Dayton and Columbus passed far beneath us … clouds appeared.

Our estimated times were right on, as was our fuel reserve. Al was unable to get the Westover weather from Pittsburgh Center. We turned north. It was twilight in Pittsburgh. The clouds below were boiling up-wards now. Rechecking navigation, fuel and time figures kept us busy in the cramped cockpit. I pulled out the letdown charts for Westover and our alternate, Pease AFB. Maps were folded and lights rechecked. My map light was out. Jolly, and it was getting dark. Bob traded bulbs with me. He could see by using his flashlight. I needed both hands to fly. The bulb broke. The clouds began to engulf us.

Al was unsuccessful again at obtaining current weather. Albany, N.Y. in 10 minutes. We closed up the formation. Navigation lights on. It was dark. Below swirled the angry clouds. Instrument and console lights were at full bright so I could read the myriad of maps, log cards, letdown charts and frequencies. I cursed Lockheed for not putting a map shelf on the instrument panel. Like a magician I had something in every pocket!

The angry clouds finally enveloped us. The Lead airplane became only three multi-colored lights. There was no silhouette. Our position report was as follows:

"Albany radio, Shorttimer, flight of two T-33."

"Over Albany"

"At :55"

"37 thousand"

"Instrument Flight Rules (IFR) to Westover"

"Estimate Westover on the hour"

"Request Westover weather and further clearance."

"Shorttimer, Boston ATC clears you to descend to and maintain 20,000 feet, report over the homer. Standby for the weather."

"Rodger Albany, Shortimer two let's go down."

"Shorttimer call Westover Approach Control for further clearance," Albany radio ordered.

"Rodger! Shorttimer go channel #15."

"Rodge," I acknowledged. Butterflies in stomach again. I always love a controlled letdown with its exactness and crisp radio communication.

Snug in our cockpits we knifed through the dark swirling mists – two sleek jets 6 feet apart, acting as one.

I noted with relaxed satisfaction time and fuel reserve were right on the money.

Our clear weather prediction was not quite right. "Shorttimer," advised Westover Tower, "ceiling is 400 to 600 feet in heavy snow and freezing sleet. Visibility is ¼ the length of the runway; 90 degree crosswind, 25 knots gusting to 35 knots. Conditions deteriorating rapidly; heavy icing reported in descent. The field is closed."

Ah, the best laid plans of mice and men, I thought, exasperated.

Lead called and asked what I thought. I barked only one word, "Pease" our alternate.

The weather forecaster did not have the current weather from Pease Air Force Base. We raced around the holding pattern sucking up precious fuel reserves. After a few minutes of this we switched to tower frequencies and tried several Air Force towers for their local and observed weather. All had the same storm report. One noted that it was dark. How inadequately expressed.

Back to the forecaster – still no weather info. Approach control did not have Pease weather but asked us for our intention. We had none yet and so informed him.

My whole world now was Lead's three multi-colored lights which twisted and turned spasmodically as we wove through the holding pattern frantically switching channels. Occasionally a shaft of light would dart from the rear seat of Al's T-bird as a flashlight moved. Otherwise, I felt as if I were a pendulum encased in a slow grandfather clock swinging at double time to catch up.

"Be advised, Shorttimer, we're unable to obtain Pease weather for you," the forecaster said.

At this time Al and I went to different channels. I went back to channel #1 and tried to contact Pease Tower.

Mitchel AFB Tower in New York answered and I was unable to read him with Pease AFB weather. The fuel counter kept relentlessly ticking away those precious gallons. Al and I finally got together again and the first thing I heard was: "Gerry, give me a heading and estimate to Plattsburgh AFB, N Y. Forecaster advises it's the only field left open."

"Rodge," I'd never heard of the place. Quickly turning the controls over to Bob, I began to look for Plattsburgh. A frantic search, all thumbs, every minute was precious … I couldn't find it.

"Say, Shorttimer, where is Plattsburgh?"

"Near Montreal," snapped Al.

Suddenly we lost power and Bob said he had become separated from Lead. I grabbed the controls, told Al to switch his navigation lights to bright. He did. Tiny pinpricks of light showed ahead. I moved back into formation. Bob found Plattsburgh using, logically, his flashlight. Quickly spinning the computer he gave Lead our Plattsburgh estimate.

Boston Center was now contacted and we were cleared direct at 30,000 feet.

After circling in the soup at night over an imaginary point with absolutely no visual references, one could almost believe we were in a huge pickle barrel. We asked for radar assistance.

"Stargazer – Shorttimer here, 30,000 feet, heading 290 degrees, request course and distance to Plattsburgh." "Rodger, Shorttimer, you have Plattsburgh, 12 o'clock, 120 miles."

Oh, what a wonderful feeling! There was someone else in the world who knew we were where we thought we were.

Radar continued to give us assistance and assurance. Finally, we arrived. By this time, my back hurt, my toes were frozen, my eyes were watering, my nose running. Nevertheless ... must stay alert ...had never been to Plattsburg before.

Seconds later, Lead chopped power, dropped his speed brakes and nosed over for descent. He was a new Lead and in his haste to get down, he forgot to coordinate with his wingman. He forgot to call! Our jet shot ahead into the night. Yanking the airplane almost straight up, I dropped speed brakes, gear, flaps to slow down. I rolled upside down and called Lead to flip his navigation lights to bright. I saw them dimly below in the clouds, I joined up from above, dropping upside down like a falling leaf. A night join-up in the clouds upside down.

The low fuel warning lights snapped on. We plummeted earthward between the Alleghenies and the Green Mountains. The letdown utilized two omni stations and was for B-47s with two radios. This was overcome by using the front and rear control panels and dexterous switching of frequencies.

The letdown did not lead us to the field. It was to a ground controlled approach pickup point. Jolly. We hadn't enough fuel now for a ground controlled approach. Mentally, I went through my bailout and survival procedure. We broke out of the clouds about 4,000 feet, saw isolated lights but no air field. Snow covered everything. Red low fuel warning lights became more significant.

"Shorttimer, Plattsburgh GCA has you in position contact on our screen. Do you wish a GCA?"

"Plattsburgh GCA negative, we do not have enough fuel. Request a straight in approach."

The town of Plattsburgh came into view – still no airfield – five minutes' fuel left now!

"Lead, let's go tower frequency and transmit for a Direction Finding (DF) Steer," I suggested.

"Rodge Two, stand by."

"Plattsburgh GCA are we still on your scope and can you give us a heading to the field?"

"Rodger," GCA acknowledged, and after a short pause, "Steer 190 degrees, field is approximately seven miles."

"Thanks GCA, Two go channel #1."

"Plattsburgh Tower, Shorttimer does not have the field in sight – request you turn the runway lights to full bright."

At 10 o'clock position, about four miles, a glow appeared.

"Shorttimer has the field, 10 o'clock, four miles," I called ... tasting sweat.

"Plattsburgh Tower, Shorttimer requests landing for two, be advised this is our second alternate, and we have low fuel."

"Rodger, Shorttimer, land runway 35 behind the B-47, winds are 300 degrees, 10 knots."

A short initial contact, a quick pitchout, and too soon I breathed a sigh of relief. The Tower called...

"Shorttimer, make a wide pattern, have a B-47 stuck in the ice on the runway." Oh! Jolly, our fuel showed ten gallons – 1 or 2 minutes – not enough to make the runway. The more accurate fuel gauge showed thirty gallons – 2 minutes. Just enough.

"Shorttimer, you're cleared ...."

I did a near vertical bank, dropped gear, flaps and dove for the runway. Al did the same. We touched down almost in formation ... three hours to the minutes after takeoff. The airplane ran out of fuel as we parked.

Fifteen minutes later came the swirling snow.

What did the new pilot learn? Well, I took him from Texas to upstate New York to Massachusetts to Virginia to Mississippi and back to Texas - showing him about real formation flying; real instrument flying; night instrument flying in weather; night penetrations; real Ground Control

Approaches (GCAs); and how to approach new, unfamiliar fields. By the end of our trip, he had a broad, wide-ranging flying experience that few of his classmates would ever have. He learned as I had learned, through several maneuvers, to become one with the airplane.

CHAPTER 7

AFTER ACTIVE DUTY

It was in the spring of 1958, after nine months of being squadron commander of the motor pool, that I was caught in the personnel reduction of the Air Force that occurred after the Korean war. So, I was released from active duty. Now what?

When I received notice that I would be ushered out of active duty in the Air Force, I had to suddenly make plans for civilian life. The question was, what plans? What to do? Where to go? Massachusetts or California? I had loved living in San Francisco and California, so I decided to go back there. But I had no family or friends there. Also, no job. I had been able to save most of my salary in Korea. I didn't have much chance to spend any money, so I saved a lot. On Taiwan, it had been the same thing. At Webb Air Force Base in Texas, I had an old used car – so no payments – not much to spend money on at Webb. So, California here I come!!

I processed out, said goodbye to my small staff at the motor pool. I took pictures of them to forever remind me of how nice and helpful they had all been to me. I went to the personnel office to get my DD-214, which was my honorable discharge – a very important piece of paper. I still remember the Captain, named

Glenn Cearfu who wouldn't let me and another officer process-ing out, make a copy of our DD-214's on his copy machine. The other lieutenant and I looked at each other – we couldn't believe this guy. He was such an unreasonable person that I still remem-ber his name.

On the road and beginning to be excited about a new horizon, I stopped on the way to California in Phoenix, Arizona. I went to the Arizona Air National Guard Building and saw that they had F-86 Sabers. I spent some time inquiring about joining the Ari-zona Air National Guard. I felt that if I could fly their F-86's, I'd stay and settle in Phoenix. But the outcome was that I had a good enough background to join their guard, however, I must know Senator Barry Goldwater or someone who had an "in" with him. I didn't know him, so on to California and the unknown.

I had corresponded with two fraternity brothers – Blair Pas-coe and Sid Hall. Blair had been in my Air Force ROTC Unit and had been on active duty in the Air Force and had gotten out early. He was my best friend at Stanford. Blair and Sid were both in graduate business school at Stanford. They said, "Come stay with us." So, I found their apartment and bunked in. I slept on their couch for a while. I don't remember how long. At this point, I still didn't know what to do. Until now, I had always had goals and planned accordingly, as follows: 1) Go to a good college – Done. 2) Be somebody and contribute to college and college life – Done. 3) Become a fighter pilot – not just an Air Force Pilot – Done. Actually, I felt that I had far exceeded each of these goals. I had gotten into probably one of the best colleges in the country. I had contributed in many ways to make Stanford a little better. I had far exceeded my academic goal with the winning Penobscot Expedition paper. As to Goal 3, I felt I had far exceeded my pilot goal as I had flown the first airplane that was capable of breaking the sound barrier. Also, I had flown the F-86 that held the world speed record.

So … again … I said to myself, What now? So far, all my previous goals and lifelong plans had been met. Now I didn't know what to do. How can I make plans when I have not set any new goals? There was an empty feeling in my stomach.

Blair and Sid were engrossed in their graduate business school studies, so not much doing around town with them. Even now, sixty-three years later, I can't recall what I did for a few weeks of this time in my life.

So, aching for the familiar, I returned to what I knew by driving up to Hamilton Air Force Base. The base was twenty miles north of San Francisco, so easily reached. I went to the personnel office to inquire about a reserve assignment and found several bureaucrats who shuffled me from one person to another. Then, with my transportation background, they found me a place at the headquarters, 4th Air Force Transportation Section. I met an old Major who was about ready to retire. I was to assist him in closing up an Air Force base nearby. Everything at the base had to be accounted for and then everything - furniture, cars, trucks and so forth – had to be offered to all other government entities in the area. If no one took all this equipment, they were then to be offered for sale to the general public. I spent one day a month at this and was obligated for a two-week active duty stint every year.

I went over to the 4th Air Force Operations Officer who had control of all the headquarters 4th Air Force Airplanes. He welcomed me with open arms. It turns out he had several C-47s (old WWII transports) for the non-jet pilots to fly and maintain their skills. Also, he had several T-33 two place jet trainers. I told him I had 150 plus hours in the T-33 and I had flown them all over the far east and all over the U.S. He called a check-pilot and immediately arranged for me to have a check-ride. So, very quickly, I became one of a stable of his jet pilots. The administrative lady who was processing my reserve status paperwork was very unhappy with me. I was already on flying status before I was officially in the Reserve. "You can't do that!" she exclaimed. "What do you mean, you're flying! You're not officially in the reserve yet."

That done, I knew that I was now happy with that part of my life.

But now what? Where do I go to earn a living? I heard about a big San Francisco rooming house called Baker Acres in the Presidio area of San Francisco, so I moved into a basement apartment, which I shared with a German exchange student. Baker Acres consisted of several multi-story buildings – men and women shared floors and bathrooms. Breakfast and dinner were served. Most everyone left after breakfast for work in town. Lots of relationships developed. Not me, yet. I had no income and no job.

An old friend who was a life insurance salesman from Duxbury Massachusetts wrote to me about a John Hancock Life Insurance Training program. I went downtown and spoke to them. I knew the senior vice president of Liberty Mutual, our neighbor in Duxbury, and also had dated the daughter of the future president of John Hancock. So, I got hired, still not certain of what I wanted or how to go about it. This was a job, and some income, but not something I had planned to do. However, the recession of 1957 and 1958 prompted me to take whatever job I could get. I was sent to the Boston headquarters for a training course. If nothing else, I learned basically about how to sell something.

Baker Acres was, in 1958, a unique living situation. Men and women were all living on the same floor and sharing bathrooms. It was a lot of fun. There were always parties and someone to talk to. In the meantime, I was selling life insurance and medical insurance – not an easy sell. I did just okay. However, I was awarded a top producer trip to the Green Briar in White Sulphur Springs, North Carolina. I was a top producer only for the first-year group. This was nowhere near an "old-hand" top producer. The Green Briar was very nice. We got more training and a lot of social activity. Everything was paid for by John Hancock.

Back in San Francisco, I was trying to sell more life insurance. I made just enough money to stay solvent but not much for partying, socializing or dating.

However, the Air Force Reserve was good. I got to fly one

of the T-33 jets as often as I wanted. It turns out that most of the officers at headquarters were Majors and above. As older pilots, they did not want to learn to fly jets. They were content to keep up their currency in the older prop-driven C-47 transports. So, there were only a few qualified young jet pilots and we could always schedule a jet flight as we were needed to keep the planes flying. In fact, sometimes the operations officer called me and said, "Don't you want to go somewhere this weekend?" I had a girlfriend in Beverly Hills and one in Denver, Colorado. I flew to see each of them occasionally. When I went to Los Angeles/ Beverly Hills, my old girlfriend, Joan Benny from Stanford and New York (now divorced), would pick me up at the base and we would spend the weekend. Then she'd drive me back to the air-field on Sunday night and I would fly back to the Air Force base and go to work Monday morning.

At Baker Acres, I met Andy Thomas, an Army pilot who was now in the Army Reserves. I flew sometimes with him in civilian Cessna 172's which were leased to the Army Reserves. One time, rather than driving, we went to the U.S. Army Airfield at the Presidio. He flew me in an Army helicopter to Hamilton Air Force base. We landed there and then walked over to the Air Force Operations area and got into my Air Force T-33 Jet. I flew him in the back seat. He was introduced to jet-flying and was so impressed that he went to United Airlines to get a job. They hired him and he quit his regular job, thanks to me. Before he went to work at United, we flew again – this time, at night, and we did acrobatics by moonlight over Northern California. Later, I was best man at his wedding in Bakersfield.

I was not a real success in the life insurance business. For one thing, I didn't like talking about death and the aftermath all the time. For some people, this business came easily. Not for me. I thought I would have to find something else to do to make a living – something I loved. So, my thought process was to try to find something interesting. One of the very older successful life insurance agents said to me at lunch one day, "In ten years, half the things that we will all be using, have not even been invented yet." Wow. That got to me. How can I possibly get somehow involved in something like this in the future?

While still in life insurance, I ran into another old friend at a Stanford Football Game. Bob Ames had been my aid when I was a cadet colonel at Stanford. He had been a B-47 pilot. I hadn't seen him since I had landed at Plattsburg Air Force Base in New York. Now he was working for Lockheed Missile Systems in Palo Alto. He had a lovely wife and four adorable young kids. His wife was from Plattsburg, where he had been stationed.

One night I arranged to take Bob up in a T-33 jet. We took off at night and were dutifully adhering to the restricted climb corridor after taking off from Hamilton AFB. Suddenly, I saw navigation lights directly in front of me. I instinctively pulled up and rolled over upside down. I saw two airplanes in formation flying down the climb corridor. This was totally against all the rules. The climb corridor is restricted air space for just leaving and flying away from any Air Force base. We were so close that when I rolled over and looked down and saw the other planes passing underneath me, I could see into one cockpit and could see his instrument lights. We weren't more than twenty feet apart. Bob saw it too. I called the radar guys and yelled at them about allowing this to happen. I got no answer.

I left the John Hancock Company in 1959 to look for something different. I met my old friend from Stanford, Howie Evans. He was living in Berkeley and needed a roommate to share expenses. He was in the UC Berkeley Law School (University of California). We got along very well as we had at Stanford. We had been part of a college crew that painted houses in the local area. While at lunch one day, I saw Kay Mickel eating at a nearby table. Kay and I had been engaged to be married while she was at Wellesly College. I had even gotten an engagement ring for her, which she wore. We hooked up again and, much to my surprise, old feelings surfaced. She had just gotten a divorce and was at law school, however, our closeness could never amount to anything since I had no job and no prospects at that time. So, after a couple of months, we parted. She found someone else and got married and left California, went to Georgetown and got a law degree. I have spoken to her over the years and several years ago, she told me she now has two children and is a Judge on the California Supreme Court.

Looking at various employment opportunities, one seemed interesting. The Stuart-Sauter Company put on conventions and trade shows, mostly in the San Francisco area. Also, some in Los Angeles. They hired me. It was very interesting work. I was busy almost seven days a week, as so many of the conventions and trade shows went on over weekends. I learned that conventions and trade shows, in many cases, took almost a year to set up. I was an assistant to a guy who flew in the Army Air Corps during WWII. He was a mentor to me, enlightening me as to how a trade show or convention is put together. It took a number of months and then, hopefully, ran well. The people who came to these conventions and trade shows never knew – nor should they know – all the things that go into making everything come together, by day and night. We worked closely with the big hotels in San Francisco. I got to see a lot of interesting inner-workings of the hotels in the city.

At the same time that I was working in the trade show industry, during my reserve duty weekend I saw an ad on the Hamilton Air Force Base bulletin board for anyone wishing to try out for the base rifle team. It instructed applicants to go see the range officer at the base range. So, knowing I had target shooting background from Stanford, I went to see Sgt. Sports at the range. I shot. I qualified. Then I was told my scores qualified me to be placed on active duty and sent to the Worldwide USAF Championships in San Antonio, Texas. Now, as this tournament went on during the week, I had to get time off from the Stuart-Sauter

Company. I took vacation time and flew to Lackland Air Force Base, Texas. On the first day of the tournament, there were over 100 people from all over the world. The first thing the head range officer asked was if everyone knew what the Crutchfield Aggregate was. I'd never heard of it, but I wasn't about to embarrass myself, so I said nothing. I guessed that if I was there, I should have known what it was. I had never done much outdoor prone shooting. The head range officer then said, "In order to get like shooters and competitors together, we would set up the firing line by competitors' average scores. First, he called out "Who has scored in the high 90's?" One guy went up to the firing line. Next, he said, "Now the mid-90's." A couple more moved up to the firing line. Then he got to anyone who had fired in the mid-80's and one more moved up to the firing line. Well, I remembered that my average score at Stanford was 385 points out of 400, so I moved up to the firing line. There were seven or eight of us there. They all seemed to know each other. I knew none of them. Then the line continued to fill out by a person's average scores.

I introduced myself to them and then said I had been on a college team but was unfamiliar with large tournaments like this one. Then I apologized for my ignorance and I said my average score was 385 out of 400, and I admitted, "I'm sorry, but I don't know what the Crutchfield Aggregate is." They said it was a several day tournament of 4,000 points – not the 400, I thought. So I told them, "My mistake. I'll pick up my stuff and equipment and move down the line where it seemed I belonged. They all rallied around me and said, "Stay here. We'll help you." I noted that they all had heavy barreled and/or custom-made rifles – and I had only a standard barreled target rifle. Well, we all shot for several days and at the end of this worldwide Air Force tournament, I came in 6th in the entire Air Force.

Sometime after that, I was approached by Colonel Joe Decker, the designated head of the USAF Reserve Rifle Team. He wanted me to be on the Air Force Reserve Team and, of course, I said yes. And he said, I'd join with Art Cook, the 1958 Olympic Gold Medal Winner, Art Jackson, a silver Olympic Medal Winner, and Vic Auer, a future Olympic Gold Medal winner. Well, my goodness, when I was on the prep school team, Art Cook had just won an Olympic Gold Medal. To those of us shooters all around the country, Art Cook was like a Shooter's God. Here, suddenly, I was his team-mate! When all the Reserve Shooters were put together with our scores, we won the 'Best Team' and we reservists won most of the trophies.

(Back L-R) **Lt Col. W. J. Ingraham**, Seattle Reserve Center; **Cwo L. G. Campbell**, Bakalar AFB, Ind.; **Capt, J.D. Hershkern**, Bakalar AFB,Ind.; **Maj. W. L. Pruden**, Denver Reserve Center; **1/Lt V.L. Hamlin**, Denver Reserve Center; **1/Lt G. S. Maloney**, San Francisco Reserve Center; **S/Sgt J.G. Morris**, 433rd Troop Carrier Wg, Brooks AFB, San Antonio, Tex; **A/1c R.W. Carson**, Pittsburg Reserve Center; **Mag Ollie E. Clark**, Ass't Project Officer, 9869th Air Reserve Sq., Del Rio, Texas. (Front L-R) **Maj Carroll R. Pusard**, Ass't Project Officer, 9869th Air Reserve Sq., Del Rio, Texas; **A/1c Robert E. Campbell**, 433rd Troop Carrier Wing Brook AFB, San Antonio, Texas; **H.H. Legg**, Bakalar AFB, Ind.; **T/Sgt Lloyd F. Smith**, 433rd Troop Carrier Wing; **Captain Edwin W. Yanta**, 9858th AR Sq., San Antonio, Texas; **T/Sgt James R. Vasquez**, 9817th AR Sq. San Antonio, Texas

The Air Force had placed ten other reservists from around the country on active duty for the match to take care of four of us. Wow, I was only a lieutenant and felt like a general. My reserve duty for the next several years was to fly all around the country and compete in rifle tournaments. For this, we got paid. We got distinctive shooting jackets and hats and all the various shooting equipment we needed. We got rifles, handguns, spotting scopes, and all the ammunition we could use. For a poor guy like me, who was using a borrowed or just standard equipment, I was in seventh heaven.

The story behind all of this activity was that General Curtis Lemay, head of the Air Force, went to the 1952 Olympics and saw that the U.S. Shooters did poorly and were beaten by everyone in the Eastern-block nations. What the Russians and other countries did was find shooters from college, put them in the Army, and pay them to only target shoot. Thus, the U.S. Shooters who only shot on weekends were up against essentially professional marksmen. So, the General established what was called an Advanced Marksmanship Unit. The Marines and the Army did the same thing. Thus, I became involved in this program, which yielded the U.S. four gold medals, two in the Army, two in the Air Force, in the next few Olympics.

Soon, Colonel Joe Decker sent word to my reserve unit that I was a member of the Air Force Reserve Rifle Team and would be put on active duty to participate in any and all tournaments I wanted to enter anywhere in the western half of the United States. So, I did. In fact, I qualified for the 1960 final Olympic qualifications – 27 through 29 July 1960. Everyone had custom-made rifles with special heavy barrels. I was very nervous. Everyone else there had been in heavy competition for a number of years. I had been in this type of competition for only one year. I didn't do as well as I could/should have. I never came close to the top two spots. I just felt so good in one way that I even qualified for the final Olympic Team Tryouts. I could have done better. I've forgotten my final score. As I went home, I left with mixed feelings – happy to be at the final tryouts and unhappy that I hadn't done what I felt I was capable of doing.

About this time, I moved from Baker Acres to a tiny studio apartment in Sausalito. There I met Walter Crump, another Easterner and "preppy" and also a sailor. We discovered a lot in common, as he, too, had won a national sailing championship. The apartment house in Sausalito was called The Portofino Riviera. This place had a dock, a small ill-kept marina, and the building faced San Francisco across the bay. I never will forget the magnificent view of the Bay with the City of San Francisco in the background. As I traveled across the Golden Gate Bridge, I always thought to myself, "I must remember this picture forever." In fact, I can close my eyes today and see the Bay and the approaches to the city by the Golden Gate Bridge and the Presidio.

Almost every weekend for the next six years, I was either flying my T-33 Jet around the country or off participating in various shooting tournaments. Thus, I got active-duty lieutenant's pay and became, I guess – a professional shooter.

And now back in the work-a-day world, I was engrossed in the convention and trade show business. The Stuart-Sauter Company also designed and built big, small, and complicated advertising booths for the large companies' advertising. Each of these came in pieces and could be set up in any city, then taken apart and shipped to the next convention or trade show.

Since I worked as often as seven days a week, I scheduled my flying at night. I'd call the 4th Air Force operations officer and ask for a jet to be made available to me on a particular evening. I'd arrive at Hamilton Air Force base, usually after dark, and there would be a T-33 Jet and its crew chief waiting for me. I'd fly all around California for an hour and a half or more, come back and land, sign off at the airplane, and go home – only to go to work the next morning.

All current Air Force Pilots, including the reservists, must meet the same minimum requirements every year. I had to fly a test of instrument flying which took most of the day, and also every year, I had to do a standard/evaluation check-ride. Here, I had to show the check pilot that I could fly the airplane in any and all situations and configurations that I might encounter. This also encompassed demonstrating my ability to cope with and control all sorts of flying emergencies. I had to take a day off from work to complete each of these, and I also had to put in one weekend a month for Air Force Reserve duty.

The Stuart-Sauter Company office manager had no use for anything military. He didn't like me taking time off and occasionally being gone on a working weekend when a convention was in progress. So, one day he told me that they were letting me go. I was nicely fired, after being with the company for about a year or a little more. My feeling when that happened was that I could fly a jet and compete as a shooter and those activities were more important to me than my job. I felt that I could get a job anytime, but that I would never be able to fly a jet like I was doing anytime anywhere.

I had some money saved. I had a used Volkswagen, which didn't cost me much, and I also had a small income from the Air Force Reserve. Since I was put on active duty so regularly and since I did so much flying, I had a minimum sustainable income, but the old bugaboo returned. I had no long-term goal. So, I began to look for something interesting to do. I had no easily marketable skill like my engineering friends, so I continued looking for something interesting. I looked here and there, answered ads, spoke to a number of persons who interviewed me, while looking for a job. I went on several interviews but saw no fit for me, nor were the companies interested in me. This was hard on my psyche – I had a feeling that maybe nobody wanted me. Then something finally turned up … a company called Telautograph Corporation. They were looking for a manufacturer's representative. They made and were beginning to market something called

FAX. This was something new – something never seen before – and it excited me!

The Telautograph Corporation, with this Fax, created a whole new industry. Now, unbelievably and suddenly, someone could send a printed page or diagram or even a picture to someone on the other end of any telephone line. I went to work at their Northern California Office helping to create this new industry. I took the Fax phenomena to the Navy at Naval Air Station Alameda and showed them that they could send complicated engineering drawings worldwide. For instance, they could get complicated engine problems properly repaired by the use of the Navy's new ability to send in-depth plans and specifications and updated current bulletins to faraway bases and maintenance depots. It was exciting! I also showed the Fax to the merchant marine ships. They could now utilize updated nautical charts. I showed people that they could send a picture, for instance, of a newborn baby, to relatives instantly. This work was new and therefore challenging to me. There were no old, long-term historical precedents to be rigidly adhered to. In essence, I could almost chart my own course based on the new capabilities of the Fax.

Central Pacific State Regional Winner - Gerry Maloney with Brig. Gen. Rollin Moore, Commander 349th Troop Carrier Wing, California - Summer 61'

About this time, Headquarters 4th Air Force was deactivated, and my assignment was now to the 349th Troop Carrier Wing. I was assigned as a troop carrier pilot flying C-119s as a Troop Carrier Wing Operations Officer and Small Arms Training Officer. However, all was not so well in the world of international politics. The Russians had secretly begun stationing intercontinental rockets on the island of Cuba. These rockets were capable of carrying nuclear warheads. President Kennedy put the military on alert. Military units of all types were moved to the Southeast of the U.S.

I woke up to my radio alarm one morning in 1962 and the announcer said that the reserve unit by the name of the 349th Troop Carrier Wing had been called to active duty, so I guessed "no work today." I rolled out of bed and promptly fell on the floor. I stood up and again fell on the floor. It was later determined that I was suffering from something called Vestibulitis (Vertigo), which meant that my inner ear, which is what makes the body have stability, wasn't working. I called Hamilton Air Force Base's 349th Troop Carrier Wing Headquarters and told them of my problem, noting that I couldn't possibly drive a car as I couldn't stand up without holding on to something. They told me they were in turmoil because of everybody reporting in but ordered me to put on my uniform and they would send an ambulance for me. I waited for two days. Sometime during the second day, a Major I knew telephoned me. He told me I'd be AWOL if I didn't report ASAP. I explained my problem and the promise of the hospital to send an ambulance for me. He said everything was in flux, but he'd call the medical people. Later that day, an ambulance arrived with two newly activated medics. I spent a dizzy week in the base hospital and was diagnosed with Vestibular Neuritis which caused my inability to stand or walk. A week or so later, I was okay and resumed my duties as Assistant Operations Officer, C-119 pilot, and Small Arms Instructor.

Previously, during our monthly weekend wing meetings, only a few came out to the shooting range to shoot or to qualify with their issued 45 caliber handguns. Now, suddenly, I and the two sergeant range officers were very popular. The squadron was scheduled to go to Florida and perhaps off to a war. Now, the range was very busy. Most of the air crews wanted to re-qualify with their issued 45 handguns or with whatever other sidearm they wished to carry. I was now in great demand.

Back to flying – all my flying career, I had been a single engine jet fighter pilot. As of 24 June 1960, I had flown my last single-engine jet flight. It was a sad day. From there, I became just another Air Force pilot, no longer designated a jet fighter pilot. Now I was assigned to fly what was known as a flying boxcar. I was not a happy camper. These things – the C-119 – flew like a boxcar. Every day, one or two of the C-119s took off with several paratroopers. We practiced the procedures for how to drop troops. I was not the best C-119 pilot. In fact, I disliked the damn things. Since I had so little time in them, even though I was a qualified C-119 pilot, I usually flew as co-pilot or third pilot. That was okay with me.

During this time, I continued to live at my small apartment on the water in Sausalito and drove the 20 miles to the base every day. The reserve call up was supposed to be for a year. I so notified my Telautograph Office. They understood.

Shortly, the wing and all of its airplanes went on a training night flight to Nellis Air Force Base, Las Vegas, Nevada. It was a night in trail sort of formation – each airplane one minute behind the other. We spent a couple of days at Nellis Air Force Base in Vegas training with new paratroopers in individual weapons. We then flew back to Hamilton Air Force Base. Shortly thereafter, as we all made plans to go to Florida, the blockade of Cuba instituted by President Kennedy resulted in the Russian ships carrying missiles and atomic weapons turn back. Negotiations with the Russians soon ended the standoff. We were ordered to stand down. The Reserve call up for a year ended after only about five weeks. I drew a sigh of relief. None of us really wanted to go to war.

When I returned to my office at Telautograph Corporation in San Francisco, I found that my office was occupied by someone I did not know. I learned that since I had gone off to war, so to speak, the company had brought in a replacement person from Los Angeles. I was devastated. The company said they knew that when a person is called to active duty in the reserve forces, or in the national guard, they must be given their old job back or be given an equal job. The law may be more complicated, but essentially, I should have my old job back. However, here was someone who had just relocated from Los Angeles and the company didn't want to send him back. So, to comply with the law, they offered me an equal position as their manufacturer's representative in Los Angeles. They had complied with the letter of the law, but I certainly did not want to move to Los Angeles. All of my friends were in Northern California. So, I was out of a job, as were many others from our short military call-up and discharge.

I had been promoted to Captain at the start of the Cuban Missile Crisis, but now I was back on the streets, feeling good and yet disappointed – good that I had participated in a successful military exercise that didn't result in war but feeling let down because I had lost a very interesting job in essentially establishing a new industry. My active Air Force Reserve role continued as did my Air Force Team Shooting.

I continued job-hunting. My criteria was still to find something interesting - something maybe as breathtaking and new as the Telautograph Corporation and the Fax was. For a month, I worked in the West Coast Volvo Car parts warehouse. I was there only because I had two friends who were Volvo executives and they needed part-time help. So, through them, I bought one of their Volvos and sold my Volkswagen. I was still looking for interesting vocations. I was almost hired by Sunset Magazine in Palo Alto but the president of the company killed the job saying something like "no budget for this now."

I remember one interview where I had filled out an application and stated I had graduated from Stanford with honors. During the interview, the interviewer questioned me about honors. I said that my senior paper had won the national history prize. He said something like, "You call *that* honors?" To him, honors were grade point averages. I defended myself and said that I thought winning the national history prize was an honor. I didn't get that job.

I had two friends working for IBM. They told me IBM was looking for people. I was interested. They told their IBM people that I was a good prospect, so I made an appointment and went for an interview. I had two interviews and then was told that I should take a test, which I took. The test was mostly about figures, percentages and so forth - definitely, not my strong suit. Of course, I flunked. In fact, it was so bad that I remember I didn't even understand half the questions. The manager with whom I had interviewed came to me looking very strange. No job offer. From his demeanor, I surmised that he couldn't comprehend how a Stanford graduate could be so stupid. Obviously, he – just like everyone else I had known, including me - knew nothing about the dynamics of dyslexia. Another person in my life disappointed in me. So, I kept moving.

I then went for an interview with 3M Company. We met in a downtown hotel conference room. 3M Company was about to embark on the establishment of a new corporate division. 3M had made music tapes for reel-to-reel music systems. Someone in management had decided that the reel-to-reel music equipment was awkward. They envisioned a tape cartridge system. 3M then developed a system where you could stack music tape cartridges in a machine that would drop individual cartridges from a stack on one side of the machine, play it and the machine then would rewind the tape cartridge and restack it on the other side of the box. This was revolutionary. This would make all records and turntables worldwide obsolete. I told them that for a year in Korea, I had put music on reel-to-reel tapes and had a stack of reels at home. I expressed great enthusiasm and further expressed a great vision for its future. This was a whole new world for the 3M Company and I wanted to be in it.

I left the interview feeling good and frankly excited. However, I didn't know the future. I waited to hear from 3M and heard nothing for a week. I screwed up my courage and called the telephone number I had used before. I didn't know whether they'd even still be in town. Well, they answered. They said that they had been waiting for me to contact them. What a surprise. They had almost given up on me. Their attitude was that if I wanted the job, I'd have to show some aggressiveness. This suddenly was something that would stay with me and guide me for the rest of my life. Go after what you want. Aim high.

We made an appointment to meet at the 3M Company office in San Francisco. I arrived there, but beforehand, I looked up the background information about the 3M Company's products. I tried to memorize a number of these products, as I felt that I'd have to show some smarts and understanding of their corporate culture. I felt I would have to know more about the company and not just their new invention. All went well, and I got hired. I don't remember all the preliminaries in the San Francisco Office, however, I do remember a good feeling of being at the very beginning of a new invention.

They arranged for me to meet two other men who were involved in this new endeavor. We were to travel to Minneapolis, Minnesota – 3M Headquarters – for a briefing on all aspects of the engineering behind the music tape cartridge system. We got to play with the thing. We learned about the promotion of a new product and our (my) part in it. Good people. Good substantial company. I couldn't have been more pleased to be a manufacturer's representative.

Back in San Francisco, I was given a new car and lots of promotional material. I was introduced to the staff as someone who was the 3M contact for the music box and all of its ramifications.

I got my sample machine and about 15 tapes which contained about 100 songs. This was only the beginning. The plan was to eventually have hundreds of songs all on tape manufactured by 3M. Now I felt like I had found a home. It was a good feeling, as I had felt like the Air Force was once my home. I got with the people at the San Francisco 3M Office and planned all of the places, stores, bars, restaurants in eleven western states that I would contact and visit and demonstrate this new phenomenon. This was the beginning of a whole new industry. We would shortly replace all the records and turntables in the whole world. This was exhilarating. I set up my own schedule from San Jose, California to Seattle, Washington and all cities in between. As a manufacturer's representative, I demonstrated the workings and the quality of the music to ship owners, ship captains, bar and restaurant owners, and everyone in between who wanted or needed music in any way. The machines and the tape cartridges were ordered directly from the 3M Factory. All who ordered and used the machine asked about when they would get more tapes and more music.

After a number of months, two things happened: 1) After many hundreds of hours of use, a tiny plastic part broke, which allowed the tape to escape its track and become tangled and useless. 2) As I understood it, the union wanted too much money for the rights of millions of songs and 3M Company balked at the cost. Thus, we were stuck with the original group of songs, so the decision was made by 3M to scrap the program and concentrate on what 3M does better than anyone in the world – that is, make the finest tape. As a result of this, 3M's leadership backed out of the machine manufacturing and thus, all other companies in the music business began working on their own types of tape cartridge music systems. 3M ended up selling all of them their tape. Thus, 3M did, in fact, create a whole new industry.

When I realized that 3M was going to curtail its new division, I knew that I'd probably be out of a job again. Friends had contacted me several months previously about something else that would fall under the category of "something new." It was the advent of computer application into the small business world. I resigned from 3M and went to see the people who were attempting to integrate computers into small business. Previously, only big businesses could afford computers. Small businesses with computers could now handle payroll, keeping track of stock, automatic record-keeping, etc. In researching this, I found this was not for me. Much of it was numbers and percentages, so I left, and contacted a friend who had worked with me at John Hancock. He had started a real estate company. We got together and had a good talk about the real estate business. He said he was a loner and did not wish to have an office full of salespeople – his main goal was to buy and accumulate rental properties. He introduced me to Billy Best, the head of Palo Alto Real Estate Company. Mr. Best agreed to train me.

Billy Best was a long-time realtor in the mid-peninsula area. I went to work there. It was all routine, mostly dealing with people – buyers and sellers. I was good at that, taking real estate courses and eventually qualifying for the designation "Realtor." Real estate, it turned out, was lucrative enough for me to actually be able to think about dating on a regular basis. I even bought an Alpha Romeo sportscar!

I was soon hired away from Best's real estate firm by Dale Denson, whose family business was Dalton Realty in Palo Alto. More on this later. Dale's family and mine became close friends and our friendship lasted fifty years.

CHAPTER 8
MARRIAGE & FAMILY

About 1961, I was still a member of the San Francisco Olympic Club and was utilizing their indoor range at the downtown club. At this time, I was still on the USAF Rifle Team and also on the Olympic Club rifle team. Also about this time, I became President of the Stanford Junior Alumni Association of Northern California. This group was well formed and attended, but not absolutely chartered with the University. I don't know how we operated without a formal University Charter before me, but I corrected this and our alumni group did become chartered.

The officers of the Stanford Junior Alumni Association met at the San Francisco apartment of Dorcas Crawford, our association secretary. While at a meeting, during a break, I went to the kitchen and discovered one of her roommates. She was quite attractive and I introduced myself to her. Her name was Minty Raymond. We found we had a few things in common. She had grown up in Greater Boston as I had and graduated from a New England Prep School, as I had. We didn't get much further than that. I went back to the meeting, thinking to myself that I should ask her out for a drink or something. When our meeting broke up that day, I left with the rest of the officers to go out for a social drink. It would be a year before I got back to that apartment for another meeting.

In 1962, still shooting at the Downtown Olympic Rifle Club and now working as a realtor with a more active social life, I attended another meeting of the Stanford Junior Alumni Association at Dorcas Crawford's apartment in San Francisco. At that meeting, I recalled the other roommate I'd met in the kitchen named Minty. I went back to talk with Minty and we seemed to really hit it off this time, discussing our similar backgrounds at length. We went out together that day and started dating regularly. We found that we were really compatible and enjoyed many of the same memories, people and pastimes. After dating Minty for another year, I proposed to her and we became engaged to be married. We were married on the 23rd of May, 1964.

Minty was given money by her dad for the wedding. She then did all the planning for the wedding and the fabulous reception at the St. Francis Yacht Club. There were probably 100 guests at the wedding and reception, and a good time was had by all. My best friend, Lt. Bud Narramore, flew all the way from Japan for

Olympic Club Party in Sausalito – Minty – front left

My Alpha Romeo Giulietta Special - white with blue racing stripes

the wedding. We spent the first night in the honeymoon suite at the Alta Mira Hotel in Sausalito. This was a wedding present from a friend who I had previously worked with. The hotel was on a hill overlooking Sausalito, San Francisco Bay and San Francisco in the distance. The planning for our wedding and honeymoon trip was wonderful and never to be forgotten. We spent the rest of our honeymoon traveling the gold route through the Sierras. Halfway through our planned honeymoon trip, Minty announced that she wanted to go home. This was a shock, but it was a harbinger of things to come during our life together. After a short rental in the heart of the Presidio district of San Francisco, Minty and I moved into a rental two-bedroom home on Oregon Street in Palo Alto. Our neighbor was also an

Pre-May Mad Marathon

It's indeed a swinging spring for Bay area party goers who have yet to see a respite from the social whirl. Events have included an immensely successful Junior League cabaret, the annual all-night Bachelors Ball, a delightful Peninsula reception and an auxiliary's kick-off party, all pictured here.

But confirmed party-goers know that these were just warm-up sessions . . . the merry month of May is still to come.

Junior League party Minty Raymond, Jerry Maloney, Dorcas Crawford and Larry Mersereau

Junior League Party in April 1964,
a month before Minty and I married.

Wedding Party (L-R front:)*Don Sandy and *Walter Crump (L-R back:) Bob Ames, Paul Livingston, Bob Aulgur, Best Man, me, Minty Raymond Maloney, Cynthia Holowell, Toni Howard and Tess Raymond, *I was best man at Don and Walter's weddings

Air Force reservist with a reserve assignment at Hamilton AFB. We sometimes traveled to Hamilton AFB together when our duty days coincided. He was a qualified Air Force navigator and worked as a navigator for Globe Airways.

Meanwhile Dale Denson was mentored me at Dalton Realty. I gradually became a success. I had a past association with the previous owner, Arthur Dalton. As a sophomore at Stanford, I had needed insurance on my Ford Station Wagon. Blair Pasco told me of an old insurance guy who headed Dalton Realty in Palo Alto. He liked Stanford students and I went to see him and got insurance on my car. Mr. Dalton was a big help to a lot of students.

Dale had bought the real estate business from old man Dalton and kept the name Dalton realty. I met Mr. Dalton and renewed my old acquaintance with him. He and I were both thrilled. I had dinner a couple of times with Mr. Dalton and his lovely wife. I believe it was either Mr. Dalton or Dale who introduced me to the

Mr. and Mrs. Robert Lovejoy Raymond

request the honor of your presence

at the marriage of their daughter

Mary Minturn

to

Mr. Gerald Stack Maloney

on Saturday, the twenty-third of May

at four o'clock in the afternoon

The Episcopal Church

of Saint Mary the Virgin

San Francisco, California

May 23, 1964

book, *How I made a Million Dollars in Real Estate in My Spare Time*. Now, this suddenly became a path for me to follow for the rest of my life.

I bought a house in an Eichler subdivision in Palo Alto, got a used Mercedes car and became successful with Dale's tutoring. A fellow realtor at Dalton Realty was a brilliant oriental man with worldwide connections named Frank Chuck. In his youth, Frank had taught chemistry at a university in China. His best friends were Mao Zedong and Zhou Enlai. He said they used to sit together and discuss communism and the future of China. Frank said he had a leaning toward a different kind of economy. He left China, I don't know when, and came to

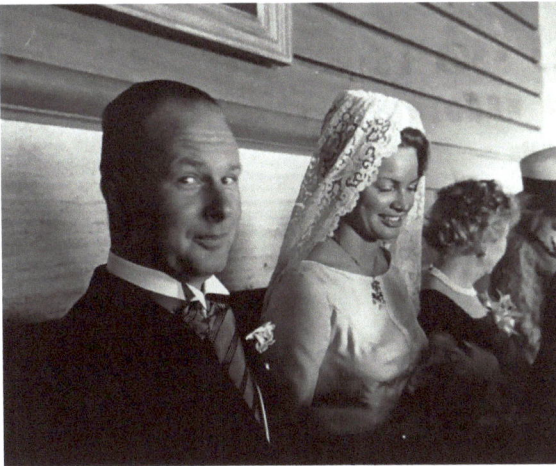

Reception at St. Francis Yacht Club, San Francisco, CA

the U.S. Frank went to work for the Carnation Company as a chemist. Eventually, I believe, Frank was their chief chemist. He developed Carnation's signature product, "powdered cream." For this, he was given much money – he never said how much, but it was enough to buy two huge apartment buildings. He then quit Carnation and went into the real estate business, working in the Dalton office.

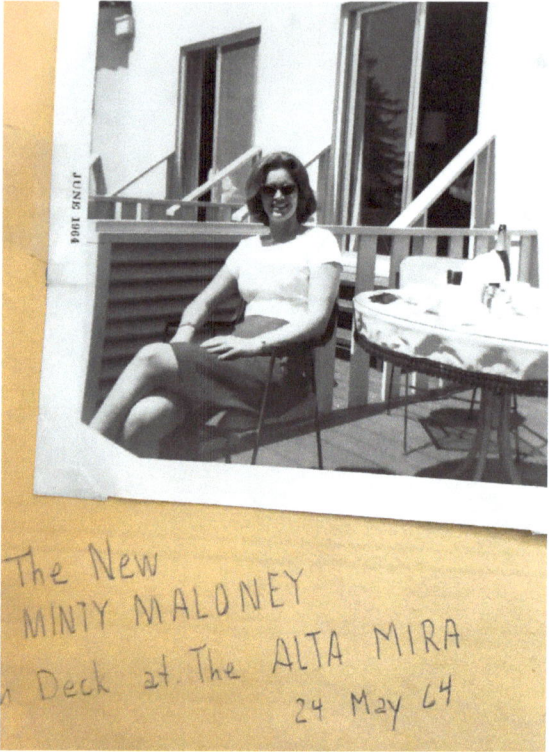

JUNE 1964

The New
MINTY MALONEY
Deck at The ALTA MIRA
24 May 64

Frank Chuck spent a lot of time and effort placing money from mainland China into U.S. real estate. I admired him. He could tell stories about Chairmen Mao and Zhou. He made the headlines about China more real and somewhat personal.

About this time, I had a discussion with several fellow realtors about our individual goals in life. All I remember was thinking that one of the group had a nice large house in Palo Alto with a two door garage that had an apartment above it. He rented the main house, which paid the mortgage and lived in the apartment over the garage. That sounded good to me, so I believe I told the group that was what I'd like to do. About two weeks later, one of our group called and told me of a house and garage rental unit that just came on the market and he thought it was underpriced. He said we'd better hurry.

Minty and I drove to see it. It was a Williamsburg Colonial, very much like the homes in New England where Minty and I had both grown up! We made an instant decision to buy it before we even saw the rental unit or the inside of the house.

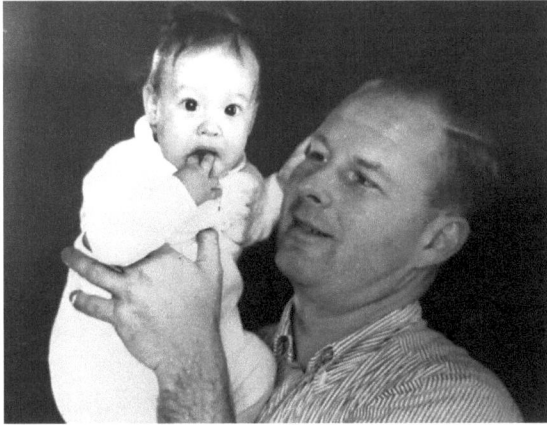
Katie and me

I went to my office and wrote up a full price offer. Then, I thought, as the house was underpriced, other people might make a full price offer, so I added $50 to the $48,000 offer.

When the owner returned at the end of the day, there were several full price offers, however, mine was $50 more! So, I bought the house. Therefore, I had fulfilled a dream from only a few weeks previously of being able to live mortgage-free. We sold our Eichler home for a $2,000 profit and moved into 749 Seneca Street in Palo Alto. I was now doing well enough in real estate to live in one of the premiere homes in Palo Alto and drive a Mercedes.

During the time we had lived in the Eichler home, Katherine Raymond Maloney was born. She was delivered by a classmate of mine from Stanford. Minty had a long, hard delivery made more difficult because the nurses at the Palo Alto Hospital went on strike. Therefore, Minty had to go to an unfamiliar Redwood City Hospital and be attended by very nice but unfamiliar nurses. Our daughter, Katie, as she has always been called, was born on August 14, 1966.

Minty called me at the office one day and asked if I'd consider getting a dog. A neighbor was moving and couldn't take his dog. I said yes and went to the neighbor's house to get acquainted with the dog. I liked him. That evening, we decided to get Rusty.

The next day after work I went to the neighbor's house to take the dog. Imagine my surprise when I found the house empty. They were gone and Rusty was sitting on the front porch all alone. I sat and talked with him for a while. He came willingly with me to our home to meet Minty and Katie and thus, a most wonderful ten-year relationship began for our whole family.

Chris and Rusty

Our son, Christopher Sean Maloney, was born at Palo Alto Hospital on July 22, 1968. Chris's middle name Sean came from my brother, Sean Maloney, who had drowned in Humrock Bay, Massachusetts at three years of age.

When we took Chris home, our dog Rusty dashed out of the house and ran up and down the whole block barking his head off, announcing to all that Christopher was home. Chris and Rusty had a close relationship always.

One of the worst days of my life was when we left Rusty at the vet's office to be put down. Minty had been told that we could not be with him for the procedure. Rusty had become ill and we'd been told he would not get better. The night before Rusty died, we had all spent several hours with him on our bed, hugging him and loving him. When I left Rusty with the vet and walked away, I turned back after about twenty paces and I will never forget the look on his face. That look said, "You are leaving me here to die alone." I am haunted by that look to this day and get tears in my eyes when I think of it. Rusty was an absolute, one-hundred percent devoted dog. He even loved to fly with me when I flew small civilian airplanes.

GERRY MALONEY, member of the Olympic Club Rifle Team, has been named coach of the State Smallbore team. He will represent California and the Club in the national championships in Ohio in August. Gerry is rated one of The Olympic Club's top shooters.

Hall and Maloney Win New Shooting Honors for Club

by Brian W. H. Taylor

The Olympic Club Pistol team made a clean sweep of the team matches at Coyote Point's "2700" aggregate matches recently. Bob Hall edged out O.C. team captain T. D. Elton for team individual honors by 13 points with 2587x2700.

Elton's 2574 plus Christman's 2523 and Jack Ahern's 2515 gave our team the overall championship at the San Mateo meet. Both Hall and Elton went home with enough prizes in Sterling Silver to give Tiffany's reason to close up shop.

Christman, shooting with borrowed guns (his had been shipped to Camp Perry for the National matches) won his share of honors along with dead-eye Ahern.

In other matches, in which results arrived too late to meet the OLYMPIAN'S August deadline, team captain Elton again was on top with the handguns, taking the Oakland Pistol Club's first 2700 match with 2577x2700. Bob Hall was close with 2569.

The Olympic Club did not enter this meet due to the entry in Richmond's match the following Sunday.

On the rifle scene, San Mateo County held a three event series of re-entry matches through May of this year on their Coyote Point Range.

Olympian Gerry Maloney swept all three matches. He beat ___ for 100 50-yard standing score with ___. In February the rafter ___ tries were forthcoming for the ___.

In March he raised ___ prone score from 99.6x100 to ___ lutely perfect 100-10x100. Thereafter there were no more entries in this event either.

In the 50 yard prone event, Maloney tied with Johnny Russell, one of the state's best shooters.

A shootoff was arranged for late May. Maloney beat Russell 200 18x to 200 15x200.

The tournament was then cancelled for the second half of the year until the County finds someone to compete with Maloney.

In June some 80 shooters met at Richmond for the annual Western States Championship tournament.

Olympian, Aug. 64

Gerry Maloney set new records ___ swee ___ San Mateo rifle events for Ch ___ ion.

Six hours and 2000 points la ___, Olympian Maloney emerged as th ___ States champion. His aggrega e ___ 1989 116x2000 topped a secu ___ ___ score of 1989 110x2000.

The lead had changed hand ___ ___ times during the five matches and was hotly contested down to the last shot as evidenced by the final score.

Maloney was first in both ___ inter national aggregate and the ___ y Sigh aggregate. He also won the ___ mete match, and in winning the 100 yar ___ ___ posted one of the few perfec ___ es fired on the Richmond range in ___ at years.

NATIONAL RIFLE

Publishers of THE

1600 Rhode Island Avenue, N.W.

During the late 1960's, I continued to sell small income properties and homes in the Palo Alto area as well as actively participating in the Air Force Reserves and as an Olympic Club Shooter. At this time, I was also coaching shooting sports at the Palo Alto Military Academy. I was a NRA Certified Rifle Marksman Instructor as well as a California Certified Hunter Safety Instructor.

Still in the reserves, I was the National Rifle Champion and my entire Air Force Reserve Group even had a parade for me one weekend. The next weekend I got rift (reduction in force). Six months later, I got a notice from Travis Air Force Base about interviewing for a reserve job. This was at the beginning of the Southeast Asia conflict in the late 60s. I went to interview with the colonel who ran the terminal. I got the job. This was a mobilization assignment. I was assigned to the transportation squadron. If or when the U.S. had to go to war, the plan was that those assigned to the reserves would be activated, thus doubling the transportation squadron. Then this squadron would split – half to go to the war area and the other half to remain at Travis Air Force Base. So, the people on both ends would have already had a working relationship.

Soon fulfilling my reserve assignment, I was running the Travis Air Force Base passenger terminal one day a month. After a couple of years, I had gained enough experience to go to the terminal commander with a problem. The problem was that at many places around the base, and especially in the passenger areas, there were confusing signage. Some signs were left from WWII – some from the Korean War – some were new – some were partially painted over. I noted that since this base was basically a transportation hub for military passengers, the people arriving here would be unfamiliar with the base and needed directions. I said, "You need some consistent signage." The Colonel agreed and told me I should do a staff study. He said, "Take your time and bring what you think to me when you finish it."

So, after some research, I discovered what I thought would be something in the order of a universal sign language. The basis of this signage was a red circle of any size. Inside each circle, would be arrows or directions – an X for do not go here – male and female figures with arrows for water closets and so forth. I presented this multi-page report with all the circles and directions in them - no language of any kind was involved. Thus, we would have a set of universal signs. The colonel was so pleased after walking around the base with this set of circles that he sent my staff study to his headquarters at the 22nd Air Force. The 22nd Air Force had control of all passenger traffic throughout the Pacific half of the world. The General at 22nd Air Force liked it. He sent it with a recommendation to the Pentagon. The Pentagon liked it and decided that they would implement my staff study on signs at all Air Force Bases worldwide. Then the Pentagon asked the General to ask me if I would go on active duty and implement this at all bases worldwide. I declined, saying that I had a civilian job and I could not take a leave of absence (not to mention that it was another temporary assignment with no guarantee, and I had a family to support).

Along these same lines, about this time, two colonels called me and asked if I would consider coming back on active duty to be the commanding officer of the Air Force's Advanced Marksmanship Unit. I respectfully declined for the same reason as above. About this time, I was promoted to Major.

Sometime later, at HQ 22nd Air Force, the General called me in and said there had been an accident. There was a big hole in an airplane. The General asked me to go down to the flight line and see what happened. I went down and was looking at the plane when the line chief came up and said, "Won't do any good, Major. This thing (the stairs on wheels that were rolled up to a plane) has made a hole in every single type of aircraft we have." I said, "Well, what do we do about it? Tell me about it." I was writing what he was saying as fast as I could. The chief actually told me what the problem was, what the fix was and how to make it happen. Nobody had ever listened to him before. I wrote up all the information I had and gave it to the General's secretary. Very shortly thereafter, the General called me into his office and said, "I don't believe this. This has been happening for years, and here in five minutes, as a reservist, you find out about it, delineate the problem and you tell me how it can be fixed." The General was amazed. When he had to write my annual evaluation, he made it as high as it could go. All this went toward higher promotion later.

While I was working at Dalton Realty, a friend inquired about my interest in construction and building. He and I had previously discussed the fact that some of my background was in the construction industry, specifically that I had worked building houses for several summers. He told me that a friend of his was looking for someone with a background in building. It sounded interesting, so I went to see this guy who was a partner in Lincoln Property Company. This was a big builder of apartment complexes all over the United States and this guy was opening an office in the San Jose, Silicon Valley area. He needed someone with a general knowledge of construction – someone who could be a Jack of all trades and not necessarily a master of any. I got hired.

I bid Dale Denson and Frank Chuck goodbye, although I still had a couple of income properties in Palo Alto so I would never be leaving the real estate business completely.

The Lincoln Property Company had already started one project in the Sharon Heights area. This area is in the foothills of the coast range directly behind Stanford University. I took over as the construction manager. This was a unique concept in apartment design, consisting of two wings of apartments each facing the other, with about thirty- feet separating them. All the entrances faced each other. Between the two buildings was the equivalent of a garden grove, a beautiful arboretum with mature trees. This one was 120 units for tree and nature lovers. All the doors, windows and decks faced a grove of minor woodlands.

I finished this project and one of the first persons to move in was my former Stanford History Professor, Dr. Miller. We had a pleasant reunion.

The next project was on quite a few acres of bushes and grassland. We planned for 680 units in eight buildings. I named each of the buildings after one of the Spanish explorers (Balboa, Cortez, Cabrillo, Serra, Coronado, etc.) who came over the mountains and camped on this very spot. An in-depth historic search pinpointed this area we were building on as the site of their encampment. Since all of the buildings were on a gentle hillside, I convened a meeting of the Palo Alto and Menlo Park Building Inspectors and public works groups to plan the roads, drainage, sewers, electrical, etc. The architect produced beautiful building plans. Since this was a garden apartment project, we moved the entire set of buildings around at different angles, much to the chagrin of the engineer, who wanted everything square and lined up precisely straight. We planned for copious amounts of greenery between all the buildings, and even moved one building so that we could take advantage of a huge old oak tree. We built a second story deck around it.

As we progressed with this huge, to me, project, the company began to hire a couple of specialists, one of whom was himself an old builder, and one who was a money manager.

About this time, Minty and I, Katie and Chris were settled in our Williamsburg style house in Palo Alto. Minty took the kids and Rusty to the local park every day. Life was good.

Minty and I thought about having a vacation place for our little family and we started looking in the forested areas of Northern California. We hoped to find some reasonably priced acreage where we could either pitch a tent and camp for a weekend or build a little cabin. We looked at several places and were not intrigued by anything until one day, while driving north on Route 1, a helicopter passed over us with a new car hanging below it. "Well," said we, intrigued … "Let's see where it's going." Following the helicopter, we came to the next sign to left and it said "Mendocino." The helicopter put the car down on a tiny island just off the coast where they were filming an automobile ad.

Looking around the town of Mendocino, we thought "We must be in Maine." We found that the history of the town dated back to the end of the gold rush when a group of farmers and loggers from Maine went around Cape Horn and came up to San Francisco and found themselves stranded as the gold seemed to have petered out. So, realizing that the logging companies needed people to cut redwood trees, they all moved north to Mendocino and there they started building houses like they did in Maine, with steep roofs and shingled sides. There is no snow in Mendocino, so steep roofs were not needed, thus the village of Mendocino looked just like a New England Village. Also, the houses appeared a little rundown and we thought maybe we could buy one there. A realtor told us that people from San Francisco and Los Angeles were coming up to Mendocino and buying them up and renovating them. Therefore, the prices had skyrocketed. We then spoke to the realtor about acquiring some land, so we went with him up into the hills of Mendocino and found 20 acres of redwood trees and a pygmy forest. We decided to buy it.

I called a friend I'd met through Lincoln Property Company with whom we had discussed buying land and he agreed to go half with us, so we made an offer on the land which was accepted. Another good thing about this was that the land had been cleared in 1860 and redwood trees grow very fast, so the forest was more than 100 years old and all the redwoods were extraordinarily tall and robust. A third of the land was filled with small mature trees called the Pygmy Forest. Some deficiency in the dirt had somehow degraded the performance of mature trees, so they became known as the Pygmy Forest. It was a beautiful piece of property.

I had joined a flying club at Reid Hillview Airport in San Jose, and was flying all types of civilian airplanes. The airport and club procedure is always to quiz a new club pilot on his experience. Then one instructor pilot always goes for a flight with a new club member. This procedure is always followed, no matter what your experience. Of course, I answered all his questions about basic flying. When we went for a flight, the instructor had a couple of hundred hours in light civilian aircraft. We joked about the vast difference in our experience, yet he was now the one in charge. I tried to fly a civilian airplane at least every two weeks. Competence was not as crucial in the light civilian airplane as it was when flying a jet. Rusty loved flying with me – turns and banks did not phase him. Once I took Katie up. I sat her in my lap and let her push and pull the controls. She "sort of" flew the airplane for a while. She was thrilled.

The land that we purchased was a quarter of a mile from the

Katie - "Pilot in Training"

Mendocino Airport. So, the next time I had some time off, I took one of the club's airplanes to Mendocino. When I landed, I went into the airport office and met an old Englishman who had been in the Royal Air Force during the Battle of Britain. He was now the county airport manager. He and I swapped flying stories at length. Then he told me of an old logging trail that led from the other end of the runway through the woods directly to our property. So, to save time, he advised me to taxi my airplane up to the other end of the runway. "There is a clearing there," he said, "so taxi your airplane over to the woods, tie it to the trees, and walk over to your property." We did this a couple of times – I even flew up there with our dog Rusty a couple of times. Rusty, as I mentioned, loved to fly. He and I could walk through the redwoods all day and never see any sign of civilization. I always kept a compass to find my way back.

Eventually, people I was working with at Lincoln Property Company built me an eight foot by twelve-foot cabin that could be assembled. They built four walls and two sides and a roof – loaned me a trailer – and Minty and I drove the trailer to Mendocino. Since the four walls were all finished, all we had to do was stand them up and nail them together. It had one window and one door. It was an enjoyable family getaway. Mendocino was a four-hour drive through back roads and many little towns, but it was only a one-hour flight. Early on, long before we bought the property, I've always believed that our son Christopher was con-

ceived at Mendocino's Little River Inn.

After about a year at Lincoln Property Company, it became obvious that the new hire was more of a building construction specialist than I was, with a more in-depth construction background than I had. So, he took over the building construction part of the company and I was moved to the job of property manager. Bad move. Here I was again, immersed in numbers, percentage, budgets, etc. I tried hard, I got others to help, but all the numbers, budgets, percentages, forecasts, etc., were beyond my comprehension for some "unknown reason," which I later found out to my lifelong relief, was dyslexia.

As this Lincoln Property Division now had more capable people in each area of construction and construction management, I was odd man out. When I got into a discussion about 200 to 300 units to manage, I found I was unable to come up with the answer to the boss's questions off the top of my head. I appeared unable to cope, so I was let go.

What now? I was 40 years old and had a wife and two children! I had no mortgage as the around the corner rental unit took care of that; I had a small income from five other rental units and a small income from the Air Force Reserve, but since I was no longer flying regularly, or shooting in tournaments, the income from the Air Force was tiny.

There was another construction company in the area that was also building garden apartments. I applied to them. They seemed interested as I had worked for Lincoln Property Company, and they assumed I knew more than I really did. I never got a chance to find out whether they would have hired me, as a better opportunity arose.

My Dad had a small general contracting company in Massachusetts. He had, on occasion, mentioned to me about the virtues of owning your own business, and he was thinking of retiring. He had said he was wanting to retire because he was not well, although he never confided his ailment to me. He wanted me to move back to Massachusetts and take over the family company.

Minty and I spent some time talking about the possibility of moving back to Massachusetts. She was always a negative person. She could find something bad about almost everything and everyone in the world every day. She didn't even like motherhood. She often said that she was a one kid mom with two kids! There was always an aura of negativity about her and this made it hard to have a deep discussion about a big move like this. Minty was sad about leaving the Junior League in which she had been active, and there were other objections, but the one overriding thing was Duxbury. Our cottage in Duxbury Bay was something we could probably never duplicate in California. Since Minty and I had both grown up in the Boston area, we already had roots there. So, after much discussion, I flew to Massachusetts and had a talk with Dad. The decision was made for us to move back to Massachusetts, although we were leaving many friends in Palo Alto.

Before leaving California, I had much to do. I put the four-unit apartment building on the market. I put our one rental house on the market. I notified our renter behind our home that we were selling. We told him he would have a new landlord. We called the movers. A classmate of mine, Ted Tanner, owned a long-distance moving company. He made all the arrangements for the storage of our furniture in the Boston area. The house we had bought for $48,000 was sold a year later for $86,000. Our renter who was living in the apartment over our garage knocked on the front door one day and said he wanted to buy the property. He said his plan was to continue living in the rental unit and rent the main house to someone. I thought this was brilliant for a young single guy.

On moving day, Dad called and said that Mom had died. She had been ill for a couple of years so this was sad, but not a surprise. Her services, we were told, would be on hold until we got back to Boston. The children were ages four and two, so neither of them was in school yet.

I signed out of my Air Force Reserve Unit at Travis AFB. Minty signed out of the junior league. We made arrangements for a fraternity brother to drive us (including Rusty) to the airport. All good things must eventually come to an end.

CHAPTER 9
BACK TO MASSACHUSETTS

Dad met us at Logan Airport, Boston, and the following day, Dad and I went to Mother's Methodist church in Waban for her services, while Minty and the kids went to her family's home. After the service, Dad and I went to Duxbury for dinner at a local restaurant. We stayed in our Duxbury Cottage that night. It was in April, so it was still chilly. I got food poisoning at the restaurant and was taken to the Plymouth Hospital the next morning. Two days later, I left the hospital under protest of the medical staff. I had been so sick from the food poisoning that I knew I had hurt my back through violent vomiting, but the doctor insisted that a chiropractor would not help me. Dad had a chiropractor and as soon as I went to the chiropractor, I was back in good shape. That is something that Dad taught me at a young age – a chiropractor can perform magic when nothing else is working. I remember that Dad used to coach the football team in Malden and he had the chiropractor set aside Monday morning for the football team. The other coaches told Dad, "You must have a better physical fitness program than we do because more of your guys are ready to play every Saturday than we can seem to muster for our teams." Dad firmly believed in chiropractic medicine and so do I. I will go to a chiropractor every month.

Minty and the kids and Rusty moved into the Duxbury Cottage with me. We had all been there on several summers, so it was easy to settle in. Katie had taken her first steps on the deck of the Duxbury Cottage. Shortly after we moved in, a cold front came through (cold for us, especially after California). There were high winds and April snow. We decided we needed some warm clothes, but the clothing store in Plymouth had put all their warm clothes away and now had only spring and summer clothing, so we borrowed sweaters and coats from Minty's family.

The next Monday I drove from Duxbury to Brookline to the G. S. Maloney Company Offices at 23 St. Mary's Court. Dad had a nice paneled office made for me in the back of our office building. For the next ten days, I went with him to meet the engineers from Shell, Mobil, Citgo, Chevron and Gulf Oil Companies. The G. S. Maloney Company did contract maintenance for all of the above oil companies on their service stations, offices and

Minty's Family "Boat House" on the Slocum River/Buzzards Bay. It slept 8 people. L-R: Rusty, Katie, me and Chris

their huge bulk plants within 100 mile radius of Boston and Cape Cod. The company also did maintenance and commercial painting on school buildings around Eastern Massachusetts during summer vacations.

The time flew by. I was engrossed in the general workload. Dad was a frustrated CPA. He could do extensive figures in his head. I bought one of the first small computers for $400.00. He was furious. He called it an absolute waste of money. Dad was always very cautious of the company overhead. He had seen runaway overhead costs put many small companies out of business. He said he could calculate and use a pencil faster than that damn computer. Then he proceeded to prove it. He did it because I was, as always, slow to tap on the keys. Neither he nor I understood that I had dyslexia. Dad was frustrated because I often took a long time doing cost estimates or job costing. It was so easy for him but proved difficult for me. Many was the evening when I didn't get home until 10 p.m., after slowly doing cost estimates in big numbers.

The Duxbury Cottage proved to be totally a loving experience. The kids immediately took swimming lessons. There would be no repeat of my brother's drowning. Dad had a beautiful 21-foot Nantucket Indian Class Sailboat – it was the fastest and best looking small sailboat in the bay. I sailed it every weekend. I usually sailed alone. Katie and Chris were too young. Minty talked of cruising with her family in the 30's but in essence, she was not carried away with hanging out over the side of a heeling sailboat in Duxbury Bay. We spent time getting settled and getting reacquainted with old friends – the Lavins – Joan and Bob, the Cousins - Charlie and Libby, and others.

Shortly after settling into our waterfront cottage, we began thinking seriously of getting a permanent house. We looked in several towns around Boston and found a great house in Newton. I had grown up in Newton, so I felt more or less at home. The house we bid on was at 63 Aspen Avenue on a one-acre property, contiguous to the Woodland Golf Course. It was perfect, especially if you were a history buff or a builder with the ability to appreciate outstanding workmanship in a home. We bought it and moved in. There was an unused tennis court because it was ten feet too short, so we eventually let grass grow there. The house was an 1880's twenty-room Victorian home that had been in the same family from the 1880's to 1968. One couple had bought it

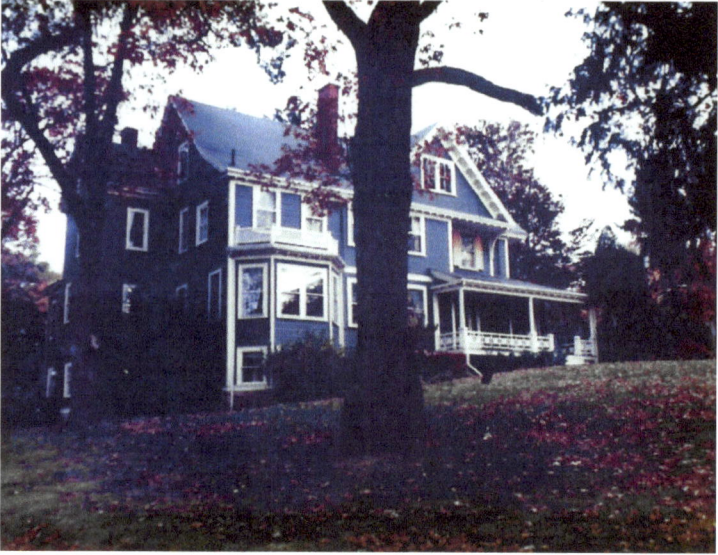

63 Aspen Ave, Newton, MA - built in the 1880s, our home from 1970-1996

two years before and then business had sent them elsewhere.

The house at 63 Aspen Avenue was magnificent. There were six separate stairways in it. One was a circular metal stairway from the dining room down to a child's theater that even had a small stage. We didn't know about the idea of a child's theater until the realtor told us about the history and things about the house. The kitchen was fairly large; the pantry the size of a small bedroom. The butler's pantry had a small wet bar. The dining room was huge and would seat easily 20 plus people, and we did quite a bit of entertaining. I had many Air Force Academy Meetings at our home (more about this later). The dining room had its own fireplace and beautiful woodwork and unduplicatable silverplate sconces. Chris (at age two) had a separate bedroom adjacent to the master bedroom. The house didn't have just a linen closet – it had a linen room the size of a small bedroom. Katie had a large bedroom, a private dressing room complete with several built-in dressers, and that was attached to her private bathroom. Off of her bedroom was a second-story screened porch. On the third floor, there were two bedrooms, a living room and a full bath which had been for the servants.

The Maloney Family - about 1975 - Newton, Mass.

The moldings, the wood floors, the light fixtures of our house, all were so perfect and beautiful that they could not be duplicated no matter how skilled the current crop of workmen were. The home was built on a slope so that half the basement was at ground level and had windows. I had my Air Force Office there. Also in the basement was a carpentry shop, the child's theater before mentioned, and a rifle pistol shooting range. We were able to purchase this home as well as two rental houses in Wellesley from the profits of the California properties.

While I worked in both the civilian sector and the Air Force Reserves, we all got to know our Newton neighbors. I loved the big house. The workmanship would be impossible to replicate, then or now.

After returning to Massachusetts from California and after settling into our Newton, MA home, I began reuniting with some Belmont Hill School friends. One was Roger Cogswell. After Yale, he had been in the U.S. Army and later with the CIA. He had moved back to Newton to enter the investment business. He was now married to Ann and they had two children, Chris and Steve. We had been on the BHS rifle team and renewed our friendship.

We established a tradition of spending Thanksgiving and New Year's Day together. In fact, one New Year's Day, all four of us cross-country skied through the streets of Newton to the Cape House. We had just had the biggest snowstorm in history. Everyone in greater Boston was stuck at home and most of the streets were not yet plowed.

I must note that I think of Ann constantly. How? Well, one day I told her there was no toilet paper in the bathroom. She dutifully replaced the toilet paper roll while noting that you should always be certain that the paper unfolds over the top. For the rest of my life, I think of Ann when I replace at toilet paper roll.

Also, I had expressed to the Cogswells that my favorite food was jam and peanut butter, so one Christmas they gave me a flat peanut butter spreader. So, as you can see, every time I eat a PB&J sandwich, I think of the Cogswells.

They remain good friends to this day.

Over the next few years, most of our energies were directed toward raising Katie and Chris. The local elementary school was only a few blocks away and Katie did alright there, but eventually, we came to the conclusion that this school was not the best fit for challenging Chris, so we enrolled Chris in a private boys' day school called the Fessenden School.

In about 1972, Dad sold the G. S. Maloney Company to me. He then left on an extended trip to Europe and the Middle East. When he returned to this country, he mostly stayed away. I paid for his mortgage, his car and his expenses. One day, a federal government auditor visited us and said he was doing a routine audit for companies that did any government work. He spent a week going over our books with my secretary. When he finished, he said we had underpaid our workers over a period of years by a total of $2,500. Dad did not believe this, so he came out of retirement and then proceeded on a deep review of our books.

Eventually, he proved dollar by dollar and date by date, that we had, in fact, slightly overpaid our workers. His figures were so carefully laid out that the federal auditor had to accept them. If it had been me, I would have paid the $2,500 and been left with the feeling that I had been screwed so the auditor could look good to his boss.

Chris was thriving at Fessenden School. His grades were good, he made many friends and played sports. During this time, Katie was doing an average job at the local elementary school. One day, in first grade, she came home and told me that she had taken some tests and been told that she had something called Dyslexia. I had never heard of it and for a moment, I wondered how a child this age could possibly have a venereal disease – Dyslexia! I asked her, "What did they tell you about it?" Katie described it as the inability to learn a foreign language, difficulty with memorization, transposing of numbers and letters. I was 42 years old, and my daughter was describing me! What she described had been my problems all my life! It was like flipping on a light in a dark room. Suddenly, so much was exposed that had been previously hidden and not understood. I had no idea that I had something that could be quantified. It had never occurred to me that I was suffering from anything.

Dyslexia was now known and understood. I suddenly realized that I was not alone in this. I told Katie that she probably inherited her Dyslexia from me. I told her of my recurring problems growing up. I told her how I never realized I had a problem. I had just worked harder and spent more time on my studies than my contemporaries in school and in other learning situations.

Upon learning this, I immediately went to Dad and told him of this wonderful revelation. I told him how I felt that a tremendous weight had been lifted off my shoulders – an unknown weight that I now knew had been there so long. I thought back about all the people – my parents, my teachers, my flying instructors, and others who had been disappointed in me. I remembered vividly the fourth grade teacher who said I was just dumb, and I suddenly knew she was wrong and uninformed. In essence, I now began to realize that perseverance had trumped adversity all of my adult life. When I told him what Dyslexia was, and how it had affected me for so long, he seemed unmoved. I almost got the feeling that perhaps he felt I was just offering him an excuse for my poor performances of the past. I thought that this would make things right with him, but I guess he couldn't wrap his mind around what seemed to him to be an excuse for deficient performances. Sometime later, without diagnosing or acknowledging dyslexia, he called me and said I had given him an incorrect telephone number. He told me rather proudly that when he realized the number was wrong, he reversed the numbers and got the correct one. So, he acknowledged that he had understood what Dyslexia meant and he was proud of that, but not of me. Our relationship never truly healed.

Minty joined the Boston Junior League and also the Vincent Club, two very social groups. Chris went to Nobles in a carpool. Kate was enrolled in a small girls school, Brimmer and May, in Chestnut Hill, MA. Every school day rain, shine or snow, she walked out the back door, across the unused tennis court, out the back fence gate, then across part of the Woodland Golf Course. She had to cross a very busy Washington Street to get to the trolly station. I marveled at her resolution as she went out and across the golf course. She was so young, but she was never worried. This, of course, was to be her modis operandi for the rest of her life – she was never afraid to venture anywhere, anytime.

In June, we always left Newton to spend the summer at the Duxbury Cottage. The Duxbury cottage was built at the end of a peninsula called Standish Shore. The pastoral nature of Standish Shore established by the pilgrim families had remained virtually unchanged for 300 years. When my father purchased our waterfront cottage in 1946, the pace of life on Standish Shore remained quite simple.

Where we lived was a part of the original land grant to Captain Miles Standish, the military leader of the Plymouth Colony. The remains of his home's cellar is now a small park several blocks away from our home. All the families on Samoset Road bonded into a tightknit community. Samoset Road was named for the Indian who came forward and befriended the pilgrims shortly after they landed. Even our dogs knew each family and their dogs. Each family had a small outboard boat and we often went boating together and sometimes across the bay to a waterfront restaurant. All of the families and all of their children on Samoset Road and next-door Elder William Brewster Road interacted. In fact, to this day, the children of the Maloneys, the Palmers, the Lavens and the Cousins still communicate and some of their children who grew up on Standish Shore have returned to purchase their own homes there.

Duxbury neighbors were all members of Wellesly Masonic Lodge (Bob Lavin, Hobard Emerson, Charlies Cousins, Phil Turner. We were all 32nd Degree Master Masons. As such, I was eligible to become and eventually became a Shriner. Every Master Mason is eligible to become a member of the Shriners. The Shriner organization exists to fund children's hospitals in the U.S. and to do many other good works to benefit the community. I think I became a Shriner in the early 1980's. In about 1995, I was asked to become the Chief of Staff of the Aleppo Shrine. The Chief of Staff is in charge of arranging and running the various parades. The cities where the Shriners parade pay a fee based on the number of units (bands, etc.) taking part. Generally, we'd have about three marching bands, three to five funny cars and at least a dozen clowns interacting with the kids, as well as a group of military precision marchers, and more.

With the help of my Duxbury friends, my job was to visit with whomever in whatever city was planning a parade. I worked out the details. I visited and walked the streets where the parade was to be held. Each side street had to be designated as a starting point for each individual unit and arranged in order. One after the other Units would leave the side street and turn onto the main parade route. All of this had to be choreographed and each unit notified of their place in line and which side street they were assigned to. After organizing all of this, I got to lead the Shriner part of the parade. After each parade, I had to work with our treasurer to be certain that each city where we participated in their parade paid the agreed amount of money. This was a very prestigious job as I was the Shriner representative to each of the area cities where we participated in their parade for over a dozen years. It was quite gratifying.

Taking care of a cottage built in 1900-1904 as only a single wall cottage was a challenge every weekend. I loved working around the house. Mom, before she got sick, had planted and maintained some beautiful gardens around the house. Dad had installed two bathrooms and rewired the whole house. However, we still had the original large black cast-iron stove. I remember cooking lobster on this stove in around 1947-48.

Our neighbors in Duxbury became our best friends. Bob and Joan Lavin and their three daughters, Charlie and Libby Cousin and their four sons. I first met Joan when she sat behind me in class at Newton High School. Walter and Ellie Palmer were across the street with their three daughters. All of the people on Samoset Road had access to the beach. Another neighbor was a retired U.S. Army Major. We spoke the same language. We were usually surrounded by our Duxbury neighbors. I took it upon myself to rake and clean the beach weekly during the summers.

I wanted a boat that all of us could spend the day on – one that Chris could fish off of and all of us could enjoy in our own way. I found one on a trailer in Dedham, bought it and towed it to Duxbury. I put out a mooring just off the beach in front of the house. It turned out to be very noisy and relatively a chore to handle, so I polished the boat and sold it.

I perused boat ads and found a model that I had been seek-

A weekend with friends on Sabia pictured in the harbor at Cuttyhunk Island, Cape Cod

ing. I bought it in Coahassett, a little town south of Boston, and took it to Duxbury. This was a small 25-foot cruising powerboat. We took it on many trips through the Cape Cod Canal and in and around the Elizabeth Isles – Cuttyhunk Harbor, Nonamesset, Weepecket, Uncantena, Naushon, Pasque, Nashawena Island, Tarpaulin Cove, Quicks Hole and the Penikese Isles. Chris caught fish, Minty cooked and we spent many very happy weekends on board this 25 foot boat. We named the boat "Rumrunner."

This summer cruising led to us wanting a more substantial boat to cruise longer than long weekends. All winter, we checked ads. I wanted to go back to sailing so we found a 33' Pearson keel/centerboard boat in Mamaroneck, New York. We drove to Mamaroneck, inspected the boat, and through a boat broker, bought the boat. It was a beautiful burgundy color. Minty named it SABIA (the Brazilian word for Robin). It had bunks for six, a spacious galley for Minty and provided a place for Chris to keep all his fishing gear. All of us went to Mamaroneck to sail it for a weekend in Long Isle Sound. The boat and family both performed most admirably. Thus began another adventure. I made arrangements with my best high school friend, recently released from the U.S. Navy and a neighbor, to bring the boat back to Padanaram. This was the name given to the harbor at South Dartmouth, Massachusetts.

We had previously arranged to have a mooring set in place. We had also applied to the New Bedford Yacht Club. I knew the past commodore and Minty's family friend was the world famous naval architect C. Raymond Hunt. We had fantastic personal backgrounds and the best sponsors. We were accepted into the Yacht Club as expected.

The trip from Mamaroneck and Padanaram took five days and it was a most enjoyable trip. The boat handled very well, so we made good time. My family was blessed. We spent several June to October months sailing on the boat. We had a beautiful home, the "big house," and thanks to my Dad, we had a five-bedroom house on a sandy beach in Duxbury Bay. In addition, we had a beautiful cruising sailboat. I utilized the navigation skills I had learned in the Air Force. It was infinitely easier to navigate a few miles at 5 or 6 knots to various harbors all over New England rather than to navigate alone in a fighter plane six to seven miles high at 500 to 600 knots per hour. We never missed a buoy even in the fog. Incidentally, before buying the Sabia, I took a boating and navigating course from U.S. Power Squadron. I did so well in the course that the commodore personally asked me to become a part of this organization and teach navigation. I declined the teaching position, but did join the organization. I flew the Yacht Club Banner, the California State Flag, and the U.S. Power Squadron Flag on the boat's yardarm. It made for a colorful boat.

We kept the boat in Padanaram and spent weekends on it, and sometimes at Duxbury and sometimes at Minty's family place on Buzzards Bay.

Minty and I continued to live in our beautiful home on Aspen

Avenue and spend summers at the family cottage on Duxbury Bay. We spent many weekends on our 33-foot Pearson Cruising sailboat. Our faithful companion dog Rusty was always with us at the cottage, but never allowed by Minty to sail with us. I always resented that.

Minty often regressed to her penchant for negativity. She seldom seemed happy when we were sailing the blue ocean with a fresh breeze ... more often, she would complain about it being too windy or too bumpy. The only time she seemed to enjoy cruising was when she was telling friends about it.

Our best family evenings came when we sailed from Padanaram to Nantucket. For several years, we docked at Nantucket Harbor the day after Labor Day. The dock fees went down by one-half on this day. Nantucket was gorgeous in early September. Katie and Chris were allowed to run all over the town. When we sailed back to Padanaram, it meant the end of another glorious action-packed summer.

Several times during the summer, we rafted up to see my friend from Newton High, Brian Mims and his wife, Susan and their three daughters. We tied up together and their kids and ours spent the afternoon on Brian's cat boat and we grownups spent the afternoon on the Sabia.

At the end of each boating season, I sailed with friends from Padanaram to either Long Point Marina in Duxbury or Great Bay Marina, Newington, New Hampshire. We brought the boat from Padanaram to Plymouth Harbor for a week or two and then to New Hampshire by way of Gloucester and the inside canal off Cape Ann. This was a gorgeous fall trip.

Another note about Minty ... I got a telephone call one day from a Colonel. He was on the USAF Major promotions board. He congratulated me on my promotion to Major. I was very happy. Minty was not. She wanted me to quit the Air Force Reserves. She was vehement about it. She had no concrete reason for this. It was just another thing that she disliked about me – whatever I thought about doing, she seemed to find reasons why I shouldn't do it.

Often, when we were going home after a party with friends, she would pick out the faults of our good friends ... "overweight, getting fat, stupid, ugly dress, food not good, too loud, too quiet, etc., etc., etc." Thus, time and time again, she had a way of spoiling what had been a good evening with good friends.

We belonged to a tennis club in Waban, Massachusetts. The club held a number of dances during the winter months. I felt right at home here because my parents had belonged to it when I was growing up. Minty would go reluctantly and then sit there with a scowl on her face. She complained that no one asked her to dance. Of course, her scowl probably turned anyone away before they had a chance to approach her. She often insisted she take her own car so she could leave right after dinner, before people started to dance.

Later, I was told that Minty had what is called a "passive-aggressive" personality. As an example, she was supposed to follow me one time in her car to Hanscome AFB where I was to give a speech and conduct a meeting. Driving behind me, she kept slowing down in order to make me slow down and end up being late. I eventually had to resume my regular speed so that I could get there on time. She arrived a few minutes later and then proceeded to claim bitterly that I had driven off and left her behind. She created a scene in front of the arriving Air Force people. She then drove off in a self-created huff! Incidents like this were just the tip of the iceberg and there is no need for me to belabor the fact that it is difficult to live with a passive-aggressive person.

We went to family counseling twice. Each time, I left with a hope that Minty would try to be more positive. She didn't change. I've discovered that people are as they are, and they don't really change. She simply had an aura of negativity about her. I felt that I could not go through the rest of my life with this negativity engulfing me. As soon as Chris left home to go to Dartmouth,

I felt now was the time to split. I spoke with a long time friend about what to do – she could advise me because she'd had three divorces.

So, a few months after Chris was at Dartmouth, I told Minty that I wanted a divorce. I simply said that I didn't want to be married anymore. This was a simple statement and didn't bring up a litany of negatives.

We went up to Dartmouth and met with Katie and Chris and told them we had agreed to split. Katie's immediate comment was, and I quote, "I wonder why you didn't do this two years ago?" Chris was devastated. He had no clue.

Minty came to me with a book that she felt I should read. It was about mitigation. I read it and it advised that we both should list all we wanted from the marriage. At the end of each chapter, the author cautioned that we should settle any differences ourselves – "Do Not go to Lawyers." We agreed we'd keep all that we each inherited and all that we entered the marriage with. Our only disagreement was the amount of alimony. Minty wanted more than I felt I could afford. So, against all the advice in the book, she went to a big law firm in Boston, and we started all over again. Her lawyer made up all sorts of allegations which then I and my lawyer had to dispute. Back and forth we went – each lawyer making out like bandits.

Two things I felt bad about were: 1) Minty had not wanted me to continue my Air Force service, even in the reserves, but upon the divorce, she wanted one-half of my hard-earned pension even though she had done absolutely nothing to foster my Air Force career. (The Air Force did not give her one half of my small reserve pension, but I wrote her a check for half of it every month, even though she was legally not entitled to it.) 2) We agreed not to go after our inheritances. Her attorney brushed aside our agreement and insisted she get half.

I must say in defense of Minty that, since I was dyslexic and terrible at figures, she very honestly handled all our bills. She never spent money needlessly and she saw to it that we always lived below our means. She managed the kids as they grew up and she instilled in them honesty and integrity.

Unfortunately, through her attorneys, Minty repeatedly came after me for more money. Due to a business recession, I made several short alimony payments. Immediately, Minty took me to court, where I was sentenced to 30 days in jail for the above short payments. For two years my business had made me no money. A court officer confided in me that if I paid her $1,000 immediately and promised cooperation, he'd see that I did not go to jail. The only good thing about all this was that Minty never spent much of it, so almost all of the money went to Katie and Chris when she died.

After my divorce, friends got my old girlfriend Joan Benny and I together. Joan had a condo in New York City and a home in Beverly Hills. Having been divorced several times, she was a pillar of support and advice for me as I navigated the last stages of divorce proceedings

So many of my friends wanted to introduce me to someone. I tried this a couple of times, but when it didn't work out, I felt that in a way I had let down my friends, who were only hoping good things for me.

I decided I'd just keep dating. I often flew to NYC or to California to spend time with Joan, although we both knew she was through with marriage. Our dating was free of worries or entanglement.

I was cautioned by some local wives that I should be most careful about making moves toward marriage. I was quite eligible. I owned a good company, I was extremely well-educated and I had one of the premier pieces of waterfront real estate in town. I had a boat and I belonged to two yacht clubs. I was warned that so many women would want to "establish themselves w/me." The words "establish themselves with you" came from a neighbor lady.

One day while walking on the beach in front of my home,

I met Elizabeth, who was also walking the beach. She looked pretty good in a bathing suit. I invited her to my home. I realize now that she cleverly invited herself to my home. (1st phase of manipulation … in order to "establish herself with me").

I invited her to dinner the next night. I was tired of four years of dating and dozens of very nice, willing women, so I sort of leaned into Elizabeth. We continued dating for a few months. I was busy with my business and with the Air Force Reserves. So she, in essence, set up our social schedule. She was divorced and had a son in Duxbury High School and a daughter at Middlebury College. Frankly, I never bonded with her son although I did, to some extent, with her daughter. Neither of my kids liked Liz. They saw right through her. Why didn't I?

We went to meet her parents and to visit with her two sisters and her brother. Now, looking back, I realize I was being manipulated into her family circle and I allowed myself to do this. It was the line of least resistance.

After about a year, I asked her to marry me and she said yes. She sold her little old house and moved into my home. Her son came with her. I provided a home for him and all of his needs, but he let me know that he did not like me asking him to help around the house and yard.

We had a big formal wedding in Duxbury, which I didn't want. I wanted blue blazers and slacks, and family only. We went to a Caribbean Resort which she picked. Then she wanted to take her kids, so we took hers and mine and the six of us went on my honeymoon. More about Elizabeth later…

CHAPTER 10

THE G. S. MALONEY COMPANY
& ASBESTOS BUSINESS

The G. S. Maloney Company did some interesting things. Our business with the oil companies was doing well. Dad had set up all the gears in motion, so to speak, and all six oil companies were ours. I had only to follow the script, which I did. The daily figures were still challenging, but my bookkeeper kept everything moving. Because I was so poor in embracing the concept of numbers, percentages, etc., I also employed a CPA to oversee, on a monthly basis, all of the work, billing, payroll, etc. She was Mary Hebditch and she worked for Dad and for me for about twenty years before starting her own CPA Firm.

I wanted to do something that was me – my doing exclusively – so I looked into the business of working with and restoring landmark properties. I took a couple of courses at Harvard/MIT in the evenings. I like the Air Force Motto: Man's flight through life is sustained by the power of his knowledge.

I have always felt the need for information in whatever business endeavor I was involved in. There was always seemingly more to know. Before the Worldwide Net, the place to go for more education was another college. I selected courses that would enhance my individual knowledge of my work. It seems to me that I was nearly always enrolled in some college somewhere. I didn't need a degree as such. I needed specific education and information. So, I took graduate level courses but never needed or pursued a degree. Some of the colleges I enrolled in over the years were: University of California - Berkeley, Harvard University, MIT, Dartmouth College, Boston University, Bentley College, the Air Force Academy, the Air War College, Northeastern University, Brandeis University, First National Bank of Boston Financial Management Course, and Tufts University. That being said, I think that each place of learning enriched me and helped me on life's path.

We restored the JFK birthplace house, the old Cambridge City Hall and the H. H. Richardson railroad depot. This would be recreating the splendor and history of these aged buildings. In preparation for this, I took courses at Harvard/MIT in the evenings. This was in-depth background of historic buildings; how to properly reclaim the original prominence of each of these remarkable buildings.

When working in the Cambridge City Hall, I looked for my birth certificate and found the original on a 3x5 index card. Also, in looking up the history of the railroad depot, I found that during the Civil War, recruits from the northeast had come to the fields surrounding this depot. They mustered there and then were boarded on a train and went South to battle.

I found these activities stimulating and creative. As a history major, these projects gave me a real feeling of accomplishment and a sense of the spirit of times past.

A friend called me and told me to read the local paper. There was an article on asbestos. Asbestos had been found in the Martha's Vineyard, Massachusetts High School and the school had been closed and sealed. The town of Martha's Vineyard was going out for bid to remove the asbestos. However, it was noted that no one had tackled an asbestos removal job of this size or any size. The article went on to warn of the grave danger of asbestosis. I went to interview the architect who was going to oversee the bidding process. He said that no one had done this kind of work, nor were there anything but vague specs. I felt that here again was something new; something that would enable me to be a leader, an innovator. My men were used to covering and sealing walls and floors when we spray-painted. Also, the men always wore masks when spray painting. The specs called for walls, windows, doors and floors to be sealed with plastic sheeting. My men already had been doing this when we painted large commercial spaces.

I partnered with a local company, and we traveled by ferry to the island. We put on masks and inspected the high school. There was asbestos-containing plaster on all of the upper walls and many ceilings. In researching the uses of asbestos, I found that in many cases, asbestos had been mixed with plaster. This softened the plaster and made it sound-absorbing. This was important in a classroom, but this material was now flaking off. Thus, the students and faculty were breathing in asbestos dust, which had stuck in their lungs. The asbestos fibers are so robust that the normal body defenses cannot dislodge or dissolve them, so these tiny fibers get absorbed into the lung tissue and eventually cause the lung to lose the ability to process oxygen. If a person smoked, the danger of asbestosis was immensely more perilous. We bid for the removal and proper disposal of all the asbestos-containing material and we won the job.

After securing the bid, we went to the isle, found a bed and breakfast and a rooming house. There was high unemployment at Martha's Vineyard during the winter, so we hired twenty local people. We had to train them in the use of masks and how to install plastic sheeting. We sort of wrote the specs as we went along, spending two and a half months on Martha's Vineyard during the winter of 1979 and 1980.

I purchased a TV camera and using this camera, took movies of all of the preparations and removal and proper disposal of asbestos. Imagine! I had just been involved in the creation of another new industry! I personally visited the head of the Northeast Environmental Protection Agency and showed the TV movie to them. They, of course, never had seen the inside of an asbestos removal project. We went over all of the safety precautions we used. The head of the NE EPA told me I had EPA#1. As far as he knew, this was the first large legal asbestos removal job in the United States. I was then requested to go to Washington DC to EPA headquarters and show the asbestos removal movie there, which I did.

I had to go to Washington DC for an Air Force Academy and Air Force ROTC Conference, so during the Air Force Conference, I went to the headquarters of the EPA and showed my movie to them. No one there had ever seen the inside workings of an asbestos removal project.

NOTE: A year later, I got together with the chemist of a paint company and we created an encapsulant for asbestos-containing materials. It was essentially liquid rubber. You could paint it on the asbestos and it acted as a prophylactic. We submitted this with specs and samples to the State EPA. We got approval.

Thus, in addition to the first movie of the inside of an asbestos job, I had also created the first state-approved encapsulant for asbestos-containing materials. This encapsulant could be applied to surfaces that contained asbestos and were in good condition. Thus, it sealed in the asbestos fibers. Now we could preserve the insulating properties of asbestos without the expensive removal and replacement. So, this was another new "first" in my life.

We finished the Martha's Vineyard job and made a handsome profit – a considerably larger percentage of profit than our usual work.

Soon, the asbestos business was consuming the company. I had to hire two new estimators. Every company in the country seemed to be suddenly aware that asbestos was bad for you. In the upper half of the country, almost every building, big or small, including houses, had asbestos covering their boilers and all of their pipes. It was good for us, as my estimators were busy every day going over bid reports from company owned buildings. In most cases, the owners were relatively ignorant of the asbestos problems. They just thought it best to get rid of it. The government was making asbestos out to be worse than it really was. The G. S. Maloney Company went from between 10 to 40 men to 70 to 150 men, depending on the jobs. My crazy partner was also bidding. He had a problem of coordination in that he spent money indiscriminately and usually spent too much of it. He liked to portray himself as a big spender, while I was the one who paid the bills and managed cash flow.

We began hearing from companies, schools, colleges all over the Eastern half of the country. I went to Florida to tell the University of Florida people what to do about the asbestos in their big power plant. We did remove the asbestos from the University of Florida in 1980.

About this time, we were producing the encapsulant that we had invented. We created a new company to market our asbestos encapsulant. We named the new company U.S. Coatings.

The EPA sent out a notice that all buildings were to be surveyed for the presence of asbestos-containing material. They didn't specify how to do the inspections. They did say, however, that every wall, ceiling, boiler, etc., must be inspected and marked. So, each wall and ceiling in every building in the country was to be inspected and every surface marked. The markings were to be noted and indexed.

Then the State of Massachusetts set up guidelines for licenses. There was an estimator's license, a foreman's license, a worker's license and a spec writer's license - all licenses that everyone had to have and all of which cost the company money. Asbestos school was established and run by people who knew less than I did. All of my workers took the course and got certificates. The State of Massachusetts got lots of money.

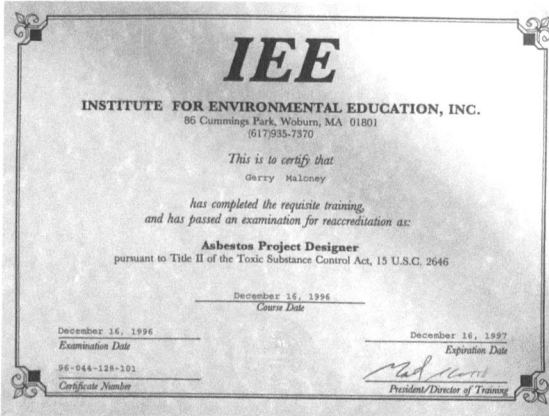

IEE

INSTITUTE FOR ENVIRONMENTAL EDUCATION, INC.
86 Cummings Park, Woburn, MA 01801
(617)935-7370

This is to certify that

Gerry Maloney

has completed the requisite training,
and has passed an examination for reaccreditation as:

Asbestos Project Designer
pursuant to Title II of the Toxic Substance Control Act, 15 U.S.C. 2646

December 16, 1996
Course Date

December 16, 1996
Examination Date

December 16, 1997
Expiration Date

96-044-128-101
Certificate Number

President/Director of Training

I went first to my prep school, Belmont Hill School, to talk about the required survey. They said all the local prep schools were getting together to research what to collectively do about this problem. I got to be the speaker. After the lecture, about twenty prep schools signed me up to do the survey and probably do the removal or the encapsulation. Those were busy days.

One of my estimators had been in the building trade and was a union man. Neither of my companies was a union company … more about this later.

Each of the schools contacted me for scheduling. Every space, including closets, attics and tunnels, had to be inspected and every surface had to have a plaster or floor covering sample taken. Each sample was to be put in a zip-lock bag and marked from where it came. All of these samples were sent to a lab to be checked for asbestos content, if any. Each sample cost about $5.00 for inspection and written report. You can see how countrywide this was. It was becoming a whole new industry. Several of my new Asbestos workers had the certificates and training that I had paid for and left to form a new company for themselves. It seemed that I was the father of most of the new companies being formed because most of the workers had been trained by me. The reports we made up contained many pages. We drew schematics of each building and noted where each sample had been taken. The reports often ran to 100 pages. The results of the sampling came back from the lab we used these to indicate whether the material did or did not contain asbestos. On the basis of this, I wrote a set of specs and costs for each company, or school.

Each job had to be reported to the State of Massachusetts before the removal process began. The Governor of Massachusetts, Michael Dukakis, was running for President of the United States. He was touting something called the "Massachusetts Miracle." Massachusetts had the lowest employment rate of any state in the country. The state had achieved this by hiring every unemployed person in the state. I don't know what the state did with most of the people, but I do know how it affected me. The state, per Dukakis, created two Asbestos Commissions. They set up offices, hired people and then began inspecting ongoing asbestos removal jobs. All of the new people began inspecting jobs and in reality, didn't know what they were doing. They were mostly a harassment. No one but a licensed worker or foreman was supposed to be in an asbestos removal job. The new inspectors hardly knew the intricacies of proper Asbestos removal and disposal. They delighted in writing up what they thought were deficiencies. They, thus, justified themselves.

As a result of this, oftentimes we put an "Asbestos - No Admittance" Sign on the front door of a building. We then closed the door or doors and chained them closed so they couldn't barge in. Then we set up a radio near the door on very loud volume, so, of course, we couldn't hear them knocking.

Both U.S. Coatings and G. S. Maloney Company were doing jobs. The encapsulant we painted on the asbestos pipes made them look new.

In several instances, I was not paid for my exhaustive inspections and reports. Two large Catholic schools with several buildings ignored my bills and telephone calls. One town on Cape Cod thanked me for my report on all of their buildings and ignored the bill.

I had been so used to dealing with the big oil companies and always having my bills paid timely, that I failed to take precautions for non-payment. We were so busy that we just ignored the non-payment. Time spent trying to collect meant time taken away from work.

The oil company business continued along parallel lines with the Asbestos encapsulation and removal as well as the sale of the encapsulant. We were not in the retail business nor did we know how to market a product such as the encapsulant. We used a lot of encapsulant but didn't independently sell much. Later, the big nationwide paint companies began providing their own encapsulant. In fact, theirs was better than what we had developed. Later, the EPA in its infinite wisdom let it be known that they thought encapsulation was a one-half measure. Without ordering it, the EPA noted that all asbestos should be removed. So, in some cases, we encapsulated asbestos and two years later, removed it.

We were busy and had a handle, so to speak, on all of our work. I had hired one of the engineers from Shell Oil Company. We had worked together for years and now he came to work for us.

My estimator with the union background kept pestering me about how much more work we could get if we were a union company. So I made a big mistake and let him bid on a removal job at the Boston Airport. To bid, we had to be a union company. I joined the union (don't remember or care which one), and the union people immediately began to dictate to the men how the job was to be run, how many men were non-working stewards and foremen. I was in way over my head – a novice.

We never finished the job and then another town where we were working was somehow invaded by the union. We were fired from the second job, so I now had purchased a lot of equipment and had a huge payroll and no money coming in. My bonding company, with whom I had had a perfect relationship for twenty years, was now called up to pay some of my debts, but not many.

I sued the town for improper dismissal. The suit cost me $100,000 in legal fees but we won the suit for wrongful termination. The City of Newton and their engineers paid me $125,000 to settle my suit. The attorneys always win. Due to not finished two large jobs, therefore, no pay.

I calculated that I owed about $850,000. My CPA agreed with me on the amount I owed. I was in a mental daze. Nothing like this had ever happened to me. There was no money coming in and I had a payroll to meet on Friday. My longtime employee and now CPA counseled me. Again in my life, the question of what to do was facing me. I knew that I had done years of good work. I had a good, honest reputation. I also had several jobs of significance that I already had contracts to do.

I spoke with Minty. She was her usual negative self. She and Katie went to England the next day to visit relatives. My attorney drew up bankruptcy papers for me to sign. I had to think this act through. I had some work in hand and more on the way. I decided not to do the bankruptcy route. My attorney pointed out that if I signed these papers, I could start over. I did not sign them.

The day before payroll – Friday – I sat at our kitchen table and cried. I apologized to Dad in heaven that it looked like I would be losing the company he had built over so many years. Chris was at summer camp. I was alone in the house. I vowed not to give up. I drove to my office and wrote payroll checks to about 50 plus employees. Then I went to my bank and wrote a check from my personal account for $200,000, depositing it into the company account. For the next fourteen years, I made periodic partial payments to those to whom I owed money. It took that long. Everybody got paid. I sold my beautiful home in Newton to pay Federal and State taxes. I went to the Massachusetts tax office and told them of my money problems. Until that time, they had had no knowledge of the situation. My CPA and I worked out a payment plan. I thought the fact that I went to them and was honest about my problem would help us work out a payment plan for the taxes owed. A day later, my banker called and said the state had raided my company account and taken all of the cash. So again, I faced payroll and other bills with no cash. Back to my bank and another personal loan. Another catastrophe prevented.

The business continued, including the asbestos business. I went to the offices of several asbestos removal jobs and asked that they pay me soon and not wait the normal thirty days. All were very cooperative and paid quickly for the work. I was, so to speak, solvent (if you can be solvent owing $850,000). Our family activities also continued unabated, except that Minty was extremely non-supportive.

By this time, Katie was at Colby College in Maine. There had been a time for a few years that her Dyslexia kept her from getting good grades, but her prep school, Brimmer & May, gave her much extra help and she was a well-rounded teenager. Fortunately, the Director of Admissions at Wellesley College, Janet Lavin, was a personal friend. She knew Katie and also knew the admissions person at Colby College, and put in a good word for Katie with Admissions. Katie did well at Colby College in spite of her Dyslexia. She even made her Dad proud when she was designated a "Senior Scholar." Senior Scholars had dinner with the College President and their names were prominently displayed on campus.

Chris had done well at Fessenden School. Minty had graduated from Milton Academy and I had graduated from Belmont Hill School. We gave Chris the choice of any prep school he wanted. Not wanting to displease either of his parents, he made a third choice, choosing Noble & Greenough School in Dedham. His grades and sports activities were so good that he could get into any prep school he chose.

U.S. Coatings and the G. S. Maloney Company continued in business. Minty and I moved to the Duxbury Cottage. I sold my home on Aspen Avenue to pay off many of my debts. Chris stayed with Minty's family for his senior year at Nobles.

I dropped out of the union and vowed never to do any more union work. The EPA reports took up much of my time. The reports were often a hundred pages or more. I got to know the business managers very well at so many schools in Eastern Massachusetts. The EPA was requiring that every school in the nation be inspected every six months to report on the condition of the Asbestos containing materials. So, I started another business – inspecting about 70 or so school buildings.

After completing the renovations work at Cambridge City Hall, we were contacted by someone who wanted to renovate a six-unit building and sell the units as condos. So, our carpenters practically rebuilt an older apartment building into condos. There were many extra requests by the new owner as we went along. Unfortunately, we never got all of these signed and approved. Also, one of the owners asked us to hire a relative who needed a job. We initially said no, but after more requests and since Mr. Cohen was the owner, we said okay. What a bad move! The guy came to work and two hours later, he came to the foreman and said he'd fallen off a ladder. Our foremen said there were no ladders up there. The guy limped off, never to return. However, he filed a claim unbeknownst to us. He had serious physical problems and now our insurance would pay for his physical problems. At the end of the year, our premiums went from $18,000 annually to $36,000 a year and the following year, $72,000. It was due to the guy who had never even had time to get on the payroll! We didn't even remember his name! We complained, to no avail. Eventually, the premiums became so high that we were out of business entirely, but before that, some interesting things happened.

Let me explain about my one overseas job exposure with U.S. Coatings. We were asked to bid on a job to clean and seal two huge, buried water tanks, two huge Jet A-1 Fuel tanks and two JP8 Fuel Tanks. We won the bid. The tanks were in Oman, a country on the southern tip of the Arabian Peninsula, and this was one of the most meaningful jobs U.S. Coatings was ever involved in.

I can't remember much of the set-up work. We signed contracts and hired sub-contractors who knew about Middle East

Work. We supplied the material and the oversight. I flew to Muscat, the Capitol of Oman, rented a car and drove all night on the one and only highway that rans the length of the country. There was only one gas station halfway in the middle of the country. All vehicles, northbound or southbound, stopped there for gas.

We arrived at the Thumrait Airbase in time for breakfast. We were assigned a guide who toured us around. There was, as you might imagine, a great deal of activity. This base was a permanent Royal Air Force bse. The USAF took over the other side of the runway. There, the U.S. built all structures that might be needed in the future to fight a war in the Middle East. There was a huge bubble - a dust-free enclosure - covering an area larger than a football field. It held, in an air-conditioned area, everything that might be needed to supply and sustain several squadrons of aircraft and support personnel.

Next, we went to the U.S. Coatings trailer office, where we saw the construction of the fuel and water storage tanks in the desert. Later, during Desert Storm, Desert Thunder and Desert Shield, Thumrait was host to every type of airplane the U.S. and the R.A.F. used. A huge tent city was constructed to house all the crews and maintenance people. The tanks we worked on supplied the water and the fuel to keep the base and the airplanes operating. Also, in 2000, Thumrait was the first place that the crew of the bombed destroyer U.S.S. Cole, were taken.

After the day's visit, we left the next morning and drove across the mountains to the beach resort city of Salalah on the Arabian Sea. We stayed at the very modern Crown Plaza Hotel. After a day on the beach and in the water, we spent a night in the Luxurious Hotel. The next day, we drove back to Muscat. All during the drive back, we saw many trucks parked beside the road with the drivers asleep in the shade out of the noonday heat.

We had scheduled a week in Spain as sort of a vacation. We landed in Seville, toured the city for two days, stayed in a small Spanish hotel. I loved that city. Then in a rental car, we drove off into the mountains to see some of Southwest Spain. I got lots of good feelings from so many friendly Spaniards as we wound through the backroads of the country. We stopped at one little café to see if we could get something to eat after the usual lunch hour. The proprietor brought his family out to talk to the Americans. A couple of old men from across the street came over to talk to us in broken English. We were then treated to a fabulous lunch in a little town stuck onto the hillside of a Spanish mountain.

Next, we visited the Plaza de Toros de Ronda. The City of Ronda is where bullfighting began. It is thought it began in around 1300 B.C. the current bullring was built in the 18th century. The town has prehistoric roots. There was no bullfighting the day we were there, but we did get into the stadium and spent some personal time thinking about all the history of that place. We then continued our tour of Span, visiting Malaga, Gibraltar, Cadiz and back to Seville for a couple of days, and then home.

An architect had drawn up specs for the removal of asbestos from the ceilings of two rooms in the Worcester Public Library. The architect had never seen the actual removal. He knew he couldn't come in to review the work, but he had one request. He asked us to please leave the plastic sheeting that formed the containment area. This we did after all the asbestos had been removed and the area washed down. An electric monitor showed us no asbestos dust.

A week later, the chief city librarian called. He said he had received a letter from the state inspector. The letter said that this was the worst asbestos job she'd ever seen. The girl inspector had personally viewed two men working on the ceiling without the proper clothes and not using the proper face masks. She also noted that there was an opening in what was supposed to be a sealed containment space.

The chief librarian said that when we completed the job, he had called the plaster company to come and replaster the ceiling. What the girl inspector saw was two plasterers replastering the ceilings.

I had to hire a lawyer to go into downtown Boston and confront the asbestos Officer with my completion date, my Asbestos dust readings of zero, and a letter from the head of the Worcester Library that said his men were plasterers working for him. He stated that the asbestos was all gone and cleaned up. Then I requested a letter from the architect stating that he had asked that we leave the containment area in place so that he would have first hand knowledge of it.

Well, we got a grudging acceptance of our place in this. A calming letter was dispatched to the City of Worcester with a copy to my company.

One more illustrative instance: A world famous landscape architect lived in Brookline, Massachusetts. His name was Frederick Law Olmsted. The state was going to make his home and garden into a park. We were to remove the asbestos from his furnace and pipes. One day, a state inspector appeared. He tried to barge in. One of my men, a 6'4" – 280-pound black man – stopped him. He said, "You can't come in unless you have an inspector's license." The inspector, a small Chinese man, said he didn't need to show any license. He was a state inspector. Our man stopped him again and said, "No Tickee/No Laundry," and shut the door.

Well, the Chinese inspector went to the EPA office in Brookline, bitterly complaining. He had lost face. The Brookline EPA guy called me and agreed with me that he should not have been admitted. He said, "You and your man made him lose face. Very bad for an oriental. This little Chinese inspector wrote us up several times at other jobs for no reason and one time actually placed some Asbestos in a completed job! We went to Court as a result of these write-ups and every time, he lost.

When my workers compensation premiums went up to $72,000 per year, it was unsustainable. I closed U.S. Coatings in 1991. This was another gut-wrenching impact on my life. I had been doing work over the years from 1980 to 1991 as U.S. Coatings. The oil company work was done by G. S. Maloney

Company. I had been so busy with the Asbestos work that we had slowly backed out of the oil company work.

In 1991, I reactivated the G. S. Maloney Company and just did the EPA regular six-month Asbestos inspections for about 70 buildings around East Massachusetts. I rented my office buildings, and this gave me rental income from five buildings, plus I rented Duxbury for one winter. I also had income from a six-car parking garage. For the next seven years, I operated as only an Asbestos inspector on the previous 70 school buildings. Thus, my business shrunk but the income from all sources was enough to maintain my standard of living, including the Duxbury Summer House and our cruising sailboat.

CHAPTER 11

AIR FORCE ACADEMY
LIAISON OFFICER

One of the first things I did, after joining the G. S. Maloney Company, was to look to the Air Force for a reserve unit. I found a local USAF Reserve unit that met one night a week. It was a non-pay unit. After a few months in this unit, I read in an Air Force Magazine that the Air Force Academy was looking for a few Liaison Officers. I quickly completed an informational background paper and mailed it to the Air Force Academy. After two weeks, I hadn't heard anything, so I then did what I had done with 3M a few years earlier. I called. I spoke with the Colonel who was the head of admissions. I don't remember the conversation, but he told me to contact Colonel Pryor who headed the Air Force Academy Liaison group in Massachusetts. I called him. He made no commitment – only told me to call his executive officer. I did. We arranged to meet for lunch and I guess I passed muster. He was a Lt. Colonel and we had a nice talk. Without committing himself, he said he'd forward his recommendation and my history to Colonel Pryor. Colonel Pryor called me and we met for lunch. At that lunch, he offered me a Reserve assignment as an Air Force Academy Liaison Officer. People, me included, think that the military simply orders you around. In my case it was not so. I was interviewed by the CO at Travis AFB before I was offered a Reserve assignment. Now, after two interviews, I was then offered the Air Force Academy Liaison Officer job.

Next was a two-week tour at the Air Force Academy. Colonel Pryor and I went together. The work was done in the classroom and with seminars by all sorts of interesting people. In essence, part of our job was to see if we could talk young people and their parents into and occaisionally out of going to the Academy. We always had to be aware that periodically the parents want to go to the academy and their child may have all the credentials, but really wanted to go elsewhere. The Liaison Officer has to be aware of this and counsel the kid separately without the parents present. All of the Liaison Officers had to write a somewhat comprehensive evaluation of the prospect. We could also make a recommendation to be offered an appointment or not.

As Liaison Officers, we were ambassadors. We worked with senators and representatives, parents and kids – touting the Air Force Academy. I got to talk to Senator Kennedy and others – got to interface with very interesting people. Most interviews were routine, but two interviews and their aftermath stand out. One: General Charles Sweeney had been the pilot of a B-29 bomber called The Boxcar that dropped the second atomic bomb that ended World War II, and he wanted his boy to go to the Air Force Academy. He called the Academy and asked who the CO of the local Liaison Group was. The General then called Colonel Pryor for a meeting. The General wanted to know who Colonel Pryor recommended to interview first him and then his boy. Thus, I got to meet and spend some quality time with General Sweeney. I guess he approved of me, so we set up an interview with his son. His son was qualified, but not outstandingly so. Nevertheless, I wrote a positive recommendation for him. He was not accepted. This did not end the matter.

General Sweeney and I were both members of a couple of Air Force groups. A year or two later, I asked the General about his

USN Capt. Tom Hudner, US Air Corp. General Charlie Sweeney & Me

boy. He told me that his son had joined the Marines and was now a Marine pilot. I got his son's address and wrote him a congratulatory letter on becoming a Marine pilot. He answered my letter and said it was a good thing he didn't get to go to the Air Force Academy. Had he gone in the Air Force, he said, he and probably others would always be comparing him to his dad. He sent my congratulatory letter to the General and the General and I became friends. I even have a picture of us together. All ended happily.

Captain Tom Hudner was the only Medal of Honor winner in the Navy during the Korean War. There is now a Navy ship, the USS Hudner, docked at Mayport. We were friends in Massachusetts. Hudner ran the Veterans Department in Massachusetts and recommended me to Governor Weld to be his Military Aide. Hudner and I led parades together. We were members, with the

General, of the Ancient and Honorable Artillery Company of Massachusetts.

The Ancient and Honorable Artillery Company of Massachusetts was formed in 1638. It was formed by a contingent of military people from the Ancient and Honorable Artillery Company of London. At the request of Governor Winthrop of Massachusetts, they came to the colonies to form the beginning of a police force. Their home was Faneuil Hall in Boston. This building has historically been referred to as "The Cradle of Liberty." The top floor of Faneuil Hall is deeded to the Ancients as their headquarters in perpetuity. The current Ancients are made up of many of the most prominent people in Massachusetts. In October of 1987, the Ancients (as they are called) traveled to London and Rome. I traveled with them as one of the Ancients. The most memorable part was having a meeting with some of the royal family inside Buckingham Palace. After the meeting, we marched outside of the palace to participate in the famous changing of the guard ceremony. We were the only group ever to march at this ceremony.

Next, our trip to Rome was planned around a special tour of the Vatican, with members of the Swiss Guard. The Swiss Guard is the oldest military organization in the world still in existence. The Honorable Artillery Company of London is the second oldest. The Ancients of Massachusetts is the third oldest military organization still in existence. We were privileged to have a private audience with Pope John Paul. When I see the picture of me holding the Pope's left hand, I get misty-eyed. My heart jumped a bit and I got very emotional after being touched by the Pope.

Another noteworthy interview and its aftermath had to do with a well-qualified black young man. I had a long talk with his parents. They did not have the money to pay for a college education for their son, but he really wanted to be a pilot and both he and his parents wanted the Air Force Academy. He was highly qualified. I recommended him without reservation. A month later, his mother called to tell me that he did not receive an appoint-

Me and the Pope

ment to the Air Force Academy, but he had been offered a full four-year scholarship to M.I.T. Wow, I thought, somebody at the Academy made a mistake!

I called the Academy and got the Chief of Admissions. After he reluctantly came to the phone, I explained that I had been a Liaison Officer for five or six years and had helped numerous men and women get into the Academy. This was the first time I had ever called about a turndown. The Colonel on the other end started to explain to me how thorough they were and that some other highly qualified people were in the incoming class. I interrupted him and said that this boy was at least as highly qualified as anyone in the class. Then I told him that "my kid" had been offered a full four-year scholarship to M.I.T.! I immediately detected a 100% change in attitude. He put me on hold and in two minutes, came back and asked me to please call his parents and tell them not to accept M.I.T. … that they would hear again from the Academy.

A week later, his mother called to tell me he had gotten into the academy. She thanked me effusively. Well, not the end of the story … about six years later, the young man called me and introduced himself in case I'd forgotten him (unlikely). He was at Pease Air Force Base in New Hampshire and he was the command pilot of a 4-engine tanker (KC135) plane on his way to Europe.

One other cadet stands out. She was a tiny 5' tall dynamo. I wrote her a fine recommendation and she was accepted and went to the Academy. A year later, her father called and said she was on the verge of leaving the Academy but still wanted to remain in the Air Force. She wanted to talk with me about the AFROTC. She and her father and I all had some input. I spoke to the Professor of Air Science AFROTC at M.I.T. and asked what he thought about taking her into his AFROTC unit. He said okay and she left the Academy in good standing. Note here that for a while, if you left the academy, even if you were academically and militarily in good standing, you could never return if you realized you'd make a mistake. This policy had recently been changed, noting that if you were in good standing, you could come back with the proper recommendations. She applied as a transfer student to M.I.T. and was accepted. That accomplished, I took her personally to M.I.T. AFROTC Headquarters and introduced her to the Colonel, who was the professor of Air Science. I cautioned him that "she belongs to me." We collaborated during the next year and she then felt that she could and should be allowed to return to the Air Force Academy. The M.I.T. Colonel and I wrote the necessary recommendations and she returned to the Academy. She graduated and later got her wings. Last I heard, she was flying a C12 Liaison Airplane and was married. Her Dad called me and thanked me for my help and guidance.

I had been a Liaison Officer for a only a few months when the Lt. Colonel Vice Commander retired. Colonel Pryor picked me for his Vice. I was very pleased, but a little worried. I was a Major stepping into a Lt. Colonel's job. Also, two of the other Liaison Officers were Lt. Colonels. A year later, Colonel Pryor was going to retire. He nominated me to replace him. This would mean that I, as a Major, would be stepping into a job which called for a

17 SEP 1982

Colonel Gerald S. Maloney
63 Aspen Avenue
Auburndale MA 02166

Dear Gerry

Since you have just "hung up your hat" from a long and distinguished career as the Liaison Officer Coordinator for Eastern Massachusetts, I would like to take the time to personally thank you for your absolutely outstanding work!

Under your guidance and direction, Eastern Massachusetts made great strides forward in the success of the Air Force Admissions Liaison Officer Program. The huge increase in effective liaison officers (from six to that Eastern Massachusetts experienced during your tenure as LOC can attributed to your superb recruitment efforts. Of course your work in area paid great dividends as the number of appointments to the Academy also reflected tremendous improvement. Our latest records reflect nearly a fivefold increase--only six appointments from all of Eastern Massachusetts the year before you assumed command to an average of approximately 30 per year over the last few cycles.

Your efforts for the AFROTC program also deserve commendation, Gerry. The 30 AFROTC scholarship winners from your area this past year must be extremely grateful to you and your LOs for all of the work you performed on their behalf. In fact, I am told that you are either directly or indirectly responsible for a total of over 29 million dollars worth of scholarships to either the Academy or AFROTC program since the beginning of your command. Congratulations!

Having had the opportunity to personally travel to your area and observe your operation, I know it is one of the best in the country. You take very special interest in each one of the thousands of young men and women you have personally counseled over the last 11 years.

For all of your hard work and dedication to the Liaison Officer Program, please accept my deepest thanks. You have been instrumental in providing us with some of the very finest Air Force leaders of tomorrow!

Sincerely

ROBERT E. KELLEY, Major General, USAF
Superintendent

My best to Mary!

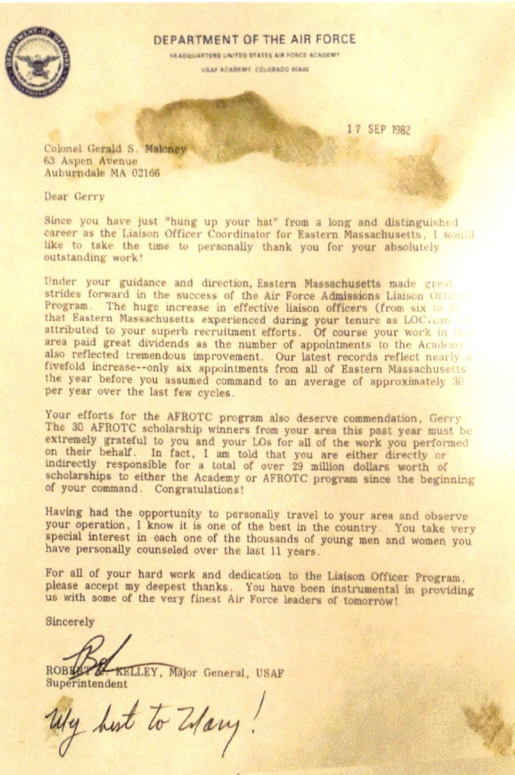

full Colonel. But first, I had to interview with the Colonel in charge of admissions at the Academy. He was in Boston for something and we had our interview. It was just me, no bullshit. Colonel Pryor called me the next day and congratulated me. I was now probably the only Major that was a Liaison Officer Director of the many Liaison Officer organizations in the U.S. All others were commanded by Lt. Colonels or full Colonels. One of the Lt. Colonels quit and went to another reserve unit. The rest remained and gave me their full support.

Our Liaison Officer unit had about ten officers. During the next twelve years, I increased my unit strength to about twenty. Note, I was made Lt. Colonel the first day I was eligible and a full Colonel the same way.

When I retired after 31 years in the Air Force and Air Force Reserves, the new Colonel tried to give me the Legion of Merit. I turned it down. I said that I felt that I had not really earned such a high medal. He reluctantly did not send his recommendation forward.

Minty's first name was Mary. General Kelly had been to my home for a series of meetings with the Civilian Head (U.S. Secretary) of the Air Force, Sheila Widnall. He had met Minty, but couldn't remember her nickname.

CHAPTER 12

MASSACHUSETTS GUARD

After 31 years in the Air Force, I retired as a full colonel from the USAF Reserves in 1985. I continued to help in the Air Force Academy admissions, but after a year, I retired from that, too. My last act was to take my Colonel Eagles Insignias and give them to my Lt. Colonel successor and a Liaison Officer nurse. I was trying to show my support for them in the promotion process.

As a member of the Ancient & Honorable Artillery Company of Massachusetts, I interfaced with many civilians, Navy retirees, Air Force and Army retirees and National and Massachusetts Guard. I got to know many of them well and I realized that I missed the camaraderie of a military organization. I asked the Brigadier General of the Massachusetts Guard if they had any openings and he said yes immediately … "Welcome Aboard!"

After I signed into the Massachusetts Guard, I now had to get an army uniform and a guidebook on the U.S. Army. This I soon did. Then I was assigned to the 3rd Brigade which met weekly in a huge old armory in Worcester, Mass. I went there and met the Colonel Commanding – he was old and ready to retire. I was to take his place. The Massachusetts State Guard had three Brigades. The 2nd Brigade was headquartered at Otis Air Force Base,

Cape Cod. They had their own building on Camp Edwards which was the Army part of the Air Force Base. They had over 100 people. The 1ˢᵗ Brigade met in an armory at Malden, Massachusetts. The 3ʳᵈ Brigade had only about fifty people on its rolls but seldom more than half came to the meetings. Then I realized that the Massachusetts State Guard and the National Guard had the same problem. Their personnel were "sort of" soldiering. Neither Guard had been called to duty in a very long time. The National Guard had a lot of members who were only showing up on their weekend duty to collect a little money. They were in no way capable of performing proper duty if called up to augment the regular army. The Massachusetts Guard, on the other hand, did not receive money unless activated. The big difference was that the Massachusetts Guard was a 100% guard for the state only. We could not be sent beyond the state. Thus, during both world wars, the National Guard was activated and sent overseas and the state guard was then activated and paid and occupied all the armories in the state. The Massachusetts Guard had about 10,000 to 12,000 people in its ranks during both world wars.

In 1918, the Boston Police went on strike. The Boston Mayor called first for the National Guard to come and restore order. The National guard was all in Europe, so Governor Calvin Coolidge activated the State Guard. Shortly after killing a couple of rioters, order was restored throughout the Boston area.

Some doctors who liked the military but needed to retain and continue their practices joined the Mass Guard. Thus, they could fulfill their interest and desire to be in the military but not be fearful of being sent somewhere and losing their practice.

When the ammunition ship in Halifax Harbor exploded during WWI, most of the city was destroyed. The Canadian government asked for help. The Massachusetts Guard sent volunteer units there with the aforementioned doctors and other medical people. There are, today, a number of pictures of Massachusetts Medical Personnel in Halifax.

This was the unit which I was now part of – a unit of somewhere around 400 people – mostly veterans like me who enjoyed the military camaraderie. However, a great number of them never came to meetings. They told me personally to please keep them on the rolls but they were too busy to come to meetings. They were, however, adamant that should the National Guard go overseas, they would immediately come to duty.

I was a retired Colonel in the Air Force and a Colonel in The Mass Guard. I was proposed by the board for Brigadier General in 1990. The promotion board was hesitant to promote a lot of its members since it seemed that all was quiet in the world, so the National Guard was planning to reduce its numbers.

Then, the 1991 Kuwait Invasion by Iraq changed things. I was shortly thereafter promoted to Brigadier General. More people started coming to meetings as they were now more meaningful.

Aide to the Governor

About this time, Medal of Honor winner Captain Tom Hudner, USN Retired, was the head of Veterans Activities in Massachusetts. He recommended me to be Military Aide to Governor Weld, and, of course, I accepted. *Liz and I and my daughter, Katie, went to the governor's chambers for a small ceremony, making me an official Aide. We had our picture taken with the Governor. The governor and I got along well since we were both graduates of local prep schools. He was a Middlesex Graduate and I was a Belmont Hill School Graduate. Every year, these schools played each other in all sports.

*I had previously been the Assistant Military Aide to Gov. King.

In July of 1992, on the 500th Anniversary of the Christopher Columbus Discovery of the New World, a flotilla of very old (tall ships) left the port of Cadiz, Spain and sailed across the Atlantic. They were coming to Boston for a few days of festivities before heading back across the Atlantic to Liverpool. Governor Weld was scheduled to meet with all the tall ship captains on board the huge Spanish Square-rigged sailing ship, Jean Sebastian De Elcano, at a very formal reception. Governor Weld couldn't go and he said I should go and read the proclamation of welcome to all the captains. One problem – the traffic through Boston at rush hour. It might be that I get there too late due to the traffic. So I called the State Police and asked for a police escort after I explained my situation, the State Police sent two motorcycles for me and we zipped through the rush hour Boston Traffic. There was much fanfare all around the waterfront when I approached the Spanish ship everybody was dressed in more gold braid than I had ever seen. All of the Captains were experienced sailors. They were in charge of the oldest sailing ships on the planet.

I apologized for the governor, explaining that he loved sailing and really wanted to meet with all of what he called "The Old Salts." But an emergency had arisen, so he sent his Aide. I read the beautifully worded proclamation to the assembled captains. They wanted me to forward copies to them, which I arranged. After the formal presentation, Liz and I had a tour of the ship. The whole crew was clad in old Spanish sailing uniforms from a bygone era. All stood at rigid attention as we walked around the ship.

While on deck, two gentlemen introduced themselves. One was Mr. Nigel Green, Chairman of the Grand Regatta Columbus 1992. The other was Captain T. F. Whiteside, Port Captain of the Port of Liverpool. They had been authorized to invite Governor Weld to the closing ceremonies of the Around the Atlantic Christopher Columbus Cruise. They asked me to invite Governor Weld on behalf of the Committee. They said if Governor Weld couldn't come, they wanted me to come.

As soon as I could, I met with the governor and presented the invitation. He said he'd love to go but the press would have a field day with him if he went all the way to Liverpool for a party. So, he authorized me to go and represent him.

Since we were going to England, I had an idea. I had heard that the Irish people were always most happy to welcome Irish Americans who had "made good in the U.S." So, hearing this, I called the Irish consul in Boston and asked him how I would go about arranging a visit to the Irish Air Corps. He seemed a little flabbergasted but said that he'd see what could be done. I didn't hear anything for a week, but shortly after that, I got a call from Colonel Mike Ryan, Military Attache of the U.S. Embassy. I said, "How did you come by my name?" He said, "Very simple. The Irish Consul in Boston called the Irish Ambassador in Washington D.C. The Irish Ambassador called the State Department who called the Pentagon, who called me to help in any way I was needed. I told Colonel Ryan I was an Air Force Fighter Pilot and I would like to see if I could arrange a visit to the Irish Air Corps base at Baldonnel. He said he could probably arrange it. I told him when we were arriving in Ireland on the ferry from England. He said he'd have an embassy car and driver waiting for us. Wow! How Nice!

Liz and I flew to London, took a train to Liverpool and checked into the Atlantic Towers Hotel. We were told everything, including meals and so forth, was covered. We began a whirlwind of lunches, dinners, excursions, etc., meeting so many interesting people. We at one time had dinner with the Chairman of the Cunard Lines, and also the Lord High Sheriff of something. We also met in the receiving line the King and Queen of Spain. The Master of Ceremonies of a Fanfare for a New World, which was a huge

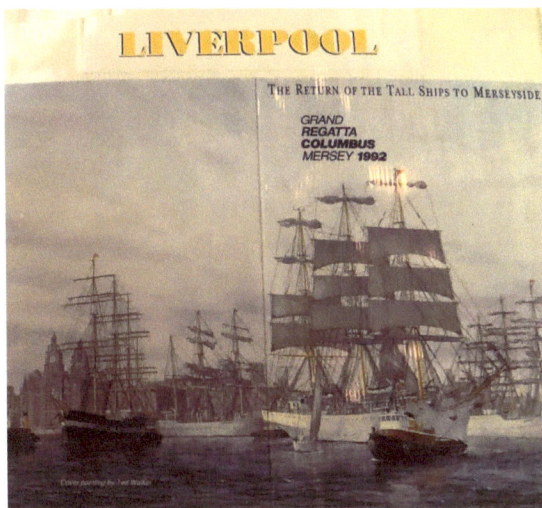

LIVERPOOL

THE RETURN OF THE TALL SHIPS TO MERSEYSIDE

GRAND
REGATTA
COLUMBUS
MERSEY 1992

celebration of fireworks on the docks – was Peter Ustinov. We were provided transportation to and from all of these events. We even had a ride with the Icelandic Ambassador to Britain. We also had a couple of motorcycle escorts to and from the hotel and the docks.

Some official representing the U.S. Ambassador was supposed to come to the Regatta and events. No senior people from the U.S. Embassy showed up. I was then told "you are the most senior American here, so you shall represent your country at these events." Well, I had represented my country athletically on the U.S. International Rifle Team – now I got to represent my country politically. All the lunches and dinners were superb.

One evening after dinner we were treated to a full-blown Tattoo – an impressive formal marching parade of military drummers which originated in Scotland.

The last event was an invitation by the British Admiral to an end of the Regatta Party on his destroyer, the HMS Brazen. This was a great party on the after deck. By this time, Liz and I had made a few new friends – one of which was the Ambassador from Ireland. We got to witness a very fine salute between vessels. Since I had been in the Air Force, I had never seen this. As each sailing ship under full sail approached the host destroyer, they dipped their country's flag. This was immediately acknowledged by the firing of one of the destroyer's guns as a salute. Then the British Flag on the big mast on the destroyer dipped – it was a beautifully done acknowledgment as each of the tall ships departed Liverpool for its home beyond the horizon.

Now, it was time to leave this wonderful, eventful and most fulfilling visit to Liverpool and Merseyside. I called the U.S. Embassy and told Colonel Ryan when we would be arriving at the Dublin Ferry Dock. He met us and drove us in an embassy car to the Fitz William Inn. Along the way, he gave us his personal embassy card. He said, "If you have any trouble anywhere, show this card to the police. After that, don't worry about anything."

After checking in at the Inn, I hired a car and got directions to the Irish Air Corps Airdrome at Baldonnel. The U.S. Embassy had made arrangements for a tour. An Irish Lt. Colonel met me at the gate. We had a short tour. He showed me where "Wrong-way Corrigan" had landed. He also showed me where the first cross-Atlantic westbound flight had departed – for this there was a large commemorative plaque set in the cement. We then inspected their airplanes. The Irish Air Corps had six third-hand jet fighters. The rest of the Air Corps Airplanes were Coastal Patrol Aircraft and trainers.

We went to lunch and I met several of the other officers. The Brigadier General, head of the Irish Air Corps, arrived from his headquarters in Dublin, and we had a nice conversation. As pilots, we had a lot in common to talk about. After lunch, one of the senior officers looked at the General and said, simply, "the book." That's all he said. It meant nothing to me. The General sitting beside me nodded and then we all left the table and went into another room. Somebody gave a key to the General. Then he called for a second key. I then realized that there must be something special in this cabinet since they all required an okay nod from the General. I thought something must be pretty valuable if even the General needed two keys. Well, out came a big thick book. This was their Distinguished Visitor Book. It seemed that not only was I going to know about the existence of it, but I was going to sign it. I looked at those who had signed it previously … Eisenhower, Churchill, Montgomery, a U.S. Ambassador, the British Admiral who headed the WWII British Fleet, General Patton, "Wrong-way Corrigan," and so forth. I didn't dare turn more pages and go back further. Wow. They were going to ask me to sign the Book! I felt quite honored. They needed a quiet okay nod from the General. Had he not nodded, I never would have realized that I did not make the grade for signing, so to speak.

After lunch, we toured one of the WWI hangars. All WWI flying movies had been made at this airdrome. The hangars and outbuildings were authentically WWI. They told me that the maintenance and roofs and so forth were all paid for by the movie companies. Fondly, I left the wonderful Irish Air Corps people and drove 'on the wrong side of the road' back to Dublin.

Our Irish adventure was not over yet. We were resting at the B&B when the manager came with the news that the U.S. Embassy was on the telephone. It was Mike Ryan calling and he invited us to meet the U.S. Ambassador. We received special instructions on how to approach the guards at the Embassy parking area. Colonel Ryan met our car at the entrance. The guards checked the car over and let us in.

The U.S. Embassy building in Dublin, Ireland is constructed in a circle. This circle represented the prehistoric fortification walls that were made from a million stones. They enclosed an area about the size of a football field. Each wall was about twenty plus feet high. The entrance was narrow and below the wall, almost tunnel-like. There are a number of these prehistoric stone-walled circles in Ireland.

We met U.S. Ambassador William H. G. Fitzgerald in his office. He was from the Boston area. We got along great! He was an Annapolis graduate and I had been on the staff of the Air Force Academy, so we had that in common. He also knew Governor Weld. He gave me a letter to Governor Weld and asked me to deliver it personally, which I did later.

After our meeting with the Ambassador, Colonel Ryan took Liz and me to see the Chief Sergeant. They wanted to know how they could help us on our journey around Ireland. First, they took us to their commissary store because Liz needed a few things. We said we planned to go to County Kerry. I wanted to see if I could find any Maloneys or Stacks. My middle name Stack was an old family name as well.

The Sergeant immediately told us of a pub in Cork that was owned by John Mansworth. He was famous throughout the whole U.S. Navy. Every U.S. Navy ship that docked in the Port of Cork got an invitation from John Mansworth for a free drink for every crew member. John's reputation spread far and wide throughout the U.S. Navy. Colonel Ryan telephoned Mansworth and told him about me and Liz, requesting that we get VIP treatment and also asking him to make a reservation for us at a local B&B that was within walking distance of the pub.

U.S. Embassy building, Dublin, Ireland modeled after prehistoric fort

After some hair-raising driving on the left, we arrived in Cork and found Mansworth's pub in mid-afternoon. The pub was not yet open, but we found a woman working in it and we mentioned that the U.S. Ambassador had called John about us. The woman called upstairs and John Mansworth appeared, all smiles and with a huge hug for each of us. We had a beer on the house while John found out all about us and why we were in England, and now Ireland. He showed us hundreds of pictures of U.S. Navy ships on many of the pub's walls. All were signed by Captains and members of the crews. True to what the Ambassador had told us, he was a man with a worldwide reputation.

Ambassador William H. G. Fitzgerald

John had already made us a B&B reservation nearby for the night. He called the B&B and told them we were on our way and to treat us like VIPs. After checking in and admiring the expansive views of the city and the port, we took a little nap. Later, refreshed, we appeared at the pub. John had made reservations for us at the Shipyard Restaurant down the hill and on the water. He insisted on personally delivering us there.

We enjoyed great food. The wait staff couldn't do enough for "a friend of John's." When we finished, there was no bill. We were then escorted out to the car that John had sent for us, and deposited back at the pub. Ensconced at the bar, we were introduced by John to his patrons. Then he called the Mayor of the City. The Mayor appeared with a dozen of his friends. We had a fantastic time, meeting so many genuine Irish people.

Next, we headed to see the "Ring of Kerry," a beautiful rich green landscape. Then we went via very narrow road to see the stone circle mentioned before. This stone circle is best described by looking at the photo below. It is believed to be about 300 AD.

"Ring of Kerry,"

Later that day at lunch in a small village, we got into a group tour. We all became quite friendly. The leader of the tour invited us to go with them to see a show by the National Folk Theatre of Ireland. We went in their tour bus to the Siamese Tire Theatre and sat with the tour group. The performance was put on specifically for the tour group. It was all in Gaelic – not a word in English. A glimpse of old Ireland, for sure. Afterwards, the tour bus dropped us off at the restaurant to reclaim our car.

A visit to the little village of Lixnaw took us to where I think my great-grandfather grew up. I have seen the form he filled out when he was at Ellis Island. At Lixnaw, we found a couple of men named Stack, but they had no interest in genealogy. I went to the local church, hoping we might look at the old church Bible or Bibles. For many years, town births, marriages and deaths were written in the Church Bible. The priest was not helpful. He informed us that over the years, Americans had come to the church looking for some record of their Irish ancestors and when they found records, they tore the pages out of the Bible. Thus, lo-

Elizabeth and I went inside Grianan of Aileach, a hilltop fort on the Inishowen peninsula in Ireland. It wasn't really a fort, but a secure homestead. Some of these stone circles are prehistoric.

cal history and many records no longer existed. He, in essence, told us to go away. At last, I took pictures of some of the farmland thinking that what I was seeing might have been where my great-granddad worked and lived. From there, we went to an old Irish hotel, the Cahernane House, circa 1877, in Killarney. It was on green acres filled with hundreds of sheep, just as Ireland should be.

Then we flew home and a few days later, I delivered the letter from Ambassador Fitzgerald to Governor Weld.

Elizabeth and I were destined to take many trips together during our marriage. We went to all the Scandinavian countries and took another trip to Paris and visited the D-Day Beaches and Loire Valley. We found that we liked France and later decided that we would later visit Provence. Elizabeth used her computer skills to arrange the whole trip, from transportation to lodging. One

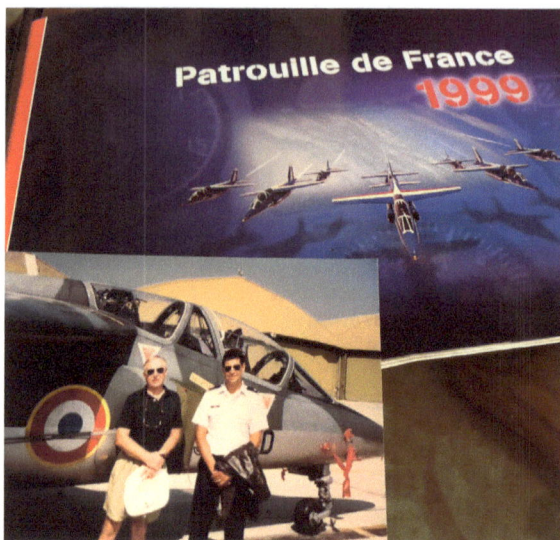

of the most memorable aspects of the trip to Provence was a short stay at an old mountainside abbey turned modern hotel. While there, as I admired the view from the mountainside, I noticed what I thought was the French Air Force Academy and accompanying airfield off in the distance. Inquiring at the hotel desk, I was informed that my assumption was correct, so we decided to visit. Following the directions, we wound up at the gate of the facility. I went into the gatehouse to try to gain entrance. The guard spoke only French but motioned for us to sit. Shortly, a United States Air Force Major arrived. He was the U.S. Air Force Academy liaison to the French Air Force Academy! The major's name was Julio Gomez. He and I found that we had previously been in the same fighter squadron (the 311th) although at different times. Major Gomez then gave us a short tour of the French Air Force Academy. He took us to lunch at the Officer's Club and introduced us to a number of the faculty. After this tour, he took us to the airfield and into the headquarters of France's Flight Demonstration team (same as the Blue Angels).

As a fighter pilot and a general, I was received enthusiastically. I met the director, Lt. Colonel Claude Saget, and the leader who flew in the Number One Flying Position, Commandant Dominique Terrier. Then I met the other pilots, all of whom spoke English - so we had a lively discussion. A photo was taken of Lt. Colonel Claude Saget and myself, and they presented me with a souvenir booklet of the Patrouille de France, their aircraft and pilots. In the course of our conversation, I pointed out the abbey, high on the mountainside, where we were staying. It was afternoon practice time for them, so Liz and I left and wound our way back up the mountain to the abbey.

This is where I have a hard time conveying my feelings about what happened next. When I think of what happened, I still get a little emotional. I was taking a nap when I was awakened by an extremely loud noise. It sounded like an airplane was coming right into the room. In a flash, it was over. About a minute later, the same thing happened. I suddenly realized that the abbey was deliberately being buzzed! I rushed out to the patio just in time to see another airplane of the Patrouille de France approaching from my left. He flew by very close and right at my eye level. As he went by, he looked at me standing on the patio and saluted. At exactly one minute later, a third flew by and the pilot saluted. One by one, each of the eight pilots I had so recently met flew by at exactly one minute intervals and saluted. I could see that they were a precise flight team made up of the best pilots in the French Air Force. As I close my eyes today, I can not only see them in my mind's eye, but I can feel the thunderous noise in my gut.

It gets even better! Exactly as the last airplane flew by me, two of the Patrouille began emitting bright red smoke. They were right in front of the abbey about two miles away and high up. While training the bellowing red smoke, they formed a huge and absolutely perfect heart in the sky. Then, without a pause, came a single airplane trailing one line of white smoke. This then formed the arrow through the heart that is a symbol of the French Air Force. This was not their normal repertoire. I guess it was only done on special occasions. I was and still am thrilled. I loved our trip to Provence, but this display - the salutes and the heart - will always be close to my heart.

Back home, I wrote them a most sincere thank you letter and had it transcribed into French.

Fast forward to 2022 … there is a group of veterans who meet every Thursday morning at 6 a.m. for breakfast at the Penman Café. One of our members is retired from the French Navy. I recently brought him my Patrouille de France book which was given to me by the Commandant. It is a 27-page pamphlet of all the best that is in the French Air Force. I showed it to my French fellow veteran and he read the letters that we exchanged and became quite emotional. I think we have established great rapport through my sharing the book and letters with him. As the oldest veteran in the group, I truly enjoy sharing special memories with the others, and this most certainly qualifies as a special memory.

CHAPTER 13
DUXBURY TO JACKSONVILLE

You may recall I mentioned a few chapters back that I read the book *How I made a Million Dollars in My Spare Time.* I was in real estate at the time and when I left California, I sold my house and rental unit, a four-unit apartment building and a four-bedroom rental house. This was the beginning of my quest for a million dollars in my spare time. When I came to Massachusetts, I bought three houses with the money from California. When I finally retired from my companies and the Air Force Reserves and the Massachusetts Guard, I sold two rental properties in Wellesley, one in Arlington, and two in Brookline. Having sold my home in Newton and my home in Duxbury, I then had accumulated about $1,900,000.00. I paid a couple of hundred thousand in capital gains taxes.

After my divorce from Minty and before Liz, I had tentatively decided to stay in the Duxbury Cottage. It was vintage 1902 and was still pretty much a cottage – just right for a bachelor. I had Katie and Chris and many good friends on Standish Shore.

Then Liz came to live in my Duxbury home. We remodeled the bedrooms from five to three and remade the kitchen. Then I had to have the whole house insulated. Liz kept on wanting new things, including cars. Her parents came to visit and they toured my homes in Weston and Duxbury. I guess they thought I was substantial. I liked them both. We also visited them in New Jersey. We helped them move to Albuquerque, New Mexico to be near their doctor son.

While I was visiting Liz's parents in Albuquerque, I called the Kirtland AFB/ 58th Wing, Special Operations. I told the operator I was a retired general who was a member of the 58th in 1956 and 57 when I was in Korea and said I'd like to arrange a tour. The operator said someone would get back to me. Shortly, the Colonel Command the 58th Special Ops wing called and invited me to visit. At the appointed time, I drove to the base. At the gate, I was accorded many salutes and led to the Base Headquarters. The Colonel met me, and we got in an Air Force car. The car had a big blue plate on the front with two silver stars on it. We toured the base. I told the Colonel that I had landed there two times while flying around the country. I was privileged to see a lot of interesting things pertaining to Air Force Special Operations. Ev-

Duxbury Cottage - Standish Shore, Duxbury, Massachusetts

erywhere we went in the car, military pedestrians saluted as they saw the two stars. Another "good for the ego" day! A lot of people were interested in hearing about their 58th wing operations in Korea in 1956 and 1957. Later, I sent the Colonel pictures of the 58th wing and its jet fighter squadron buildings in Korea.

Elizabeth loved living in my beach house. She invited all of her friends over for sunbathing and swimming. She joked that a number of her friends said she married me just to get into the Duxbury Yacht Club. She said this so often that I think this was part of our whole relationship. None of her friends were Yacht Club members. A big mistake I made was entrusting her to pay our bills and use our credit cards. I had been used to Minty, but Liz overspent from day one. We always seemed to have high credit card bills. My company was doing well and I was busy as a Commander of the Air Force Academy Admission Group in Massachusetts, so I did not focus on the money flow.

Liz also loved cars. She was always wanting another car – a different one. Well, it turned out that we were married for about ten years, and I bought her 8 cars!! Shortly after we were married, she wanted to revamp the house and kitchen. I spent $20,000 on this, and then she wanted to move to Florida. Over six years, during the winter months, Liz had often talked about moving to Florida. Well, in the winter storms of 1996-97, we experienced 120 inches of snow. Usually in Duxbury, we had about 24" to 30" of snow. With snow up to my eyeballs, I said "Let's go to Florida and look at real estate."

So, we flew to Florida. We started in Key West and worked our way through Florida. We rented a car and stayed at Distinguished Visitors Quarters on Patrick AFB. Our quarters were right on the beach.

Once we were given a house with five bedrooms, five bathrooms, a huge kitchen and dining room. This was the place that visiting dignitaries from all over the world stayed when they came to watch the shuttle take off or land. The guest book was filled with very high profile people.

Another time we went to Naples and almost bought a new house there, but thought better of it. On one trip, we ended up staying at NAS Jacksonville. We liked Northeast Florida. It was more like Georgia- real trees and lush greenery.

On a second trip, we went to Charlotte, South Carolina and loved it, but when you can move anywhere, why move into a hurricane area. Finally, we ended up in Jacksonville. We loved it. We divided our time between Jacksonville and Massachusetts.

Back home, we decided to put the home in Duxbury on the market. I was advised it took an average of three to four months to close. I had told business associates, friends, the Guard and the Shriners that I'd probably be going to Florida in the fall ... about five months from the 30th of May. Realtors said the house was worth $750,000. I put an ad in the Sunday paper for $850,000. On Sunday, I spent the day leading a big Shriner parade. When I got home after the parade, Liz said "I sold your house today." She handed me a full price offer, no contingencies, 30 day-close. Of course, I accepted.

We made plans rapidly. How to leave a family home you have occupied for 51 years. Now, I had not the five-plus months I had anticipated, but only thirty days. Quickly, we flew to Jacksonville, contacted a realtor and decided to get a condo first. Then if we liked Northeast Florida as much as we thought we did, we'd buy a house after a year or so. We bought a condo in Sawgrass. It was a quick trip down and back – some furniture moved into storage and some we took. This was a frantic last month. I think many of our friends may have thought that we just disappeared from the face of the earth, since we'd told everyone that we'd probably leave in the fall.

The weather was just one of the contrasts between Florida and Massachusetts. When Liz was with me in Duxbury, she had a premier piece of property, a prominent husband who was a Major General in the Massachusetts National Guard, and friends who admired her as well as her circumstances. She truly enjoyed basking in the glory of her position. It had satisfied her ego, but Duxbury was behind us now.

After we got settled in Florida, Liz realized that we were among many retirees on the first coast and had no special recognition. She didn't like being anonymous, so she spent even more money and kept wanting to move to huge million-dollar houses and get bigger, fancier cars. Finally, her overspending was so extensive that she went through our $15,000 savings account and when we needed a new refrigerator, we didn't have enough money to buy one. We had to use a credit card! I learned later that, in anticipation of divorcing me and going on to "greener pastures" (men who hadn't yet been fleeced), she racked up $20,000 in credit card debt buying a new wardrobe, new dishes, etc., and, of course, the new Jaguar was in her name as well. When we were finally divorced in 2001, I felt a great sense of relief.

Queens Harbor Yacht Club

We moved to Queens Harbor mostly because it was built around a golf course and a marina. Before I had my boat shipped from Duxbury, I received a visit from the Yacht Club Commodore. He didn't have to convince me to join. I had already been a member of two large old-line yacht clubs in Massachusetts. I ordered my 25-foot power boat to be shipped to Jacksonville. When it came, we docked it in Queens Harbor Marina. This was not quite as good as having it moored 100 feet from my house, as it had been in Duxbury Bay. Now, it was only five minutes away. I must note here that this was a good-looking boat but mechanically left much to be desired. One day, when everything ran okay, I sold it. Then I bought a used 36-foot Twin Diesel Mainship. It was a good boat – perfect for us. We cruised all over Florida's east and west coasts. After about a year, I became the Commodore of the Queens Harbor Yacht Club.

One of the things I mentioned early on is that I should always try to make better any organization of which I was a member. I got to pick my three other officers. Together, we set about reorganizing the yacht club. The club had no bylaws, so I personally copied and edited a set of bylaws from my two previous yacht clubs. Normally, the yacht club went somewhere one weekend a month. We left on Saturday, returning on Sunday. I changed this schedule. I set up a new schedule where all the boats left Queens Harbor on Friday. We then got to spend all day Saturday wherever we went. This new schedule was enthusiastically embraced by all our members. Next, I instituted a Commodore's Cocktail party on Friday evening. The Commodore provided all the drinks. My attitude was that all the yacht club dues should be returned to the members in one form or another. We tasked the wives to bring the food for the Friday afternoon cocktail party. This schedule continues to this day … twenty-one years later.

Next, I personally took the individual yacht club crests which could be reproduced to a company that makes drinking glasses with a crest or logo encased within the glass. I had a supply made and set up a rule that each boat got one for each and every weekend cruise they participated in. Later, I designed two plaques to hang on the yacht club wall. One was called "Inadvertent Immersion" – this was an award for anyone who fell overboard. They got their name put on the plaque. The other was called "The Bent Prop Award." Anyone who ran aground during the year got their boat name on this plaque. In some cases, several people fell overboard and/or ran aground. The intercoastal was very tricky. These awards were given at the annual Commodore's Ball. I established uniform rules that in essence came from my old-line New England yacht clubs. All the yacht club officers would wear white pants, blue blazer with yacht club crest on their pocket, white shirt and blue tie. The officers were to wear these on semi-formal occasions.

The yacht club held an annual Christmas boat parade. This was really a disorganized gaggle of beautifully lighted boats jockeying for position in the harbor. I organized the annual boat parade into numbered groups and aligned them just as I had done with the numerous Shrine parade groups. This organization was controlled by me by radio to each group so as to process the boats in an organized, properly spaced parade through the two-mile long Queens Harbor. I organized and ran this boat parade for eight Christmases. I am now Commodore Emeritus.

While living in Queens harbor, I realized that there were a number of retired veterans in our community. There was, however, no veterans group or organization. My thought was that there should be a place or time when this special group of people could get together on a regular basis. I spoke to Vice-Admiral Mike Kalaras and he agreed that it was a good idea. So, I said to him, "Most of the veterans in Queens Harbor have Navy backgrounds. You're senior. Do you want to start something?" He said, "No, not me," but sort of in gest, he said, "I'm your senior. You go ahead and do it!" Very few people ever call a two-star general subordinate or order them around... but, anyway, I obediently contacted several vets that I knew. There were several Navy Captains and one Rear-Admiral, as well as many other ranks. We got the group organized and a roster set up. So, we did form a luncheon veterans group that met monthly in the Queens Harbor Clubhouse. Somehow, even though I was Air Force, I got elected as the Chairman. This group was established in about the year 2000. As of 2022, we still meet at least quarterly. I still go but I have long-since relinquished the chair. There are about twenty members of all ranks in the group.

One day when I was the Yacht Club Commodore, someone from the Jacksonville Marine Institute came to me and asked what I thought of a fundraiser utilizing the two-mile long harbor and the Club. So, I visited the Jacksonville Marine Institute Building and talked with everybody there. They are a high school/junior high school for wayward kids – female and male. It gives them a chance to be crew members on a boat. As crew members, each of them has a duty such as tying the bow line, tying the stern line – this is a very simple exercise in learning responsibility. If you miss the line or don't do it properly, it is immediately obvious. I wanted to help this group. After much planning, I set up the following: We secured the use of three forty-foot motorboats. We then got three well-known Jacksonville restaurants to donate food. We then got three harbor-front houses with docks. We then set up the restaurants in each of the three houses. Our idea was that we would sell tickets to the event – as all the ticket money was deductible due to the Jacksonville Marine Institute being a 501c(3). People from all over Jacksonville came to see and participate in this event. The Queens Harbor Barefoot Classic – conceiving, organizing and coordinating – began April 29, 2000.

This is how it worked: In the evening, People went to the Queens Harbor Clubhouse and got a glass of champagne. They then exited the back of the clubhouse and walked to the club dock. There, about a dozen people boarded a boat – that boat, number one, went to the first house, docked, let everyone off to view one of the Queens Harbor beautiful homes and they then enjoyed a delicious dinner. While this was happening, Boat number 2 took a dozen people to house number two. Then Boat Number 3 took a group to House Number 3. Then all three boats began what amounted to a rotating trolley service, each boat stopping at a dock, picking up passengers, cruising the harbor and docking at the next house discharging its passengers. They then picked up anyone who had eaten their share and took them to the next house. Thus, we had three forty-foot boats doing a round-robin, picking up and dropping off people all evening.

We had contacted all of the Queens harbor homes facing the harbor and asked them to turn on their houselights and landscape lights. From the water, all were seeing a beautiful nightscape while getting rides in great boats and eating their fill of exotic food. What a way to spend an evening! I was at the Clubhouse dock with the Marine radio directing the boats to keep them moving and properly spaced. At each dock, I had placed one seasoned U.S. Coastguard auxiliary member as a dockmaster. This auxiliarist was augmented by two or three Naval Sea Cadets. Each boat had a radio and each dockmaster had a radio. Thus, we were able to control the proper flow of the boats and their passengers. After visiting three houses and having three boat rides around the harbor, they were deposited back at the club and then they were ushered into a silent auction. We organized and did this for six or seven years. I believe we made over $100,000 for the Jacksonville Marine Institute. Everybody was very impressed. Most of the people had never seen the inside of Queens Harbor or the actual harbor. It was just gorgeous.

After several years of doing this, I tried to hand it off to a commercial captain who worked in the area. He said he'd do it. I forgot about it and about two weeks before it was supposed to happen, I got a call from the Jacksonville Marine Institute the captain had let them down and couldn't put it all together. I went back for one more year, reorganized the whole thing and ran it one last time.

Back in 1997, after moving into Queens Harbor and becoming a member of the QH Country Club, I went to a new member reception. How disappointing. All the new club members were given a free drink and told to introduce themselves. My thought was "what kind of new member orientation is this?" Shortly thereafter, I referred to a previous new member orientation script that I had experienced in other organizations. I wrote this up and went to the club director of membership. I soon found myself as chairman of the membership committee. It was now up to me to plan the program for new members. So monthly, I got all the new members together. The program was that each was asked to tell where they came from and what they did for a living and what their hobbies and interests were. This new member meeting was held before all the regular members, so there were several hundred current members present. New members were thus exposed

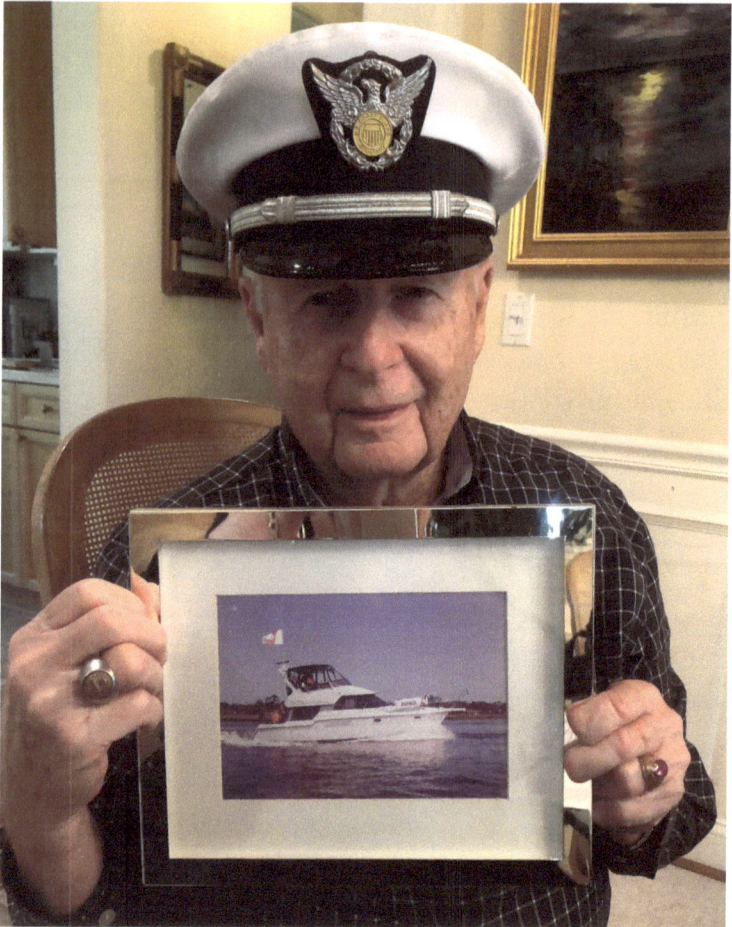

Patrol Boat

to other members who had like hobbies and interests. My hope was that immediately, associations would form.

Case in point: I met a man who was a member of the Coast Guard Auxiliary. I too had a background in boating. We got together. Later, he brought me to a U.S. Coast Guard Auxiliary meeting. Without hesitation, I decided to join, however, joining was not automatic. I had a U.S. Coast Guard Auxiliary book to read, then I was tested on all the aspects of the U.S. Coast Guard Auxiliary operations. I passed this test and was welcomed into the group. The Coast Guard Auxiliary of the Beaches was officially known as Flotilla 14-4. We met in a conference room of the local U.S. Coast Guard Building. There were only about a dozen members. Two of the members had boats that they used as patrol boats. This group, Flotilla 14-4, patrolled portions of the Intracoastal waterway weekly. Occasionally, we were called upon to look for a body, pull debris from the waterway, or rescue a boater who was in trouble. Often, however, we spent the day as a crew of between three to six people enjoying an uneventful cruise, in essence, showing the flag. Each boat, while on patrol, had a large two foot by five-foot sign on the side of the boat saying Patrol. We also flew a large Coast Guard flag on the masthead.

I had to take a two-month extensive course on seamanship in order to be a crewman on even my own boat when it was on duty. I was quizzed by a Senior Auxiliary member who had achieved the distinction of "Coxwain." As a Coxwain, he alone assumed the responsibility for each of our boats while we were on patrol. When I passed all the Coast Guard tests in the book, I received the designation of "Crew." I volunteered my boat to be what was called a "Facility." In order to be a facility and be utilized by the Auxiliary as a patrol vessel, we had to have on board two first-aid kits (one to carry to a distressed boat), a second anchor, extra bottles of water, six lines (each labeled as to how they were to be used when towing a disabled boat). We needed four extra life preservers, a hand-held radio capable of being carried to the boat in distress so that we could communicate with our Facility. We also carried a couple of extra sweatshirts and blankets.

The first boat I volunteered on was the 36-foot Aft Cabin Mainship. My next boat Facility was a 42-foot Twin Diesel Carter. Each of these required a minimum auxiliary crew of four – preferably more. Each crew member should be Coast Guard qualified as "Crew." At least one crew member must have the Coast Guard Designation of Coxwain. Our cruising and patrolling area was about forty miles of the Intracoastal waterway north and south of Queens Harbor. Due to my background, I was asked to become

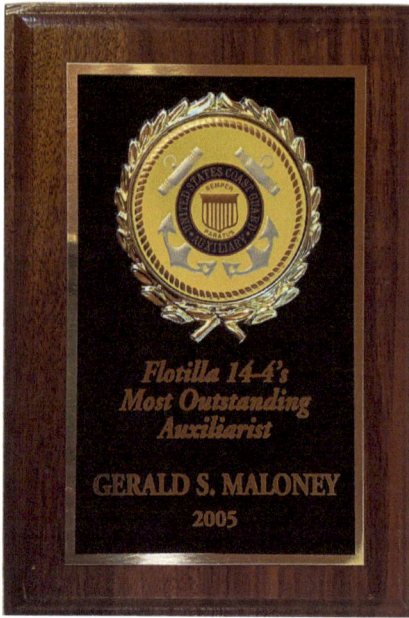

Flotilla 14-4's
Most Outstanding
Auxiliarist

GERALD S. MALONEY
2005

the Flotilla Commander, which I declined. I felt I had enough of taking the responsibility for running things.

The Auxiliary also ran boating classes. I was in the Coast Guard Auxiliary for 16 years. In addition to patrolling, my biggest duty was teaching. Eventually, over the years, the courses that I ran got good reviews from the local boat community. After a couple of years, my classes went from 8 people to 30 to 40 people. Each student paid $25 to the Coast Guard Auxiliary for the six- week course. Up until I took over the position of Public Education Officer in 1999, we had only a few hundred dollars in our bank account. While I was running the program, we had so many more people, we made much more money during this time. We even had enough money for a $10,000 CD. We also bought a lot of equipment for our Flotilla. Often, someone taking my class would wish to join the Auxiliary. Thus, after several years, we doubled and then tripled our membership. After retiring from running the boating classes, I remained in the Auxiliary and occasionally went out on patrols. All told, I spent 16 happy productive years in the Coast Guard Auxiliary of the Beaches and probably taught more than 1000 people about basic boating.

The last time I taught, there was a class of 15 people. I told them I'd been doing it for eight years – this is my last class. At graduation, they brought a big cake and gave me hugs and kisses and a nice thank you card. I see people all around the state who remember I taught them the various categories of sailing.

Lighthouse – 2007-2011

A good friend, Greg Streeter, Captain USN retired, helped to decorate my 42-foot twin diesel aft-cabin Carver for the yacht club Christmas parade. He told me of his work with the St. Augustine Lighthouse. He knew of my work with the restoration and preservation of older landmark properties in Massachusetts. He suggested that I'd be a good fit for the Board of Trustees of the St. Augustine Lighthouse. After a short visit there, I became a board member. After several meetings, I was asked to head the Board of Trustees. I was surprised, as all of the board members were from St. Augustine. Kathy Fleming, the head of the lighthouse, thought that my maritime experience with my restoration of landmark properties background made me more than qualified to be the Chairman of the Board. This was most pleasing to me as I also thought

Maloney Family at the Lighthouse, 2022

my background would be of value to the Lighthouse and its museum. I spent every Tuesday for four years at the Lighthouse. My tenure was for a year, with the option for a second year. During this time, I took all the office staff to lunch individually as I wanted to find out their backgrounds and where they thought the Lighthouse could grow. I had grown up in Duxbury, Massachusetts – across the bay from Plymouth. One of the first things I noticed was that almost none of the millions of souvenirs sold to the vast army of daily tourists, featured the date of 1565. Everything and anything that came out of Plymouth prominently displayed the date 1620 on it. I felt that 1565 should be, somehow, on everything that sold at the Lighthouse and in St. Augustine. I had always personally felt that living in Duxbury and growing up on the farm of the military head of the Plymouth Colony, Captain Miles Standish, had put me in the middle of the history of the United States. Now, I realized that St. Augustine was established 66 years ahead of Plymouth by the Spanish. This, too, was real history, but had never been written about as extensively as had Plymouth in our history books. I checked on several U.S. History books and most allowed only one or two sentences about St. Augustine. Obviously, in my opinion, the British prevailed … therefore, they wrote the history books.

My next endeavor was how to expand on the rich history of St. Augustine. The original Lighthouse would seem to have been first noted about 1586. A pictoral of a 4-legged tower is plainly shown on a chart made by Baptiste Boazio of Sir Francis Drake's attack on St. Augustine of 28 May, 1586.

If this tower was used as a watchtower, it most probably was used as what would amount to a Lighthouse. If the Spaniards of the 1500's followed the Mediterranean model, they would have built a fire in a pit on top of the tower. This would be a very good 1500's lighthouse. During the day, the smoke would amount to a very visible

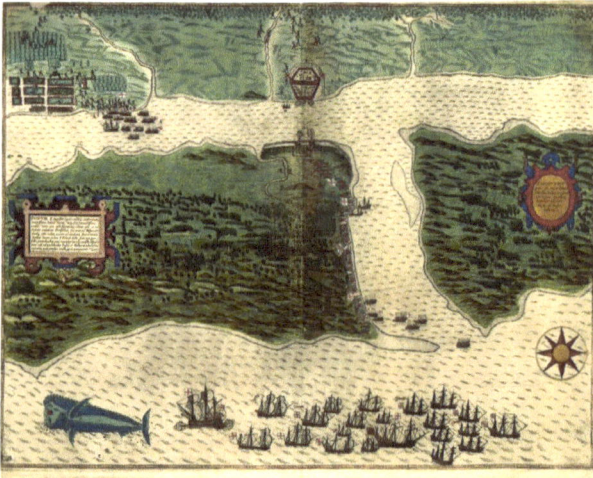

Sir Francis Drake's 1586 attack on St. Augustine

day beacon. I used my knowledge and experience with the Plymouth Colony to infuse into the Trustees and all the employees the unique significance of the St. Augustine Light Station as the oldest by far in the nation.

As Board Members rotated off the board, I tried to get new members from the Jacksonville area to spread awareness of the Lighthouse and its historical significance. I reached out for prospective new Board Members with interdisciplinary backgrounds. The Lighthouse had used its full name (St. Augustine Lighthouse and Museum). I added "Maritime" to the Museum. Consequently, from that point on, it would be St. Augustine Lighthouse and Maritime Museum. This distinguished our museum from the larger Flagler Museum and more aptly described its collection.

When my two-year tour as a Trustee was coming to a close, I was asked to stay on for another year. This required a change in the Junior League and Lighthouse Bylaws. I actually did two

JACKIE ROONEY/For Shorelines
Lighthouse Archaeological Maritime Program Director Samuel Turner (from left) and First Light Maritime Society Chairman Maj. Gen. Gerald Maloney showed Granaderos President Robert Champion and Mauricio Gonzales a replica of a 1760 yawl boat being built at the St. Augustine Lighthouse & Museum. The boat will be given to the Spanish, who are building a replica of Bernardo Galvez's flagship the Galvestown, which will visit St. Augustine in 2012.

more years. I think I left everyone with a more worldly view of the Lighthouse and its place in U.S. History.

One area of the Lighthouse and Maritime Museum was the group of Marine archaeologists. This group was separately incorporated as LAMP (Lighthouse Archaeological Maritime Program). Three maritime archaeologists joined the staff to seek out and dive on the wrecks of about 400+ ships that had floundered at St. Augustine over the more than 450 years of the port. I spent a great deal of my Tuesday visits with the archaeologists. What they were doing would bring national recognition to the Lighthouse organization. Occasionally, I went out on their boat to see the raising of long-submerged objects from one of the 400-year-old wrecks. I had four wonderful, fulfilling years working with Kathy and all the other people there. I am now, it seems, Chairman Emeritus of the St. Augustine Lighthouse and Maritime Museum, which is officially recognized by the Smithsonian Institute.

UNF Veterans Group

One day in about 2007 Dr. Anne Flipse on the UNF Board invited me to lunch. I met with her and with Kathleen Leone, the administrator for the UNF Student Affairs Council – Chair of Student and International Affairs @ UNF. They wanted to recruit me for a group they were starting at UNF. It was to be a group to help veterans transition from the military to civilian life and, to be specific, to transition into the UNF student body. Immediately, I agreed to help. Shortly, I met with the creator of the concept of helping all the vets who matriculated to UNF. At our first meeting, they elected me as the Chairman of this Committee. We named the group The Military and Veterans Resource Center, hereafter known as "MVRC." The UNF administration gave us three tiny offices. We at first only had one secretary/administrator. I spent a number of afternoons there during the next few months. Soon, we had a full-time director paid by UNF. He was Captain Ray Wilkstrom, USN (retired). He was a 100% full-time director. Ray and I met monthly to go over the plans and programs that Ray was busy developing. Eventually, due to the large number of veterans accessing our services, the MVRC got a much larger set of six offices, and a dozen full-time people. We also had a computer room that was for use by any veteran. Very important, I think, was the lounge. Here, veterans of all services could relax among other vets. Eventually, the veterans who were older and much more worldly-wise than their college contemporaries could freely move into the UNF student mainstream. Thus, over the years, the MVRC, thanks to Ray, became an integral part of the UNF campus. I had very little to do with the development of the MVRC on the campus. In my monthly meetings with Ray, I was in reality a sounding board for his plans and programs. During these years, I also met with and offered my support to the Army ROTC Unit. I was once honored by them at the annual Army ROTC Military Ball.

As the Chairman of the Veterans Group, I automatically became a member of the Council. This Council was a group of about thirty people, many of whom were grads of UNF, some on the President's Master Board, and several other members were volunteers at other UNF entities. The Council elected me the Chairman after my first year. So now, I was Chairman of the organization that oversaw all student activities at UNF except academics. I worked closely with the Vice president for Students and Foreign Affairs and his administrator, Ms. Kathleen Leone. I met weekly with them and we developed a warm close relationship. We invited monthly speakers from every activity on campus, such as LGBTQ, Disadvantaged Student Group, and other such. There was even a group that provided free food and a free kitchen to poorer students who didn't have access to the food ticket. They told us about that situation and it was just one of the areas where we tried to help. Part of the council's job was to go out into the community and tell people about all the happenings and opportunities at UNF. I personally visited a number of student organizations during my tenure as the council chairman. This was a very fulfilling job. The vast majority of UNF students seemed happy and outgoing. I also made many friends in the university administration including the last three presidents. To this day, I remain active in the Veterans Group.

Sandalwood High School

In 2017, while reading the local newspaper, I read that Sandalwood High School Air Force Junior ROTC was planning to form a rifle team. I thought that perhaps I could help in some way. I wrote a general letter to the high school stating my qualifications in this area. For four years, I heard nothing and forgot about my offer. Then, one day in 2021, a Sergeant Gote called me and reminded me of my offer to help. He said he had kept my letter for four years in the office of the Air Force JROTC Staff, which he directs. I was invited to meet them and since then, I met with the Sandalwood High School Principal, and I guess I got his blessings. Recently, I have spoken to and mentored six separate classes of about thirty cadets each. I have also coached some of the cadets at their rifle range. Much as I did in 1968 and 1969 at the Palo Alto Military Academy in CA, the JROTC has tentatively scheduled me to come at my availability to continue coaching the rifle team. So now, instead of one day a week at the Lighthouse in St. Augustine, I will be spending time coaching the Air Force JROTC Rifle Team. The commander also wishes me mentor the cadet corps, which I am happy to do.

On April 22, 2022, I was honored to be invited to be the keynote speaker at Sandalwood's AFJROTC 28th Annual Military Ball, held at the University of North Florida. I arrived at the ball and was greeted by Major John C. Coveney, USAF(retired) who is the AFJROTC Aerospace Science Instructor at Sandalwood. My biographer, Susan D. Brandenburg, was on hand to make

Maj. Gen. Gerald Stack Maloney, Jr. and Major John Coveney (USAF-Ret)

a record of the event, and she was invited to join us at the head table. It was a memorable evening for several reasons – number one being that the keynote speaker had laryngitis! With the help of the Major, I managed to convey a couple of important remarks to the assembled cadets, including the advice that they should always be proud of whatever they do, and they should Aim High! Another memorable part of the evening was that I was honored with a plaque of gratitude for my service to the AFJROTC and, despite her absence at the ball, they also honored Ambassador Marilyn McAfee for her service to the United States of America. There was a tall, slim African American cadet named Elizabeth Green sitting at our head table. When asked why she was a cadet, Elizabeth confided that she wanted to be a jet pilot. When asked why she wanted to fly a jet, she noted that she had been watching the Blue Angels all her life and wanted to be one. Not surprising

… Elizabeth Green was one of the most accomplished cadets, receiving award after award during the Awards Ceremony. As one retired jet pilot to a future jet pilot, I was proud to pose for a photograph with Elizabeth.

Elizabeth Green and me at The Military Ball

CHAPTER 14

MARILYN AND ME ...

I had met a lady decorator who had been employed to do some work at my Queens Harbor Home. While in a general discussion, the decorator mentioned something called The World Affairs Council. I asked her to tell me more about it. Shortly thereafter, her husband mailed me an application, which I completed. I was informed of a World Affairs Council dinner at the Marsh Landing Country Club. I attended and met lots of new, interesting people. The leader of it was a retired U.S. Ambassador named Marilyn McAfee. She was the organizer and president. We met, but at that time I was with a new girlfriend. Over the next couple of years, Marilyn and I often spoke at World Affairs Council meetings, but we were never able to get in more than a few words. She was busy.

When my girlfriend and I dissolved our relationship, a couple of our friends, the Joneses, invited me to dinner with Marilyn. Good, I thought. I've admired her and her work developing the World Affairs Council for several years. Now, I'd be able to interface with her. We had a nice dinner. We went to a local movie the following week, and then dinner. I have never dated another woman to this day.

There was something more that developed than had been present with either of my former wives. Each of us had our own lives and history. We were both volunteers and public servants in many areas.

At this time in my life, I was Commander Emeritus of the Queens Harbor Yacht Club, current chairman emeritus of the St. Augustine Maritime Museum and Lighthouse, and chairman of the Veterans Resource Center at the University of North Florida. Marilyn was the President of the World Affairs Council and a member of the Foundation Board of UNF. Immediately, each of us folded effortlessly into each other's lives and activities. This was in 2005. She was the recipient that year of the Florida Times-Union annual Eve Award. This award was for "bringing world figures to the Jacksonville area." Shortly thereafter, I moved into Marilyn's house, but kept my Queens Harbor home to use as an office. I was on six boards at the time and I still go to my Queens Harbor home to do board work and association correspondence.

I had always wanted to regularly attend a church, but neither of my wives was interested in church. Marilyn, however, was a church goer. So finally, after all these years, I became a parishioner of Christ Episcopal Church and a regular attendee. Shortly thereafter, I was asked if I would like to join the Churchmen of the Beaches. I already knew a few of the members, so joining was easy. I went to a few monthly luncheon meetings and almost before I could meet all the members, I was appointed the next Chairman. Since I hadn't been a member very long, I had no knowledge of member capabilities. So, I asked past-chairs, secretaries and treasurers to stand up. They all agreed to assist me and since then, we have become good friends.

Now, as prospective chairman, I had to find ten interesting luncheon speakers (no summer meetings). Between Marilyn and me, we were able to get ten very interesting speakers. Heretofore, the Churchmen's secretary would mail out meeting notices every month. By this time in our lives, I thought probably everyone had a computer or cell phone, so we began sending information and notices electronically. This radically improved the workload for the board. I announced that if we went to all email, we would save enough money in stamps to pay for the increase in our food prices at the Sawgrass Country Club. So, dues remained the same.

The Treasurer and I went over the budget and we increased "Honorariums" for our speakers from $100 to $200. Soon into my tenure, I realized that all the retired chairmen had a special table only for them. With consideration and agreement of the retired chairmen, I deleted the practice of a special table for past chairmen. If they wanted, they could sit anywhere or with each other. There would be no special designated table for us.

Upon discussions with many of the past chairmen, I found that when their year was completed, they got nothing in the form of any kind of recognition for their year's work. I felt that they should get something as a recognition for all their efforts and work. After some discussion with the officers, we settled on a plaque with a gavel on it and wording as follows:

The Churchmen
This gavel is presented to (name) in grateful appreciation
For your service as our distinguished Chairman (year)

We had twenty of these made – one for each of the last twenty living chairmen. I personally presented each one during one of our

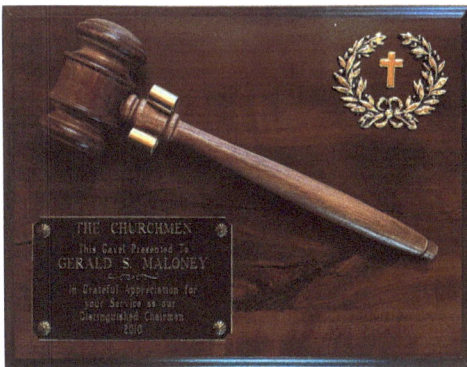

monthly luncheons. With this I hoped to establish a tradition whereby each retiring chairman would receive some sort of memento as appreciation for a year's service. This practice continues. I am now Chairman Emeritus of the Churchmen.

Marilyn continued to expand the World Affairs Council and I was one of her big supporters. With her push, the WAC has grown from about forty people to over 1,500 in the last few years.

From the beginning of our relationship, I felt that this was togetherness until we die. We love one another and we have elected to stay together in her home and not move to any of the local retirement homes in spite of the fact that so many of our friends have moved into them. At this point, we still own both of our homes and are quite satisfied with the arrangement we have.

Marilyn, for a few years, went on cruise ships as a guest speaker. I went with her. A few of the places we went were Suez Canal, Egypt, Sicily, the entire Mediterranean, Spain and Portugal. Another cruise was to visit all of the oldest historical ports along the West Coast of Europe. Another trip was to Latin America. I usually went along at no cost. On the Latin American trip, I went for half-price if I would give a lecture on the Argentine-Falklands War. I spoke to the group in our hotel in Argentina. Afterwards, some of the Argentine hotel staff who had overheard the talk spoke to me about the war. I was surprised they were unaware that Argentina had lost.

As I write this, Marilyn and I are in our seventeenth year together. We have friends all over the Northeast Florida area. She established the Council's practice of inviting well-known speakers of national or international quality. Active fundraising covered honorariums. Attendees range in age and political affiliation.

One of the most interesting speakers was Dennis Ross. He was President Clinton's Chief Negotiator for the Middle East. He recounted the occasion when Palestinian Chairman Arafat met with the Israelis at Camp David. This meeting was hosted by President Clinton. Because I was with Marilyn, I got to spend some quiet time with Dennis Ross. From him, I heard the inside story of why these talks seemed on the verge of getting an agreement between the Palestinians and the Israelis. He spoke about the Camp David Accords and why they broke down at the last minute. Less than a month later, when Marilyn and I were in Cairo and the U.S. Ambassador hosted a luncheon for us, I was to hear the other side of the story. The U.S. Ambassador invited a number of other officials and ambassadors, one of whom was Mohammed Rashad. He was the number two Palestinian to Chairman Arafat. We were introduced and I told him that I had spent an afternoon talking with the U.S. Negotiator Dennis Ross. Mohammed immediately said he wished to tell me Arafat's side of the Camp David Accords. We sat on the deck of the building overlooking the Nile River. He then gave the Palestinian view of the Accords. Imagine, thanks to Marilyn, I was probably one of the very few (if not the only one) who got to have an in-depth conversation with both of these men about the hopes for the Camp David Accords and the eventual breakdown. Sometimes, I think the title of General allows one a more in-depth analysis of a problem. People assume you are intelligent and perhaps worthy of their closely held information and, hopefully, you are wise enough to understand their position.

Here's how we got to Cairo: One evening Marilyn and I were at dinner when we got a phone call from Egypt from Mrs. Mubarak's office (wife of Egypt's President Mubarak). Marilyn was invited to come for dinner the following Saturday. She asked if I could come and the next day, after some vetting, I was included in the invitation. We flew to Cairo. When we landed, we were escorted by several Egyptians from the airport out the side door, bypassing the customs lines and check-ins. Our baggage was taken care of – we were shown a vehicle and told we had a driver and a guide 24/7 as long as we were in Cairo. They took us to the hotel where we were to stay, signed us in, sent our bags up to the room, and welcomed us. We then joined guests at a private dinner with Zahi Hawass, the world-famous archaeologist in charge of Egyptian antiquities. He was so impressed with Marilyn that he asked us to take tea with him in his office the following Monday morning. During tea, he summoned his number one assistant and told him to show us several sites that were not open to the public. I did not at that moment understand the significance of this. So, with Mr. Hawass's blessing, we proceeded on a monumental trip back in history. First, Marilyn and I went to the Pyramids. The man who was the head of the Pyramids and all of the activities there came to meet us at our car and insisted we join him in his private office. We took tea again while he gave us an in-depth history lesson on these famous Pyramids. Imagine, I thought to myself, learning about the Pyramids not from a history book but from the very person who is charged by the government of Egypt with their oversight. Our guide said not to bother getting any closer to the Pyramids. He had much better things to show us.

Next, we went to the Sphynx. We went through a wire entrance and enclosure with guards and we proceeded down a wooden stairway. About the time we got close to the Sphynx, I asked our guide "where are all the people?" I said, "We passed several busloads of people coming here. He said, "Oh, they can't get in here. Look up at the surrounding wall. See those people?

Egyptian Tomb

That's where they are. They are wondering who you are." So, we were alone with the Sphynx. I even got to sit on one of its paws. I have often wondered what the hundreds of people looking over the wall thought about the two of us there.

Next, we went to a very special private tomb. We went down a giant steel door which seemed to be inbedded in the side of a hill.

Our guide produced two keys which unlocked gigantic locks. He swung the heavy door open and we entered. It was a room about the size of a large western style master bedroom. The walls and ceilings were covered with Egyptian hieroglyphics. In all the beautiful large sprawling tombs where tourists are permitted, no flash photography is allowed. There are plexiglass barriers protecting the hieroglyphics so no one can touch them. For us, our guide slid the glass back. He told me, "You may touch the wall and the hieroglyphic paintings." He explained that this is a privilege accorded to only someone by specific authorization from Zahi Hawass. He said, "You are extraordinarily privileged." He said it would be alright for us to take a photo of me actually touching the hieroglyphic paintings. He noted that they are 4,600 years old. I still get chills thinking of it. Our guide then said, "Here is the sarcophagus of an ancient priest/general. Since you are general and the mummy is that of a general, ZH has authorized me to allow you to go down into the sarcophagus to inspect the priest/general mummy. Our guide opened a large glass cover of the sarcophagus and I descended by a very old ladder and came within inches of the mummy, which looked like a big shriveled up doll about four feet long. There was a glass in front of it. I said a little prayer and then climbed back up. When our guide closed the glass top, he asked me if I wanted to be immortal. I didn't know what to say to that, but before I could answer, he said, "From General to General, wet your finger and write your name in the thick dust on top of the glass." He said, "Your name will be here for another hundred years, because no one ever gets to enter here." Other names were on the dusty glass top, so I printed in small letters, *General GSM* on the glass. At that point, I reverently said Hello to his soul.

Marilyn and I were both deeply touched that we had been allowed into such an historically significant private burial chamber. My heart still skips a beat when I think about it. I thought and hoped that the general's soul had been with us.

Next, we went to what is known as The Step Pyramid. Instead of having smooth sides like the other pyramids, this Pyramid has terraced sides, thus the name. When we arrived there, we walked through a hundred yard long courtyard. Then as we arrived in front of the Pyramid, we descended down a walkway to what appeared to be a cellar door entrance. This door was also massive and I think again required two keys. Once opened, we descended along a narrow dimly lit tunnel. At the end of the tunnel we were faced with a huge cavernous space. The inside of this huge Pyramid was hollow. I commented to Marilyn that you could put a ten-story building in here. The walls were steep and I felt like I was standing on a cliff. Our guide pointed out some holes along the ground floor. These holes resembled cave openings. He said each hole led to a deep underground tunnel. He pointed out that each of the tunnels had been opened and excavated a short way but they were not yet cleaned out and explored. Then, seemingly lost in thought, he said, "we know not what secrets remain to be excavated and uncovered." I thought to myself that I'd love to be able to be one of the Egyptologists who would someday be tasked with opening one or more of these mysterious underground tunnels. That completed our mesmerizing journey into the world of ancient Egypt.

The next evening was the dinner to which Marilyn had been invited. What I had forgotten was the fact that Marilyn was to be one of the featured speakers. She, along with Julie Eisenhower, was to speak of the roles that NGOs (Non-Governmental Organizations) play in a country's governance. Our driver had to stop as we approached the palace on the Nile where the festivities were being held. We all were carefully inspected. The driver, the guide and I were all inspected. We easily passed inspection, as we were expected. Next, our vehicle was thoroughly inspected, including underneath. After the inspections, a second gate opened and we entered what looked like about a 100-yard, well lighted driveway. This driveway to the palace was paved with Persian carpets. I repeat – Persian carpets! The entrance was up a set of very wide, well-lighted stairs and into what appeared to be a ballroom. It was beautifully appointed and the other end from where we entered was open to the Nile.

We joined a large reception and numerous delicious food trays were passed among the guests. There appeared to be about 100 people, a majority of them Egyptian. The food trays were voluminous, with hot and tasty morsels of every description. After about thirty minutes of mixing and enjoying the food, a uniformed man tugged at my shirt sleeve and quietly said, "Mrs. Mubarak will see you now." Marilyn and I were discretely led through the crowd to a small side room. Mrs. Mubarak was seated on what almost appeared to be a simple throne. Other than a couple of advisors to Mrs. Mubarak, we appeared to be her only guests. Marilyn had met Mrs. Mubarak previously in her capacity as a U.S. ambassador. I was so in awe that I can't remember anything of what was discussed. Marilyn, as always, was very well composed. After a few minutes, we returned to the ballroom. I noted there were quite a few men in suits with big bulges in their suit coats. In fact, one of the men had trouble keeping his Uzi sub-machine gun from slipping out from under his clothes.

Ms. Eisenhower spoke to the gathered guests for a few minutes. I don't remember a word she said. Then Marilyn spoke. She spoke about the important role NGOs can and do play in the exercise of governance. Marilyn knew that NGOs were considered meddlesome by the GOE. Soon, the evening ended and we departed in our van, driving silently over the Persian carpets. Next, on to Luxor.

We flew to Luxor and were met by a woman who told us she was our guide for the next few days. Again, we had a driver and a vehicle exclusively for our use. We checked into the St. George Hotel in Luxor with a suite that had a view of the beautiful Nile River. We visited Luxor, which was the largest temple complex on the east bank of the Nile. It was breathtaking – huge columns and huge statues everywhere. I thought of the thousands and thousands of man hours it took to create this place.

Next, we were taken to the Karnak Temple Complex. It was not as well preserved as Luxor but it was larger. It was/is, in fact, the largest complex ever constructed for religious purposes. It was known by Egyptians as "Most Selected of Places." Marilyn and I wandered around and if it weren't for our tour guide, we would have gotten lost in the midst of this vast mixture of decaying pilons, chapels and other buildings. Included in this complex, was also a huge reflection pool. I thought to myself, "this reflection pool has reflected my face and millions of other faces for over 4,000 years." Chills ran down my spine. The entrance to Karnak was guarded by about twenty-four stone lions. There were twelve on each side of the boulevard-like entranceway.

Next, we visited the mortuary temple of King Hatshepsut. This was the site of the king's burial. Unlike the pyramids, this burial building was a masterpiece of ancient architecture built into the side of a cliff. It was very well preserved. I'm not sure how I can convey my feelings standing in this place. It gave me a primeval feeling. There, as a few days before, I was intimately face to face and feeling the presence of a soul. It's hard to express the feeling deep down in my gut standing in this place and looking at where this king was buried.

During all this time, our guide gave us a running description of the buildings and ruins and special obelisks throughout this area as we drove around.

Next, she took us to the Valley of the Kings and then the Valley of the Queens. There were many huge burial tunnels and rooms beautifully decorated. Having been in the construction business, I had only an understanding of the aengineering achievements – accomplished on each of these vast undergound chambers.

I was in awe of the amount of work and obstacles that each of these burial vaults represented. The majesty of these places has never left me.

248 Major General Gerry Maloney, Jr.

CHAPTER 15

AWARDS – RECOGNITIONS

AWARDS:

Order of the Paul Revere Patriots from Governor King.

Best in Asbestos Industry Award from Governor Dukakis

National Champion Rifle: 1961, 1963 and 1965

U.S. International Rifle Team, 1959. 2nd in World Competition

National Shooting Records: 34

National sailing Championship, Annapolis, 1950

Recipient National History Award,
Best Undergraduate History Essay in U.S., 1954.

Past President, Standish Shore Neighborhood Association,
Duxbury, MA

AUTHOR:

The Penobscot Expedition - 1778
"First definitive historical account of America's worst Naval Defeat.

Passenger Traffic Flow – A universal signage system adopted worldwide by the U.S. Air Force for the efficient and expeditious movement of military personnel.

PERSONAL:

Commodore Emeritus – Queens Harbor Yacht Club, Florida

Local President – Past Yacht Club Commodore's
International Association

Past Member Board of Governors –
Queens Harbor Yacht & Country Club

Member U.S. Coast Guard Auxiliary - Public Education Officer

Outstanding U.S. Coast Guard Auxiliary Member 2005

Fleet Landing Board Member

Past President Queens Harbor Veterans Group

Chair Emeritus of St. Augustine Lighthouse and Maritime Museum

Chair of All Student and International Affairs,
University of North Florida

Chairman Emeritus, "The Churchmen" – Ponte Vedra Beach, FL

Chair Emeritus of the Lighthouse Architectural Maritime Program

Board Member – Naval Order of the United States
Northeast Florida Chapter

Mentor and Coach of the Rifle Team of the Junior Air Force ROTC –

Sandalwood High School, Jacksonville, FL

Chair of the Military and Veterans Resource Center
at the University of North Florida

Chief of Staff of Aleppo Shriners of New England

AIRPLANES PILOTED BY GERRY MALONEY:

F86 Saberjet .... Korea, Japan, Taiwan

TF80 .... Korea, Japan, Taiwan

T33 ....Korea, Japan, Taiwan, USA

U3 .... Hamilton AFB, CA

L20 Beaver .... Korea

Otter .... Alaska

01 Birddog (Army L19) .... Korea – 24 Inf. Div/Demilitarized Zone

C45 .... Hondo AB, Texas

C46 ....Taiwan, Hong Kong

C47 .... Hamilton AFB, CA

C119 .... Hamilton AFB, CA

T6 .... St. Augustine, FL/Hondo AB, Texas

Bell H47 (Army) .... Presidio of S.F.

Sikorski H19 .... Big Spring AFB, Texas

Super Cub.. Hondo AB, Texas

Stearman .... Duxbury, MA

Schweitzer Glider...S. F., CA

Navion (Army)... Presidio of S.F., CA

Stinson... Marshfield Airport, MA

Luscomb.. San Francisco (S.F.), CA

Cessna 150 .... S. F., CA & Jacksonville, FL

Cessna 172 .... S. F., CA

Cessna 180 .... S. F., CA

Cessna 182 .... S. F., CA

PA 28 .... Ga. To Ohio Cross Country

PA Cherokee... San Jose, CA

Chipmunk (RCAF)..St. Augustine, FL

P51-Mustang (WWII) .... Nov '13 – Naval Air Station – Cecil Field

Aronka .... Plymouth, MA

CHAPTER 16

REFLECTIONS

On boating ... I have boated the east coast from Halifax Nova Scotia to Key West, Florida (the entire east coast of the U.S. and Canada). I had a 33-foot Pierson/cruising sailboat. Also, I was crew on a friend's 40-foot sailboat that twice went to Nova Scotia. Some of this cruising was by sailboat and some by power boat.

On flying ... I have written much about my flying adventures. I still fly with friends occasionally. The Confederate Air Force has kept a lot of the WWII planes flying. For example, they will send a P-51 to a private airstrip and advertise $1600 for 30 minutes flying time. On November 3, 2013, I flew a WWII P-51 Mustang. I wore my General's flight suit and people wanted pictures with the General. It was good for the ego. The P-51 did everything I wanted it to do. I felt right at home flying it up or down or inverted. The Mission of the Confederate Air Force, now called the Commemorative Air Force is to maintain as many WWII planes as they can and keep them flying. Thus, the $1600 charge.

On the Military ... The military has impacted me greatly. I have worn the uniform of my country for six decades – ROTC – Air

Force – Massachusetts Guard - Coast Guard Auxiliary. I wish other people could experience something like what I've experienced. It doesn't have to be military – but something they can always feel a part of.

On Success ... In order to do well, you have to figure out what you want to do and work at it and try to be better than anybody else and then you'll get ahead. I've always had to work hard - Dyslexia has always been a cloud over my head. Very few things have been handed to me. Learn what you're supposed to do and do it. A lot of people don't know what they're doing. I've never done drugs or smoked. I've done a lot of firsts:

- Flew the first airplane to break the sound barrier.

- Flew the first airplane that flew faster than sound.

- Completed the first large legal asbestos removal job in the U.S., starting a whole new industry.

- Made the first movie on asbestos removal.

- Developed the first government approved encapsulant for asbestos.

- I was a manufacturer's representative for the first fax ma chines, starting another new industry.

- Was a manufacturer's representative for 3M Company for the first music tapes/cartridge system - starting a third new industry.

- Uncovered and authored the first account of America's worst naval defeat - the Penobscot Expedition of 1779.

- Scored the first perfect score ever on the 50-foot Olympic Shooting Target

Always search for something new - you cannot be afraid.
Aim high.

On my daughter Katie... Katie was born in the Redwood City, California Hospital and she was everything her mother and I had dreamed about. She developed an adventurous personality early on. When she was about three years old, Katie disappeared from our Palo Alto home. We looked everywhere. A few frantic moments later, I spotted her turning the corner at the end of our block. She had walked herself all the way around the block.

Katie almost at the controls of a Piper Cherokee Airplane on the way to our property in Mendocino, CA.

At age 16, Katie (a natural artist) applied to the Parsons School of Design for a summer program in Paris. She fearlessly left home alone and returned from Europe a much more mature and worldly young woman. Minty and I must take some credit for having enough confidence in Katie's innate ability to function in the world to let her go on her own.

Katie was born with the same love of sailing that I had. Helming a 33-foot sailboat under sail in cross currents and wind changes is difficult. Katie easily seemed to master that. Like me, she loves time on the water and being at the helm.

Due to Katie's obvious reading problems (dyslexia), we eventually found her a small, private school where she would receive personal

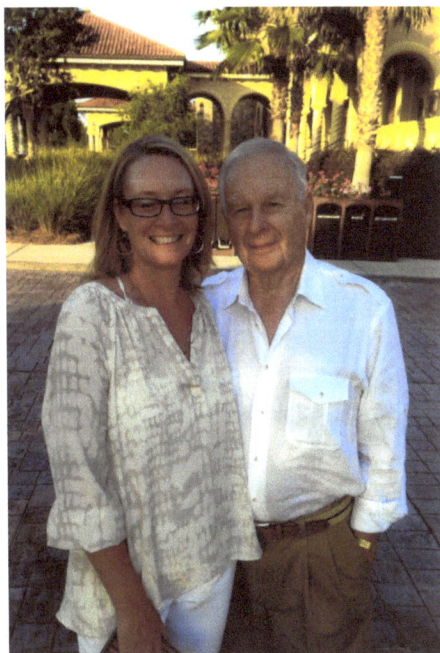

help. Although we had been advised that Katie might never be able to go to a regular college, she worked hard and, with the support of a caring faculty, had achieved a credible enough record by her senior year in high school that she was accepted at Colby College in Maine.

Katie had about the same dyslexic problems at Colby as I did at Stanford. Unlike Stanford, the language department at Colby refused to acknowledge the existence of dyslexia. Therefore, in order to graduate with the language requirement, Katie spent a semester of her last year immersed in Spanish while living in Mexico. In spite of dyslexia, Katie was named a "Colby Senior Scholar," which allowed her to create her own curriculum.

After college, Katie remained in Maine for thirty-plus years. She worked at the Portland Museum of Art, the Children's Museum, and numerous other creative self-employed pursuits.

She purchased her first house - fixer-upper - by herself and this was the beginning of a new passion that I believe she also got from me. Over the years (and two marriages), she purchased and fixed up four houses in Maine.

Having lived and worked at a ski area for seven years, Katie and her then husband purchased a 42' sailboat to pursue her passion for travel and sailing. The 40 year old boat and a disintegrating marriage made that dream short-lived, but led her to her current fixer-upper on the water in Florida. She now lives three hours from me, which allows us to see each other very often. She sails, paints pet portraits, practices canine massage and is finishing her home.

She is warm, thoughtful, makes friends easily and is fun to be with. Proud Daddy thinks Katie is a beautiful woman inside and out.

Christopher and Katie, flanking their father!

On my son Christopher ... In thinking of my beloved son, Chris, his vivaciousness, spirited effervescence, brilliance, and his eventual diagnosis of bipolar disorder, it reminds me of the famous Churchillian comment about Russia: a "riddle wrapped in a mystery inside an enigma."

As a youngster, Chris was intellectually bored at the local elementary school, so we sent him to a private school where he prospered in academics, sports and social life. He thrived in this structured environment.

After the Fessenden School, he chose a fine local prep school, Noble & Greenough. Here, too, he prospered. He enjoyed four years of great grades, good sports and made good friends. However, looking back, I realize that he was unable to organize himself outside of school. He often failed to do the chores assigned to him to keep the household, cars or boats in good shape. If he did not do them, we did them for him. Minty and I failed as parents by overlooking his inability to organize his homelife. Neither Minty nor I had ever heard of something called bipolar dis-

Chris and Katie

order, which we later discovered that Chris had (just as we had never heard of dyslexia until Katie was diagnosed).

Chris did well enough academically to go to Dartmouth. I was so proud. My Dad, his grandfather, was Dartmouth Class of 1924. Chris would now carry the Dartmouth torch. Minty and I drove Chris to Dartmouth and settled him in and did not hear from him for months. Finally, after several months, I drove to Dartmouth and found him. We went to dinner and had a couple of beers and he was as vivacious as ever. When confronted with our anxiety about his total lack of communication, he hung his head for a moment and promised to do better. He never did. I have one of his few letters. It was a heartfelt letter about his inability to get his life and school all lined up and executed in a timely manner. Sadly, when I read that letter, I felt that Minty and I had truly failed him. This letter was a plea for help … help he did not get from us.

It was a special moment for both of us when I gave Chris my Dad's Dartmouth letter sweater. When I was in high school, and played pick-up hockey on the local pond, I noticed a number of other kids wearing letter sweaters, so I asked Dad if I could wear his big green "D" letter sweater. He said, "No. You didn't earn it." Chris had a number of problems throughout his years at Dartmouth because he had difficulties organizing himself. Though he left Dartmouth, he later returned and graduated. Chris spent four years on the varsity rugby team. Thus he certainly earned his grandfather's big green D letter sweater which I presented him with on graduation.

For a few years, Chris lived with his mother (we were divorced by then). Eventually, he moved to Oregon and got a job, but once again, we heard nothing from him. After much networking, Katie re-established contact and visited him. He moved back to Mas-

Chris in South Dartmouth, MA

sachusetts and took a job at B.U. While living in Boston, he got married and had a daughter.

During this time, Minty died. The Boston University job dried up and Chris didn't seek further employment. His marriage ended in divorce. Then he disappeared for several years again. He made no contact with anyone except his daughter Lillian. Hing spent all of his money on legal fees in the divorce, the only money he had came from walking dogs around the Providence, Rhode Island area.

One day, a local social worker asked him if he would walk her dog. She immediately realized that he was a well-educated man. She had a long talk with him and sent him to a doctor. Between the two of them, he was diagnosed bipolar-2. He had no idea – nor did we – what bipolar was. It was a revelation to him, just as my dyslexia discovered in my 40's was a revelation to me. He was treated and we began to connect again. Marilyn and I flew to Providence to see Chris and his daughter Lillian. Chris now has a job taking care of dogs in a veterinarian's office. I bought him a car and still provide him with some income. I feel sad that he still has problems and seldom communicates. He does occasionally communicate with Katie. I worry about what he will do when I'm gone. My wonderful granddaughter Lillian is 16 and lives with her mother in the same area as Chris. He sees her regularly and they are very close. I am proud to say he is a wonderful father.

I'm grateful to have a relationship once again with my son. He is a good man who has faced many challenges and, like his Dad, has achieved much in spite of those challenges.

On my dear Marilyn ... After admiring her for three years across a crowded room at the World Affairs Council, I finally had the opportunity to dine with her at the home of some friends and for the first time, we had the chance to really talk. This was a glorious night for me. The following week, we went to a movie and dinner. I never looked back. We were almost immediately a couple. I had always wanted to go to church, but it hadn't been a priority with the other women in my life. Marilyn and I have gone to church ever since we became a couple, and I pretty quickly joined the Christ Episcopal Church in Ponte Vedra and soon thereafter, I became an usher and have been for 17 years. In fact, after realizing that there were no directions for ushers to follow at the 7:30 a.m. service, I wrote a set of standard procedures for all the new ushers to follow. These are still in use today.

Marilyn was asked often to go on cruise ships as one of the celebrity lecturers. She got to take me with her! A few of the places we visited during various cruises were: All of the old European Atlantic Ports, the Red Sea, Cairo, Suez Canal, Siracusa, Sicely, Alexandria, Carthage, Malta, Crete, Lisbon, Majorca, etc.

As a retired U.S. Ambassador, Marilyn usually spoke about the history and governments of countries on the itinerary. As

Deputy Inspector General of the State Department, she had been in many countries to conduct or oversee inspections, and knew them in some depth. When she was President of the World Affairs Council – or as the speaker on a cruise ship – I always assumed a supporting role. When I participated in military events, she had a secondary and supporting role. Marilyn comes from a military family so she was very comfortable in those settings. She especially enjoyed my help in chatting ("charming", as she says) with members and cruise guests. Thus, we have a very comfortable, long-term relationship. We have maintained that wonderful, fulfilling relationship for 17 years.

On my granddaughter Lillian ... Lillian was born in Boston, Massachusetts on November 23, 2007. She is the only child of my son Chris and my only grandchild. Most unfortunately, I am not able to spend much time with her. She lives with her mother in Rhode Island, not far from Chris. I did spend a few glorious days with Chris and Lillian in Providence, Rhode Island a couple of years ago. I also visited her at her elementary school several years ago. She was the tallest, prettiest girl in her class and also the smart-

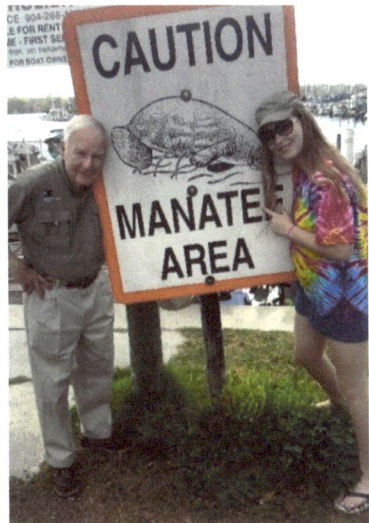

Lillian and me

est. She was very popular there. I enjoyed her immensely when she and her Dad visited in April of 2022. We visited some of my special places in St. Augustine and beyond.

Lillian is as tall as I am and superbly well-adjusted for one who has grown up in a split family. She has a bubbly personality and is a beautiful young girl. Lillian and Chris are as close as a father and daughter could ever be. Seeing them together makes my heart sing.

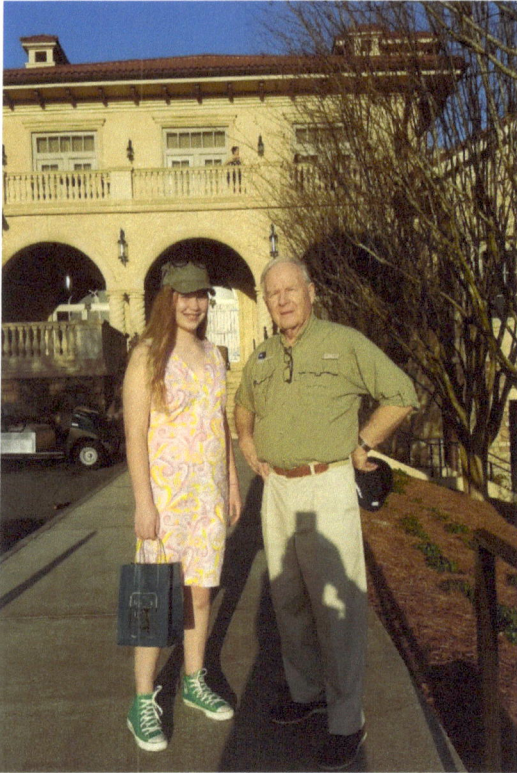

Lillian visiting St. Augustine with me in 2022

They sometimes seem to almost finish each other's sentences, and there is obviously great understanding between them. Both of them are absolutely brilliant, and they recognize that quality in each other and glory in it. She calls me Grandpa. She has also won a couple of science projects and has had some writings published. Chris is always kind, compassionate and forgiving with Lillian. He is a superb guide for her, and I feel he is a superb dad. They see each other every week. Lillian is, in respect to her loving father, a very fortunate young lady. When she was here in April, we had a heart to heart talk. I told her, "You're the last Maloney and I'm hoping that when you get married, you'll keep that name or possibly have a hyphenated last name." She just smiled and informed me that she'd already thought about that.

On the Present ... 2022 ... Over the years, I've collected fabulous memorabilia of my Air Force Career and other activities

Memorabilia - Holder presented by Sandalwood AFROTC - 2022

including interesting headgear. As Chief of Staff of the New England Shriners, I led parade routes through Boston and Cambridge, walking several miles several times – wearing the Shriners hat below:

As a member of the USAF Rifle Team, we all were given (WWI-like) Air Force Hat after our Air Force Rifle Team won the national championship. I was proudly wearing the hat one day as I walked down the street on base and a military police car stopped. The young MP got out and saluted and said, "Sir, what is that hat? I've never seen anything like it!" I informed him that this was the hat the Air Force Rifle Team wore – and there were very few

USAF Rifle Team Hat

of them in the Air Force, but they were authorized headgear.

As Commander of Air Force Academy Liaisons, I supervised and oversaw the recommendations of the members of the Massachusetts Congressional Delegation for applicants to the Air Force Academy. I supervised the counseling of applicants and worked closely with senators and congressmen and their staff members.

During this period, I maintained close personal contact with Senators Brooks, Kennedy, Tsongas and Kerry concerning Air Force Academy matters. Thus, I was responsible for bringing over $29 million dollars of Federal Scholarship monies to Massachusetts students.

Governor King awarded me the "Order of Paul Revere Patriots." hat below:

Governor Edward King, Boston, Massachusetts

Throughout this book, I've referred to my father often and not always in favorable language. Dad got Oat Cell Cancer (Carcinoma) at age 75 when he still lived at 592 Chestnut Street. He spent the next two years in remission, traveling to Europe and the Middle East. He was a good grandfather to Katie and Chris when he lived nearby. He didn't want any help while he was ill. He made a bedroom downstairs and had several male friends in town and a male nurse came by. I visited him weekly. He was Catholic and considered himself to have been living in sin for many years because he and our mother didn't raise me as a Catholic and didn't attend church together. He went to the nearby rectory and there was a new young priest there who absolved him of all sin. He received communion the following Sunday. Katie, Chris and I went to church with Dad that day and when he entered the church, I asked Katie and Chris to hold his hand on either side and march him to the front pew so that the whole church could see him with his grandchildren receiving communion. I can still close my eyes and see him walking down the aisle of the church with two little kids holding his hands. He was failing physically but still sharp enough to continue berating me up to the day before he died. He called me on the telephone and asked me to make arrangements at a local nursing home. The next morning, I went to the nursing home and they said, "Your Dad called already." He died a week or ten days later, and our differences were never completely resolved. I loved him, despite the vivid memories of his mental and physical abuse of me. Dad was an incredibly tough taskmaster and was probably the reason I have had the determination to do what I've done with my life. It's been an amazing journey – looking back over my life as I have written this book - and realizing that I've accomplished so much more than Dad ever expected of me. Life has been good. I've aimed high and, more often than not, thanks to God and the best of intentions, I've hit the target.

BIOGRAPHER'S NOTE

After nearly two decades of being peripherally acquainted with "Marilyn McAfee's Main Squeeze," that smiling man with the bushy eyebrows, I am humbly grateful to now count him as my dear friend, Major General Gerald Stack Maloney! My humility is prompted by the awe that Gerry's incredible story has inspired in me, and my gratitude is due to the fact that he has entrusted me to help him write that story. "My General" as I now fondly call him, is a man of heroic determination in the face of insurmountable odds; a man who has achieved great success and yet remains unpretentious and even self-effacing when describing his achievements; a man who loves his country and his family and gives God the credit for everything. My General has soared in the air as a pilot, navigated the waters as a sailor, traveled to the depths of the earth as an explorer, hit the target accurately and repeatedly as a champion shooter, earned his leadership position in myriad organizations, used his intelligence, imagination and energy to bring about improvements in every community graced by his presence, and generously extended his powerful love and support to family and friends without exception. My General is an extraordinary man, and this biographer is thankful to God for placing me in his life.

With love and admiration,

Susan D. Brandenburg

MG – Major General Maloney and his biographer, Susan D. Brandenburg
My Award-Winning 1955 MGTF-1500 - the last of its kind

CAPT. MALONEY, USAF CHAMPION

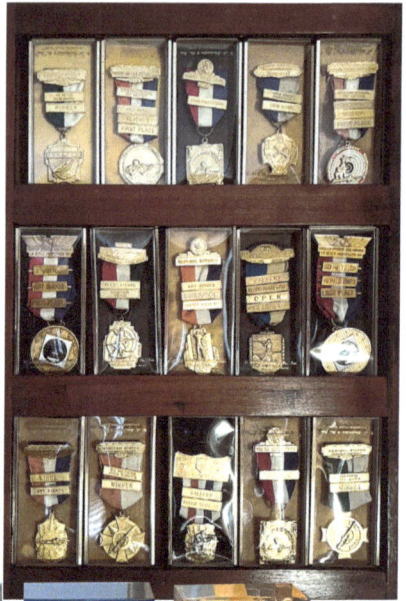

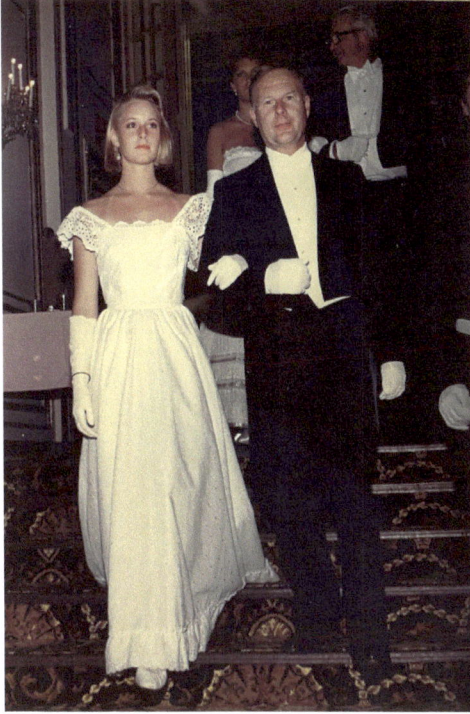

The Florida Times-Union

Gerry Maloney's war-era posters are subject of new exhibit at Cummer Museum

Posters created to inspire nation and saved by Gerry Maloney as a kid are now in Cummer exhibit.

Charlie Patton
Published 12:30 a.m. ET Oct. 2, 2010

For Gerry Maloney, the memory remains vivid 70 years later.

He was standing on a bluff looking out toward Cape Cod Bay, where a convoy of ships was forming.

As he gazed out to sea, a P-40 Warhawk, a fighter plane that would see heavy service in World War II, flew along the coast at Maloney's eye level. The plane passed him, then turned and flew past him a second time.

As their eyes met "he waved and I waved," Maloney remembered.

He knew instantly: "I want to be a fighter pilot." Eventually that would happen.

"Award for Careless Talk," 1944, Stevan Dohanos.
Florida Times-Union

THE ART OF WAR
OCTOBER 1 THROUGH NOVEMBER 14, 2010

The Cummer
MUSEUM of ART & GARDENS

THE ORIGINAL WORLD WAR II POSTER COLLECTION
OF MAJ GENERAL GERALD S. MALONEY

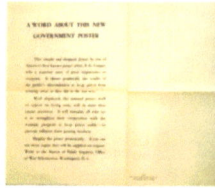

1918 / 1944
64.6% / 25.9%

85 MILLION AMERICANS HOLD WAR BONDS

a careless word
...another cross

A GOOD SOLDIER STICKS TO HIS POST!
—AND THAT INCLUDES SOLDIERS OF PRODUCTION!
Your War Production Drive
LABOR MANAGEMENT COMMITTEE

An Exclusive FILM for War Workers!
AAF REPORT
The official Film Story of the Army Air Forces packed with actual combat scenes

AIRCRAFT INSIGNIA

AMERICAN JUNIOR RED CROSS

American Labor
...PRODUCING FOR ATTACK

AMERICANS SUFFER when careless talk kills!

CZECHOSLOVAKS

DUTCH

GREEKS

NORWEGIANS

POLES

...and bless those back home who, knowing of our sailing, kept that knowledge to themselves

ANOTHER ENEMY TO CONQUER
FOREST FIRES
9 OUT OF 10 CAN BE PREVENTED

ATTACK ATTACK ATTACK
BUY WAR BONDS

AVIATION CAVALCADE

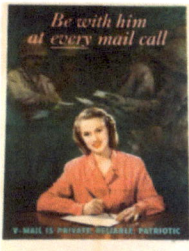

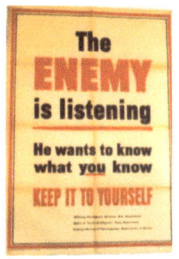

Enlist in a Proud Profession...
U.S. CADET NURSE CORPS
A LIFETIME EDUCATION FREE!

Enlist in a Proud Profession!
U.S. CADET NURSE CORPS
A Lifetime Education FREE!

"Even a little can help a lot-NOW"
Buy U.S. WAR STAMPS & BONDS

EVERY CHILD NEEDS A GOOD SCHOOL LUNCH
SCHOOL LUNCH PROGRAM

EXTRA WAR BONDS
5th WAR LOAN

FARMERS!
Uncle Sam asks you...
to get ready for the census taker

FILL IT!
HELP HARVEST WAR CROPS

FIRE AWAY!
BUY EXTRA BONDS

FISH IS A FIGHTING FOOD
WE NEED MORE

FOLLOW SAFETY RULES!

FOOD IS A WEAPON
DON'T WASTE IT!
BUY WISELY—COOK CAREFULLY—EAT IT ALL

FOR A SECURE FUTURE
BUY WAR BONDS

For Health...eat some food from each group...every day!
IN ADDITION TO THE BASIC 7... EAT ANY OTHER FOODS YOU WANT

For Liberty and Peace on Earth
Give WAR BONDS

FOR VICTORY — AND MY PERSONAL POST WAR WORLD
I'M FOLLOWING THE 7-KEY PLAN TO HOLD PRICES DOWN

FOR WAR SERVICE
SEEING IT THROUGH!
are You?

GET 'EM INTO THE FIGHT!

"A BRIDGE OF SHIPS IS THE SHORT LINE TO TOKYO"
GET 'EM OUT FOR YOUR NAVY!

GIVE 'EM
BOTH BARRELS

"Give 'em the stuff to fight with..."
SACRIFICE FOR FREEDOM!

"Give 'em the stuff to fight with..."

GIVE IT YOUR BEST!

GIVE WAR BONDS
The Present with a FUTURE

GIVE YOUR GOOD BOOKS TO OUR FIGHTING MEN
TO GIVE

Going our way?
BE A VICTORY FARM VOLUNTEER

GROW MORE...
CAN MORE...
in '44
GET YOUR CANNING SUPPLIES NOW!

GROW YOUR OWN
Be sure!

HELP SEND THEM WHAT IT TAKES TO WIN

HERE'S HOW TO HEAD OFF RUNAWAY PRICES
FOLLOW THE 7-KEY PLAN TO HOLD PRICES DOWN

HEY GANG!
keep on licking war savings stamps
-they're full of VITAMIN V

I need you on the job full time...
DON'T GET HURT

I need your skill
in a WAR JOB!
See your nearest U.S. EMPLOYMENT SERVICE

I'll carry mine too!
TRUCKS AND TIRES MUST LAST TILL VICTORY

I'M COUNTING ON YOU!
DON'T DISCUSS:
TROOP MOVEMENTS
SHIP SAILINGS · WAR EQUIPMENT

I'M OUT TO LICK RUNAWAY PRICES
LET'S ALL FOLLOW THE 7-KEY PLAN TO HOLD PRICES DOWN

I'm proud of YOU FOLKS too!

"I've found the job where I fit best!"
IND YOUR WAR JOB
n Industry – Agriculture – Business

If it'll save a second
IT'S A GREAT IDEA-
let's have it!
SHORT CUTS CAN SHORTEN THE WAR

If you tell where he's going...
He may never get there!

The Jap way-
COLD-BLOODED MURDER
We'll make them pay if you keep up
PRODUCTION

EEP IT UP BROTHER

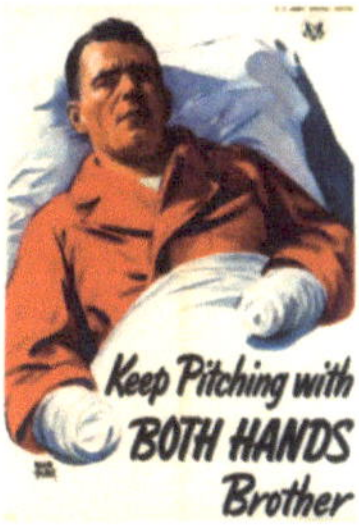
Keep Pitching with
BOTH HANDS
Brother

KEEP PUNCHING..
EVERY DAY!
Your LABOR-MANAGEMENT PRODUCTION COMMITTEE

Keep the home fires burning
MORE PRODUCTION!

KEEP THE
HOME FRONT PLEDGE
Pay no more than Ceiling Prices
Pay your Points in full

COST OF LIVING IN TWO WARS
Keep up the good work
Keep down living costs

LESS DANGEROUS
THAN CARELESS TALK

LET 'EM HAVE IT
BUY
EXTRA BONDS

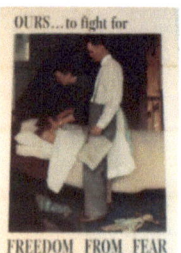

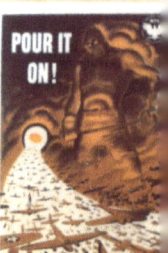

SAVE YOUR CANS
Help pass the Ammunition

PREPARE YOUR TIN CANS FOR WAR

See "Here's Your Infantry" and Buy that Extra BOND

She's a swell plane—give us more!

MORE PRODUCTION

She's a WOW
Woman Ordnance Worker

The Sky's the Limit!

KEEP BUYING WAR BONDS

SMACK THEM AGAIN, BROTHER

SMOKEY SAYS—
Care will prevent 9 out of 10 forest fires!

SOMEONE

TALKED!

...the state of this nation is good the heart of this nation is sound the spirit of this nation is strong the faith of this nation is eternal.

FRANKLIN D. ROOSEVELT

STOP HIM
AND THE JOB'S DONE

Symbol of Life

U. S. ARMY NURSE CORPS

Thank God for American industry—labor and management—which has given us the weapons and the equipment with which to conduct our North African campaign.

Thanks, Buddy!

NEWSPAPER BOYS HAVE SOLD OVER 1¼ BILLION WAR SAVINGS STAMPS SINCE PEARL HARBOR

the five Sullivan brothers missing in action off the Solomons

THEY DID THEIR PART

THEY STAKE THEIR LIVES ON YOUR ORDNANCE

They've got more important places to go than you!...

Save Rubber
CHECK YOUR TIRES NOW

THIS IS THE ENEMY

"THIS WORLD CANNOT EXIST HALF SLAVE AND HALF FREE"

FIGHT FOR FREEDOM!

Time saved on YOUR job SAVES LIVES ON HIS!

Turn in your ideas to do it BETTER, FASTER

To Have and to Hold—

BUY WAR BONDS

TOGETHER WE WIN
Get behind your labor-management committee

TOOLS ARE WEAPONS!
USE THEM WISELY...
7 TIPS TO SAVE YOUR TOOLS

BETTER CARE MEANS LONGER WEAR

TWICE A PATRIOT!

"Sometimes I feel my job here is as important as the one I had to leave."

www.ingramcontent.com/pod-product-compliance
Lightning Source LLC
Chambersburg PA
CBHW040940100426
42812CB00026B/2729/J